Invisible Countries

INVISIBLE COUNTRIES

JOURNEYS TO THE EDGE
OF NATIONHOOD

❁

JOSHUA KEATING
MAPS BY BILL NELSON

Yale
UNIVERSITY PRESS

New Haven and London

Yale University Press books may be purchased in quantity for educational,
business, or promotional use. For information, please e-mail sales.press@
yale.edu (U.S. office) or sales@yaleup.co.uk (U.K. office).

Set in Adobe Garamond type by IDS Infotech Ltd., Chandigarh, India.
Printed in the United States of America.

Library of Congress Control Number: 2017958268
ISBN 978-0-300-22162-6 (hardcover: alk. paper)

A catalogue record for this book is available from the British Library.
This paper meets the requirements of ANSI/NISO Z39.48-1992
(Permanence of Paper).

10 9 8 7 6 5 4 3 2 1

For Miranda and Thomas

Contents

Author's Note

The goal of this book is to explore how we wound up with the current arrangement of countries on the planet, why that arrangement has stayed relatively static for so long, and whether changing the arrangement would be possible or advisable. The book looks at some of the forces keeping the current map of the world in place as well as some of the forces—economic, cultural, and environmental—pressuring it to change. The idea to write a book about why it's so hard to start a new country—or alter the shape of an existing one—came about long before a confluence of events driven by Vladimir Putin, Xi Jinping, Donald Trump, ISIS, and Brexit made the topic far more timely and applicable to some of the world's most pressing ongoing crises than it had been.

The case studies in this book are examples of places, both real and virtual, where our comfortable view of the world's landmass as divided into neat, mutually exclusive territorial units called countries breaks down.

Each of the five "countries" (all of which I traveled to in 2016) described in this book's main chapters illustrates a problem with the world map as currently drawn. Abkhazia, a Russian-backed breakaway enclave, recognized by most of the world as part of Georgia, shows how geopolitical rivalries shape which countries achieve full independence. Akwesasne, an indigenous political community that straddles the U.S.-Canadian border and predates the countries that have emerged on either side of it, challenges the notion that only one kind of nation can be sovereign. Somaliland, a semi-autonomous region in northern Somalia, has achieved all the trappings of country-hood but is simply ignored by most of the international community. The same can't be said of Iraqi Kurdistan, a place regularly in global headlines but continually frustrated in its efforts to challenge the Middle East's geographical status quo. Finally, Kiribati, a small island country in the central Pacific, has become a poster child for the imminent political disruptions caused by climate change, raising the question of whether a country can continue to exist when the piece of land it is associated with no longer does.

Interspersed with these primary chapters are small sections I call "outliers": examples of people refusing to be confined by the world map as currently constructed. They discuss the Sovereign Order of Malta, Estonia's electronic residency program, the free-market utopi-an political experiment known as Liberland, and the struggles of stateless people to have their human rights recognized in a world where national citizenship is all but mandatory.

My hope is that these examples, some well known, some obscure, will lead readers to think more critically about the contemporary map of the world and to consider more creatively what it might look like in the future.

Invisible Countries

What Is a Country?

It was close to dusk on the Black Sea coast when the parade of imaginary countries began.

On the surface, it was an event not unlike the opening ceremonies of any other international sporting event. Sequined divas belted cheesy inspirational pop ballads. Choreographed masses of dancers performed a tribute to the glorious history of the host nation. Athletes, most with little hope of making it past the early rounds of competition, mugged for selfies and proudly waved their flags.

But the twelve teams that had made the journey to the World Football Cup in Abkhazia in June 2016 were representing countries that are not at all like the countries at the Olympics or the World Cup. And none of the flags paraded through the stadium that night are on display outside UN headquarters in New York City. These were countries that most people don't consider countries at all.

The World Football Cup, organized by the Confederation of Independent Football Associations (ConIFA), is where countries compete when they don't meet the threshold of statehood required for membership in bodies like FIFA (the Fédération Internationale de Football Association), the International Olympic Committee (IOC) or, for that matter, the UN General Assembly.

Some were the type of places that are described in news reports by dismissive phrases like "breakaway," "semiautonomous," or "self-proclaimed." The host country, Abkhazia, was one such: de facto independent since breaking off from newly independent Georgia in a devastating civil war that ended in 1993 but today recognized by only Russia and three other countries. As far as the United States and Europe were concerned, this event was being held in Georgia. (The Georgian government grumbled publicly about the event but made no effort to stop it from going forward.)¹ A team represented the Kurds, the largest ethnic group in the world without its own state but one that is now tantalizingly close to achieving the dream of independence. Somaliland, the unlikely and unrecognized beacon of stability in the Horn of Africa, was also represented, as was Northern Cyprus, the Turkish-dominated northern half of the Mediterranean island.

Some teams represented groups wronged by history. The "Western Armenia" contingent represented a Turkish Armenian community decimated during World War I. The Chagos Islanders, originally from a small archipelago in the Indian Ocean but now living largely in the Crawley area of London, were evicted from their home islands by the British government in 1971 so that the United States could build a military base on Diego Garcia, an expulsion the islanders continue to challenge in domestic and international courts.

Other teams represented ethnic minorities who've found themselves on the wrong side of international borders, such as the Koreans of Japan or the Hungarians of Romania. A Punjabi team purported to represent not only the historical region today divided between the countries of India and Pakistan but the global Punjabi diaspora. A Saami team represented an indigenous group living in northern Scandinavia that has achieved a significant level of political autonomy in recent years. Rounding out the competition were some European regions—Padania, or northern Italy; and Raetia, the Romansch-speaking region of Switzerland—that seemed less interested in making a political statement than in just playing some football. "This team is not like a political thing. I think Italy is fine the way it is," the Padania goalkeeper told me at the opening ceremony.

At the opposite end of the intensity scale was Harpreet Singh, a thirty-three-year-old London accountant who quit his job and poured his life savings into building the Punjabi team. He told me, "I don't consider myself to be Indian. The Indians have perpetrated atrocities against Punjab. I don't consider myself British. I don't hate them, but I choose not to be associated with being British." After asking me to imagine how I would feel if my own family were murdered in front of me, he said, "If you ask me now, 'What is your family?' my family is all Punjabis worldwide. They are my family. They are more important to me than my own wife and children."

I spent most of my time at the tournament following the team from Somaliland, an unrecognized autonomous state—considered northern Somalia by the rest of the world—that I would visit later that summer. Most of the team's players live in Britain. The team's director, thirty-two-year-old Ilyas Mohamed, said he wanted to build pride among the citizens and diasporic community of a place few in the world have heard of. "I feel obliged. Somaliland was where I was born. Somaliland has a lot to offer, but it's got a lot to learn from others."

Only the hardiest fans of esoteric international soccer made the long trip to Abkhazia to watch the tournament, but a fair number of foreign reporters were in attendance, attracted by the quirky spectacle of a World Cup for countries that don't exist. The event was also a blatant propaganda exercise for the host country, Abkhazia, a place that doesn't rate highly for news coverage even compared to other participants in the frozen conflicts of the post-Soviet world. It was easy to be skeptical about the event and ConIFA, an Isle of Man–based body staffed by a skeleton crew of volunteers, but I appreciated the open-minded approach to nationhood taken by the event.

Many of the participants hope that their membership in ConIFA is only temporary, a way station on their path to eventual membership in FIFA. While FIFA's bylaws allow for membership for regions that are not independent, membership applications must be approved by the association's executive committee, and world soccer's premier governing body has fairly vague criteria for membership. FIFA's rolls include some tiny, only semi-independent places like Montserrat, an island in the Caribbean, and Niue, a territory fifteen hundred miles northeast of New Zealand in the South Pacific. Palestine is in FIFA, though not a member of the United Nations. As of May 2016, so is Kosovo, also not a UN member state.[2]

ConIFA currently has forty-seven members—and no, you can't just declare your local pub an independent nation and start a football team. New members are decided on by a vote of the existing members and generally have to be semiautonomous states or minority groups recognized by international NGOs. Still, a few members, such as Cascadia—a region of Oregon, Washington, and British Columbia—seem dubious to me.

More than any other activity except perhaps war, for which they often serve as a metaphor, sports bring the world's countries into contact with each other. You don't have to buy the kumbaya platitudes of glorified criminal rackets like FIFA and the IOC to acknowledge that the appreciation of athletic competition, particularly the world's most popular sport, has a rare ability to cut across national boundaries even as it incites national pride.

Because a national team is often seen as the proxy for a country's ambitions on the world stage, events like the World Cup and the Olympics serve to reinforce the international community's narrow definition of national legitimacy. Only "real" countries need apply. Whatever your views on the current borders of the Caucasus, central Europe, or the Middle East, ConIFA's more open-minded approach is refreshing: an acknowledgment that most countries start out as a dream before they become widely acknowledged reality. Nations have been referred to as "imagined communities" for good reason. What countries aren't "self-proclaimed," after all?

There was also something undeniably poignant in the alternate history of the world that the event displayed. If a few battles, peace conferences, and revolutions had turned out differently, it's not at all hard to imagine an alternate historical timeline in which Punjab, Padania, and Kurdistan are established countries with seats at the United Nations and teams in the Olympics while Pakistan, Italy, and Iraq are merely the fanciful notions of dreamers and fanatics. The event was a useful reminder that the map of the world we all know today is the product of a series of accidents and historical processes that could just as easily have gone another way.

That's a useful truth to keep in mind in a world where the borders and countries we currently have increasingly seem permanent and immune from challenge or questioning.

When I was about ten, my prized possession was a five-hundred-page *Encyclopedia of World Geography*. It was an invaluable resource, the kind of item curious children depended on in the pre-Wikipedia era. Each of the world's countries and a handful of territories and dependencies had a separate entry that included a capsule history and notes on geography, economy, culture, and political system. The world portrayed by this book was a tidy one, with every country falling into its place as a self-contained unit of information. The cultural, political, and historical entity that is Italy, to take one example, from Rome to the Risorgimento, da Vinci to Fellini, fits nicely in an illustrated five-page write-up in the Europe section between Ireland and Latvia.

The book still sits, gathering dust, in my childhood room. When I thumb through it today, I find it striking that although the encyclopedia is nearly two decades old, it really doesn't feel that out of date. Yes, there are new heads of state in all but a few of the countries, new economic powers have risen, autocracies have become democracies and vice versa. But only three new UN-recognized countries have been created—South Sudan, Montenegro, and East Timor—and the rest are all essentially the same shape and size they were in the mid-1990s. By and large, a kid in 2018 could still easily depend on the book as a resource, so long as she wasn't assigned a paper on East Timor.

This level of stability is a historical anomaly. Someone who bought such a book in 1960 would have found himself continually scribbling in the margins over the next decade, trying to keep up with the wave of newly independent African states shaking off European colonialism. The first half of the twentieth century, with two world-reshaping global wars, the rise of Communism, and the slow demise of European imperialism, was not kind to writers of geographical reference books. If I'd come into possession of the encyclopedia just a few years before I did—say, in 1990—it would have been useless to me within five years as the Soviet Union splintered into fifteen independent states and Yugoslavia exploded into five.

In the early 1990s, the world was in the midst of a new springtime of nations; at the time, it certainly would have been logical to believe that nascent nations would continue breaking up "artificial" states and what remained of multinational empires into units based on ethnic self-determination. It was a time when popular opinion in the West rallied around the Dalai Lama and Tibet's independence struggle, when the Oslo Accords seemed to set in motion a process that would lead to a two-state solution for Israel and the Palestinians, when a new doctrine of humanitarian intervention was eroding traditional notions of sovereignty on behalf of threatened groups in places like Somalia and the former Yugoslavia, and when transnational human rights organizations were gaining in influence and power. While long-marginalized groups from Kurdistan to Abkhazia to Nagorno-Karabakh may have viewed these developments with excitement, for others, the emerging new world order was a cause for concern.

"The creation of new states has been so common that it is increasingly difficult to counter demands for the establishment of yet other states, especially when the demands are pressed by peoples with a high international profile," wrote Gidon Gottlieb of the Council on Foreign Relations in his 1993 book *Nation against State,* lamenting, "Many states that do not 'deserve' to be states have been created in the past few years." Going forward, he predicted a grim scenario: "Granting self-rule or statehood in a given area to most of the nations and peoples that want it now, would result in scores of new sovereign states. While the creation of some new states may be necessary or inevitable, the fragmentation of international society into hundreds of independent territorial entities is a recipe for an even more dangerous and anarchic world."[3]

The popular culture of the era reflected this mindset as well. In the classic 1992 science fiction novel *Snow Crash,* author Neal Stephenson described a near future in which the United States had been balkanized to the point that the federal government's authority extended only to its own headquarters building and most people lived in neighborhood-sized, politically autonomous, usually ethnically homogenous "burbclaves" with their own laws and security forces. (Oddly enough, Abkhazians make an appearance in *Snow Crash,* having apparently cornered the San Fernando Valley pizza delivery market in Stephenson's dystopian future.)[4]

Today, these fears seem misplaced. For all the political tumult of the last quarter century, the number, shape, and arrangement of countries on the world map has remained remarkably unchanged.

What happened to slow the process of country creation down? Since the end of the Cold War, a global norm has prevailed enforcing *cartographical stasis,* a freezing in place of the map as it existed at the end of the twentieth century. This norm prevails even as ethnic and religious conflicts rage within the countries on the map.

In fact, we can even think of the map of the world itself as an institution, an exclusive club of countries, the majority of which were created over the course of the twentieth century. The club only rarely accepts new members. Its existing members are not always friendly with one another, but they tend to follow a certain set of rules. If we imagine the map as a club, its bylaws might read as follows:

Rule 1: A country is a territory defined by borders mutually agreed upon by all countries.

Rule 2: A country must have a state that controls (or at least seeks to control) the legitimate use of force within its territory, and a population of citizens.

Rule 3: Every spot on the earth's landmass must be occupied by a country.

Rule 4: Every person on the planet must be a citizen of at least one country.

Rule 5: On paper, all countries have the same legal standing—Tuvalu has just as much right to its countryhood as China, Somalia just as much as Switzerland—even if they are politically and economically highly unequal.

Rule 6: Consent of the people within each country is preferred, but not required. Tyranny or de facto anarchy within a country is not grounds for loss of club membership.

Rule 7: Under some circumstances, one or more countries may invade or occupy another country, but not eliminate its countryhood or redraw its borders.

Rule 8: The currently existing set of countries and the borders between them should be left in place whenever possible—that is, the club prefers not to admit new members.

These "bylaws" are fairly durable and are backed to a great extent by the rules of our era's most important multinational institution, the United Nations, and the foreign-policy stances of its preeminent superpower, the United States. An enormous amount of political and military capital is invested in preserving the world map's current stasis. Sometimes, as in the First Gulf War, following Iraq's invasion of Kuwait, military force has been used to enforce the rules. But before we get to that, it's worth spending a little more time nailing down just what we mean when we talk about countries.

One universal truth in the modern world is that wherever you are on the earth's landmass, you are in a country. And while these countries differ significantly from each other, they all have fundamentally equal status as "political" units. The vast majority of humans are defined by citizenship to a particular country, whether due to an accident of birth or a conscious choice to seek naturalization.

What we're not talking about when we talk about countries, or at least not precisely, are "states" or "nations," though the three words are often used interchangeably and I will sometimes use the other two terms in this book when it's more appropriate. A state, according to

Max Weber's famous definition in his essay "Politics as a Vocation," is "a human community that (successfully) claims the monopoly of the legitimate use of physical force within a given territory."[5] That's a useful and durable definition, though minimal. The "physical force" component, expressed in some versions of the definition as "violence," gets most of the attention, though the "given territory" part is equally important, making clear that a state's political power, which "grows out of the barrel of a gun," as Mao Zedong memorably put it, has limits in physical space.[6]

Statehood also has an international legal definition, set forth in an otherwise obscure treaty called the Montevideo Convention. In 1933, the U.S. government under Franklin Roosevelt signed a treaty with the governments of Peru and Brazil upholding the "good-neighbor policy" of noninterference in the internal affairs of Latin American nations. Among its other provisions, the treaty includes a definition of a "state" as an entity possessing "(a) a permanent population; (b) a defined territory; (c) government; and (d) capacity to enter into relations with the other states."[7] Though it was never originally intended as such, the Montevideo Convention has come to serve as international law's go-to definition of statehood. It's not a document that most Americans are likely to have heard of, but in interviews for this book, officials in aspiring states including Kurdistan, Somaliland, and Abkhazia referred to these criteria unprompted to argue their case for international recognition. In fact, a number of governments that meet the criteria are not internationally recognized, including several of the examples explored in this book, but the definition works for the vast majority of states in the world. Conversely, some states still enjoy international recognition despite violating one or more of the Montevideo rules. For instance, Ukraine's government is not in full control of much of the country's land area. Syria's population has been displaced to the point that it can hardly still be considered permanent. For much of the last twenty-five years, Somalia had no central government. All are widely recognized as sovereign countries.

The idea of a "state" is easier to pin down than a "nation," which is more a cultural than political concept. Weber wrote that a nation is a "community of sentiment, which could find its adequate expression only in a state of its own, and which thus normally strives to create one."[8] A "community of sentiment" can be defined by language, religion, ethnicity, or none of the above. The political theorist Benedict Anderson described nations as "imagined communities" in his classic book of that name. Anderson argues that the ancient cultural identities that bind nations together are in fact "imaginary," in that they are often retroactively developed by elites for political or economic goals.[9] Most of these identities are far more recently created than their adherents believe.

What separates a nation from a culture or ethnic group is the aspiration for political self-determination. A people becomes a nation when it achieves political sovereignty of some form. Catalonia and the Mohawk are nations, though not independent states. A nation need not necessarily have its own politically sovereign state, but it usually strives to. This striving we call *nationalism,* defined by the philosopher Ernest Gellner as the "political principle which holds that the political and the national unit should be congruent."[10]

When nationalism is successful, resulting in what sociologist Anthony Smith calls "the conquest of the state by the nation," we refer to the resulting political form as a "nation-state." But this commonly used term has its own flaws—namely, an implication that, as Smith puts it, "a single ethnic and cultural population inhabits the boundaries of a state."[11] Only homogenous island nation-states like Iceland and Japan come close to fitting this bill, though not entirely, as the presence of the United Koreans of Japan team at ConIFA demonstrated.

The vast majority of countries have at least one significant minority group or immigrant population. Some European countries, particularly those in eastern Europe that until very recently had extremely low levels of immigration, are also fairly homogenous, though that may not last long if current rates of migration into Europe continue. Writing in the mid-1990s, Smith estimated that less than 10 percent of UN members are truly nation-states in the sense that they are overwhelmingly inhabited by a single cultural group.[12]

For the purposes of this book, I will usually call the entities we're talking about *countries*. This is both for simplicity's sake and because of the territorial connotations of the word. A country, fundamentally, is a piece of land that has been separated from the rest of the earth's landmass by political boundaries agreed upon by the world's countries as a whole. Within that piece of land, there can be democracy, tyranny, monarchy, or near anarchy, but it is still recognized as a country. These two factors, division and recognition, are what define a country as a country. What makes a country, in other words, is its place on the mutually agreed-upon map of the world.

Countries aren't merely parcels of land, of course. They also divide human beings, the economic activities they pursue, their cultural institutions, and the media they consume into separate territorial units. But while these divisions have been blurred substantially by mass migration, economic globalization, and modern communications technologies, the territorial divisions—the actual lines demarcating different realms on the physical space of the earth—have only become more fixed and unmoving. Despite decades of predictions that these territorial divisions would simply wither away into irrelevance thanks to globalization, they still play a major role in defining the lives and livelihoods of the vast majority of people on the planet.

The map of the world is still relevant and will continue to be. But current arrangement of that map is under remarkable pressure from new nationalist forces, revisionist global powers, and even the changing environment of the planet itself. We've had our current map of countries, give or take a few small changes, for more than twenty-five years, but that doesn't mean it's going to continue to persist in its current form forever.

When I first conceived of the idea for this book, years ago, it seemed like a niche topic or thought experiment. But recent events have made it far more pertinent. In February 2014, shortly after the overthrow of Ukraine's pro-Russian government, Russian special forces troops annexed the Russian-speaking peninsula of Crimea. The next month, the territory was formally annexed by Russia after a controversial referendum. In June 2014, the group once known as al-Qaeda in Iraq, rebranded as the Islamic State of Iraq and Syria (ISIS), stormed across the Iraq-Syria border, capturing a wide swathe of territory in both countries, pledging to eliminate the artificially drawn boundaries of the Middle East in order to build an apocalyptic caliphate governed under its own unforgiving and genocidal interpretation of Islamic law.

In 2015 and 2016, competition over jurisdiction of the South China Sea heated up with China's ongoing construction of artificial islands meant to extend its exclusive economic rights to disputed reefs claimed by Brunei, Malaysia, the Philippines, and Vietnam. Beijing has claimed the development of these islands has no military purpose, but satellite imagery shows the construction of airstrips on several of them.[13] The United States has objected to the island-building project, and the presence of the artificial structures has heightened the risk of confrontation between the Chinese and U.S. navies in one of the world's most volatile regions.

In June 2016, British voters shocked observers and world markets by voting narrowly to pull the United Kingdom out of the European Union. The result not only cast doubt on the future of one of the world's strongest multilateral institutions, a unique and mostly successful experiment in breaking down national borders, it also called into question the United Kingdom's own future as one country: immediately after the vote, leaders in Scotland, which had voted strongly against "Brexit," threatened to call a new referendum on withdrawing their country from the UK. Catholic leaders in Northern Ireland suggested they might reopen the question of reuniting with the Republic of Ireland, more than two decades after the region's sectarian violence mostly came to an end.

And all that was before Donald Trump arrived on the scene. At the November 10, 2015, GOP primary debate in Milwaukee, candidate Trump was asked by CNBC's Maria Bartiromo about the economic costs of his immigration plan. Trump replied, "I will tell you, we are a country of laws. We need borders." He compared his plan to build a wall between Mexico and the United States favorably to Israel's separation barrier. Pressed by Bartiromo on the economic impact of deporting 5 million people, Trump returned to the theme: "Maria, we're a country of laws. We either have a country or we *don't have a country*."[14]

The notion that being a country requires maintaining national borders and having a defined citizenry is certainly not controversial. But from Trump's statement we can infer that his notion of what a country is takes the idea to its logical extreme. The "great" nation that the president envisions is a hermetically sealed box whose borders are permeable only to those the government chooses to allow in: religious or national background are eligible criteria for exclusion. The response to danger from abroad is to "close up our borders." Trump's response to the pressures of economic globalization is old-fashioned mercantilism enforced with punitive tariffs on countries like China and Mexico that don't bow to America's interests. His repeated suggestions that the United States should have "kept the oil" in Iraq after the 2003 invasion suggest a sympathy with centuries-old notions of conquest and war spoils.

Trump's statements suggest that he does not hold the view, shared by U.S. presidents since the Second World War, that the territorial sovereignty of existing countries is an inherently important norm that warrants protection. Rather, it's something to be negotiated. As has been well covered by the media, Trump has expressed sympathy with Russian president Vladimir Putin's worldview. He has publicly suggested that Russia's widely doubted denial that it is supporting separatist rebels in eastern Ukraine is correct, and his campaign reportedly pushed to remove tough pro-Ukrainian language from the Republican Party platform in 2016.[15] Newt Gingrich, then a surrogate for the Trump campaign, even went so far before the election as to dismiss Estonia as a "suburb of St. Petersburg" when asked whether eastern European countries warranted protection from Russian aggression.[16]

After breaking precedent by taking a call from the president of Taiwan prior to his election, Trump mused that he might be open to abandoning America's long-held "one China" policy that recognizes Beijing's sovereignty over the island.[17] (He later backed down under Chinese pressure.) A few months later, he went to the opposite extreme, telling an interviewer that he had learned during a conversation with Chinese president Xi Jinping that "Korea actually used to be a part of China," a historically dubious claim that's understandably controversial in South Korea.[18]

The former senior Trump administration foreign policy advisor Sebastian Gorka, according to one report, advocated partitioning Libya into three areas based on Ottoman provinces, drawing his proposed new map on a napkin in front of an apoplectic European diplomat.[19] In December 2017, Trump announced that the U.S. government was formally recognizing Jerusalem as the capital of Israel, ending decades of formal neutrality on the disputed city's sovereignty. After a quarter century of the United States mostly fighting tooth and nail to keep international borders in place, Trump and his advisors have indicated he's open to changing them.

Judging by his shocking election victory, Trump's ultra-sovereigntist worldview obviously appealed to many voters made uneasy by the de-stabilizing impact of globalization on the American economy, the changing ethnic composition of the country as a result of immigration, and the threat (real or perceived) of nonstate entities like ISIS. This is hardly a uniquely American phenomenon. The unprecedented refugee crisis of 2015–16 vastly improved the electoral prospects of nationalist European parties from France to Germany to Hungary that cam-paigned on explicit promises to restore national sovereignty. For over half a century, the prevailing trend supported by Western governments has been that borders should gradually become more porous, allowing the flow of both capital and people, while their physical shape should be unchanged. Trump's ascendancy to the most powerful office in the world threatens to overturn both norms.

All of a sudden, stories about the control of territory and border disputes seem to be everywhere. To a greater extent than at any time since the breakup of Yugoslavia, the future shape of the map of the world is being questioned. It's looking likely that this period of stasis the world has recently enjoyed is less the endpoint of a historical pro-cess than merely a brief lull in the map's ongoing turbulence.

These developments are part of what brought me to Abkhazia and the World Football Cup. The best way to understand a system is to view it from the outside, and getting an outside perspective on the world system of countries is not easy, given that most places on earth are in some recognized country or another. It requires going to some pretty out-of-the-way places. To get a better sense of the rules that underlie the current world map and the pressures it is under, I wanted to go to the rare spots on earth where those rules don't apply, where the system breaks down—places where what country you're in is an open question. The places profiled in this book may be exceptional outliers, but perhaps those of us who live in more "normal" countries have something to learn from their position on the outer edges of the map.

This book will start with a short historical overview of how countries emerged as the predominant form of political organization on the planet and took over the world's landmass, and how Abkhazia somehow got left out of the club. Chapter 2 will look at the Mohawk community of Akwesasne, which straddles the border of the United States and Canada but is heir to a political tradition that predates both. Akwesasne has managed to survive as a very different kind of independent nation in a world system that doesn't generally tolerate difference. Chapter 3 focuses on Somaliland, a textbook "limbo world" country, autonomous and possessing all the qualities we associate with countries—and more of these, actually, than Somalia, the country it is nominally part of—but nonetheless remaining unrecognized and invisible to the outside world. If Somaliland isn't a country, a visitor is forced to ask, then what is? Chapter 4 looks at Kurdistan, perhaps the most likely to emerge as an independent country in the coming years. This case underscores the cruel absurdities of the current map of the Middle East as well as the unignorable dangers that accompany proposals for changing the status quo. Chapter 5 takes a look at Kiribati, a small island country in the Pacific whose very existence is threatened by rising sea levels, and whose people may soon face the dilemma of whether a country can continue to exist as a political unit in the absence of the physical territory it is linked to. A concluding chapter will ask whether the current age of stasis is coming to an end in the era of ISIS, Brexit, China's island building, and Trump. Interspersed with these chapters, I will profile some smaller cases of anomalous countries: an ancient Catholic order that challenges everything we think we know about sovereignty, Estonia's "e-residency" scheme, the attempts of a hardy band of libertarian dreamers to build a utopian society on unclaimed territory in the former Yugoslavia, and the challenges faced by stateless people in a world where citizenship in a country is essentially mandatory.

I don't intend to issue proposals for redrawing the world's borders—past efforts by outsiders to redraw maps in eastern Europe, the Middle East, and Africa haven't turned out so well for the people who actually live in those regions—but I do hope to illustrate both the problems with the current map and why changing it is so difficult. While some argue that countries and borders are increasingly irrelevant in an interconnected global economy—an argument that's in fact far older than the Internet, the World Trade Organization, or even the jet engine—I believe countries are and will continue to be the best protectors of the individual and collective rights of the people who live in them and the optimum system to preserve worldwide peace. But just because we need countries doesn't mean we necessarily need the current arrangement of countries or that our ideas about what countries are shouldn't be subject to question.

Rather than function as an argument for the irrelevance of the world's countries and borders, this book will, I hope, contribute to a conversation on how to make them work better for the people who live within them.

1

How Countries Conquered the World

Crossing the border into Abkhazia, viewed by most of the world's governments as a Russian-backed outlaw enclave, is not as forbidding as you might think.

The country has an airport, but Georgia doesn't permit commercial flights in or out, so the only planes that use it are Russian military transports. Travelers looking to enter are advised to choose one of two land crossings. The players and officials at the ConIFA World Football Cup crossed the internationally recognized border with Russia, a bit south of the Olympic city of Sochi. Most of the journalists covering the event, including myself, looking to avoid the expense and hassle of acquiring a double-entry Russian visa, opted for the much more controversial crossing on the Georgian side.

I reached the Inguri River, which forms the western border between Georgia and Abkhazia, on a cloudy and blustery day, feeling very much as though I had blundered into a bad Cold War spy movie. I had taken the night train from Georgia's capital, Tbilisi, two hundred miles west to the grim border town of Zugdidi, where I caught a *marshrutka,* one of the routed minibus taxis that are the preferred mode of public transportation in the Caucasus, to the border—or "the border," if you prefer. In keeping with the Georgian government's attitude toward this frontier, there's nothing along the road indicating that you're approaching an international boundary.

The marshrutka lets out at a Georgian police roadblock manned by one bored police officer and a few stray dogs. I had been advised by the organizers of the tournament not to identify myself as a journalist to the Georgian authorities and—more important—not to in any way suggest that Abkhazia is not part of Georgia. Thus as far as this gentleman was concerned, I was simply a backpacker touring the Caucasus. If the officer were to ask me why on earth an American backpacker was trying to get into Abkhazia, I was to say, "If I am in Georgia only once in my life, I want to see all of it, including Abkhazia!"

This subterfuge proved unnecessary. The Georgian police officer, seemingly drunk at 9 a.m., simply gave my passport a quick once-over and waved me through. From the checkpoint, it's about a two-kilometer walk to the potholed Inguri Bridge, where Abkhaz-controlled territory begins. Cars aren't allowed across the bridge, so horse-drawn carts are available to transport travelers and their luggage. I didn't have much baggage so opted to walk.

Cared for by neither government, the road is rapidly deteriorating. Small herds of cows wander aimlessly, oblivious to the geopolitical fault line beneath their hooves. On either side of the road, the marshy no-man's-land looks overgrown and verdant. It reminded me of how the DMZ between North and South Korea has become an unofficial wildlife refuge, used by a number of endangered bird species as an unmolested habitat.[1] In those rare spots on earth that politics prevents humans from claiming, nature stakes its own claims.

On the other side of the rusting bridge is a metal fence and a sign in three languages welcoming you to Abkhazia. Here is an inspection point run by the FSB, Russia's internal security service and one of the successor agencies of the KGB. We were shepherded into a holding area to await questioning.

The setup was sinister enough. The armed guards summoned us one by one for individual questioning in a trailer surrounded by a maze of barbed wire at the border crossing. At the back of my mind was an incident caught on video the month before in which a Georgian man was shot by border guards under mysterious circumstances.[2] But then my inquisitor, a baby-faced teenager, started quizzing me about hotel prices in the capital city of his own country, then asked for my Facebook address, and I realized that he was more interested in staving off boredom than in sussing out potential national security threats. The guard was also particularly interested in whom I had seen and what I had been asked on the other side of the bridge, as if one day an oblivious backpacker would inform him that there was a Georgian tank battalion just over the horizon preparing to roll in.

We may have been only a kilometer away from Georgia proper, but it felt like another world entirely. The vast majority of the planet is divided into well-defined and mutually recognized countries, but I had just crossed into a gray area.

Abkhazia is a distinct cultural region with its own language. It existed as a sovereign kingdom from the eighth to the eleventh century, though the degree of that kingdom's independence from Georgia is disputed. It has been under Georgian, Ottoman, and Russian rule, as well as semi-autonomous. In the mid-nineteenth century, the Russian government forcibly deported tens of thousands of Abkhazians to Turkey. During the Communist era, it was, confusingly, designated an autonomous republic within the Georgian Soviet Socialist Republic. After Georgia split from the Soviet Union in 1991, Abkhazia demanded its own independence, which resulted in a bloody civil war that ended in Abkhazia's de facto autonomy, the killing or displacement of tens of thousands of civilians, and the expulsion of nearly a quarter of a million ethnic Georgians from the territory.[3]

Abkhazia

After the 2008 war between Russia and Georgia, which took place primarily within fellow breakaway republic South Ossetia and mostly spared Abkhazia, Moscow formally recognized both regions as independent.[4] This was partly a tit-for-tat response to the U.S. recognition of Kosovo over Serbian and Russian objections. But Abkhazia has been much less successful than Kosovo in getting the acknowledgment of other governments; besides Russia, only Venezuela, Nicaragua, and Nauru recognize its independence.

Abkhazia is usually dismissed in Georgia and the West as a Russian-occupied puppet state, and there's certainly some truth to that. From the FSB officers at the border to the long train carrying tanks and artillery I saw a few days later while driving up the coast, the Russian military presence in the territory is as palpable and as highly visible as the Russian tourists who pack the beaches in the summer and the Russian businesses that dominate commerce in the major towns.

But most of the Abkhazians I spoke to were fiercely defensive of the independence that had cost so many lives, opposing integration either back into Georgia or into Russia, viewing the heavy Russian presence in the territory as a necessary evil to ward off Georgian aggression. In a 2008 poll conducted by American researchers, the overwhelming majority of Abkhazians said they favored full independence, a result that held even among ethnic Russians in the territory. This is in contrast to opinions held in South Ossetia and the Russian-supported breakaway region of Moldova, Transnistria, where strong majorities favor integration with Russia.[5] This is not to say that Abkhazians are anti-Russian, just the opposite, but they tend to bristle at the notion that they're merely a tool of Russian foreign policy.

That said, sooner or later, all conversations about Abkhazia seem to turn into conversations about Kosovo. The predominantly ethnic Albanian former Yugoslav republic that declared its independence from Serbia in 2008 and has been recognized by 114 UN member states, including the United States and most of the European Union, but *not* Russia or most of its allies, is in many ways Abkhazia's mirror image.[6] (Only the tiny Pacific island of Nauru has chosen to play both sides of the fence and recognizes both.)

For Abkhazians, the West's recognition of Kosovo against the will of Serbia and Russia while they languish in limbo because of pro-Western Georgia's objections is proof of Western hypocrisy. This was underlined a few weeks before my visit in the summer of 2016 by FIFA's decision to admit Kosovo to global soccer's premier governing body. Kosovo may still not be a UN member, thanks to Russia's veto, but clearly U.S. support gets you much closer to the table. Kosovo, which gained de facto independence after a NATO-led bombing campaign justified as a humanitarian intervention, benefited from the presence of a UN peacekeeping mission and the support of the United States and European Union. Abkhazia, on the other hand, is widely viewed outside the region as merely a Russian project propped up by Vladimir Putin to punish Georgia for defying Moscow.

"Your government is very effective. Congratulations!" then foreign minister Viacheslav Chirikba told me when I asked why more countries had not recognized Abkhazia. "Every time there's any sign of anybody looking positively toward Abkhazia, the State Department calls and threatens them with sanctions. We are on the wrong side of the barricades. We are pro-Russian and the Kosovars are pro-Western. I think it's very easy. It's a black-and-white picture." However, the former linguistics professor turned diplomat maintained, "Recognition is not critical to our welfare. We can survive without it like Taiwan and other places." Nonetheless, the disparity between the Abkhazia and Kosovo situations rankled. "We are living in a world of double standards and hypocrisy. Kosovo never had a state. Abkhazians always had some kind of nation, either independent or autonomous within another state."

Chirikba voiced a recurring theme. Wherever I went in my research for this book, I was told that the world's powers were ignoring the clear historical reality of various groups' nationhood. Where territory is concerned, the past is never past. Americans tend to scoff at these "ancient grievances," as Bill Clinton once described the motivations for violence in the Balkans.[7] This is a luxury made possible by living in a youngish country with no history of foreign occupation. But in places that feel wronged by the current map of the world, there's usually an insistence that the present predicament can't be understood without centuries or millennia of historical context.

Historical claims to any given piece of land can be impossible to adjudicate. Most patches of land on earth have been occupied by more than one group of people and many are of great historical, political, or religious significance to more than one. One man's Temple Mount is another's Noble Sanctuary.

"Abkhazia has always had a form of statehood and nationhood," Chirikba argued. "It was a kingdom, it was a principality. In Soviet times it was a republic. After the end of the war with Georgia, we became an independent state."

This rationale is a bit beside the point. Plenty of other places, from Ruthenia to Punjab, have likewise been independent at various times in their history, but it doesn't follow that they have contemporary claims to political independence. The suggestion that because a country was independent in the past it ought to be independent now ignores the myriad of potential statehoods all over the world that never came to pass.

But it is true that the current arrangement of countries on the map, despite its recent period of stasis, is not in any way natural and shouldn't be viewed as sacrosanct. It is easy to imagine the map looking quite different if a few turns of events had panned out differently. So how exactly did we end up with this particular map rather than any of the infinite alternatives? How come Georgia and Russia are countries but Abkhazia is not? And for that matter, why do we even assume that every space on earth has to be occupied by a country?

Filling in the Gaps

It's still possible, as I did several times while researching this book, to visit places where it's not quite clear what country you're in. But visiting a place that's not in a country *at all* is a lot tougher. One particularly remote slice of Antarctica is still unclaimed, but north of that, and everywhere that someone might conceivably visit or inhabit, almost every piece of land is claimed by one country or another. The map of the world is all filled in. It's been this way since February 8, 1920.

Svalbard, an archipelago in the Arctic Ocean about halfway between Norway and the North Pole, is around 23,500 square miles in area, roughly twice the size of Hawaii. Today, it's best known as the home of the Global Seed Vault, a backup repository of seed samples from around the world to be used only in case of global catastrophe.

The uninhabited islands were discovered in 1596 by the Dutch explorer Willem Barents. The area was used by British, Dutch, and Danish whalers in the seventeenth century and then by Russian and Norwegian fur trappers in the eighteenth. But by the mid-1800s the island's animal population had been badly depleted and hunting tapered off. The islands were mostly abandoned, leaving them as *terra nullius,* land claimed by no country.

The concept of terra nullius dates back to the Roman Empire. During the Crusades, the Catholic Church endorsed it as justification for seizing lands occupied by non-Christians in the Middle East. This right to conquest was put to full use by European powers in the New World during the age of exploration. In most cases, the idea of terra nullius was used to deny the sovereignty rights of the people already living in areas that had been "discovered" by Europeans, but Svalbard was a purer example: it really was uninhabited by humans, and for much of its history no humans expressed interest in inhabiting it.

That began to change in the late nineteenth and early twentieth centuries, as several European countries set up coal-mining operations on the islands. Svalbard's anomalous political status began to be seen as a problem. By this point, nearly all the rest of the world's landmass was either part of an independent nation-state or a colonial possession of one.

In 1917, future U.S. secretary of state Robert Lansing described Svalbard as "a unique international problem . . . to which a parallel will be hard to find in modern times."[8] A 1919 article published by the *Geographical Review* noted that the archipelago was "one of the last remaining territories on the face of the globe to be unclaimed by any state." The implication was that in the modern era, such an anomaly was no longer acceptable. (The article also predicted, dubiously, that the isolated, frigid archipelago "bids fair to become not only a great mining country but the grandest playground in Europe."[9] This was a little optimistic. To this day, Svalbard is home to more polar bears than people.)

On the sidelines of the 1919 Paris Peace Conference where, with the encouragement of U.S. president Woodrow Wilson, the modern nation-state was becoming a universal ideal, a commission was formed to deal with this last holdout of the pre-national world. The Spitsbergen Treaty, developed by the commission and named after the archipelago's largest island, granted Norway sovereignty over the islands so long as it preserved commercial fishing and mining rights for other countries. It's remembered today as the first legally binding treaty dealing with the administration of the Arctic.

It's also still controversial: in 2015, Norway lodged a diplomatic complaint after Dmitry Rogozin, then Russian deputy prime minister, flew to the islands, exercising what the Russian government claimed was its right under the 1920 treaty to "free access to the archipelago for signatories."[10]

But less discussed is the larger historical significance of the treaty: the elimination of the world's last significant patch of terra nullius. In *Heart of Darkness*, Joseph Conrad's narrator recalls that when he was a child, "there were many blank spaces upon the earth," including the North Pole, various places scattered about the equator, and in every sort of latitude all over the two hemispheres.[11] There may have been people living in these places, but what Conrad essentially meant was that there was still space on the earth unclaimed by countries recognized by European governments. By the time Conrad wrote the novel in 1899, those spaces were getting fewer and smaller. Today, they are all but nonexistent. Every spot on the earth's landmass, outside of Antarctica, is claimed by a country—and sometimes, as in Abkhazia, by more than one. The map is all filled in.

What Was the First Country?

So we have an approximate date of when the process of filling in the map with countries ended. When that process began is a tougher date to pinpoint. The traditional storyline is that the nation-state model was developed first in Europe and then exported to the rest of the world via colonialism. But this ignores both the premodern predecessors of contemporary countries and the fact that the countries of North and South America have proven more durable as political units than most of those making up Europe.

Governments have ruled over territory since the city-states of Sumer, in modern-day Iraq, in the fourth millennium BCE. Ancient Egypt was a unified territorial state whose people shared a government and a distinct ethnic identity.[12] Imperial Rome helped develop a concept of citizenship conferred by a government, as distinct from simple membership in an ethnic or geographical identity.[13]

We tend to think of these as "civilizations" rather than modern-style countries in which government, national identity, and citizenship are bound together. It's very difficult to know today to what extent the peasants who made up most of Egypt's population, for example, identified with the culture propagated by the religious and political authorities. A better case for premodern nationhood might be made for China, which was unified under the Qin dynasty around 221 BCE. China had a policy of universal military conscription for men as early as the second century BCE, something that wouldn't appear in Europe until the nineteenth century. By the time of the Tang dynasty (618–907 CE) China was ruled by a bureaucracy of Confucian officials whose authority and decrees spread to the farthest regions of the country.[14]

Most modern countries have little political continuity with the ancient governments that occupied their territories. Few would argue that modern Italy is the direct political successor of imperial Rome or posit a direct link from the Mayan kings to the Mexican government today.

As an illustrative point, consider the controversy in the world of archeology and antiquities over who "owns" cultural heritage. In the past few decades, conservators and archeologists have mostly worked under the model of repatriation, which holds that antiquities are the property of the state governing the territory in which they were found, a reversal of the previous practice in which antiquities were routinely removed to the country of the discoverer who dug them up. The dispute between Greece and Britain over the repatriation of the Elgin Marbles, now at the British Museum, is the most famous case. Some museum directors have pushed back against repatriation, arguing that modern nation-states should not have exclusive right to the antiquities of ancient civilizations they have little connection to, other than sharing the same physical territory.[15] In other words, why does the contemporary country we call Greece have any more right to the marbles found on the land it now inhabits than Britain? Neither country existed at the time the marbles were produced. And if modern Greece is considered the successor state to ancient Greece, should it also have claim over Greek antiquities found in contemporary Turkey? The debate reemerged when ISIS began its campaign of destruction of "un-Islamic" antiquities in Syria and Iraq, calling into question whether modern states are always the best custodians of their geographical heritage.

To avoid getting too far into the weeds, we can make a distinction between countries' geographical birthdays, meaning the earliest point at which their current core territory was a distinctive political unit not ruled by a foreign power; and their political birthdays, the point at which the government currently ruling the country came into being.

Going by the helpful index of countries' independence days in James Crawford's book *The Creation of States in International Law,* Japan is arguably the world's oldest country still existing in something resembling its original political form.[16] It has had a unified central state since around the seventh century BCE as well as a sense of cultural separateness from nearby countries. While its unity has been threatened by feudal fragmentation and civil war on numerous occasions, the emperor's authority has remained in place.[17] Japan's imperial family has ruled the country since the, perhaps mythical, Emperor Jimmu united the country in 660 BCE and his descendants still reign, even if the emperor's role is now almost purely ceremonial.

The Aksumite kingdom of Ethiopia was formed around 300 BCE, and except for a brief annexation by Italy during World War II, Ethiopia has been an independent territorial unit since then, though its monarchy was finally overthrown in a 1974 coup, so it's not exactly the same country today. The People's Republic of China was established in 1949, but there has been a distinctive country of China since the second century BCE. The modern French state was born in 1789, but on land unified by Clovis back in the sixth century CE. The Russian Federation, born out of the disintegration of the Soviet Union in 1991, is also in some sense the political successor to a country dating back to the founding of a principality in Novgorod in 862 CE.[18]

But these governments, however much they resemble modern countries in some respects, didn't recognize themselves as part of an international system of states until the modern era. The ancient Romans didn't consider the Germanic tribespeople they encountered to be citizens of a nation in the way that Romans were citizens of Rome. Likewise, the ancient Chinese never thought of themselves as a distinctive, territorially bounded country among other countries—they referred to their country as "the Middle Kingdom," believed the emperor ruled "everything under the heavens," and looked at neighboring peoples as dependents and satellites.

As noted in the introduction, what makes a country a country is, in large part, recognition by other countries. It is also recognition *of* other countries. Being a country requires having other countries to differentiate oneself from. When people talk about the nation-state system emerging in Europe at the end of the Middle Ages, what they mean is that there were a number of countries that each recognized each other's countryhood.

How Westphalian Was Westphalia?

The 1648 Peace of Westphalia is so closely identified with the idea of national sovereignty that the current international system of nation-states is often referred to as "Westphalian," and arguments periodically emerge about whether we are moving into a "post-Westphalian" era in which the sovereign nation-state is no longer the defining unit of international politics. One historian called the Peace of Westphalia "the majestic portal which leads from the old into the new world." Jean-Jacques Rousseau predicted that "the peace of Westphalia may well remain the foundation of our political system forever."[19] He may have been right about the system, but he was wrong to imply that it had anything much to do with Westphalia.

The peace, actually two treaties, one negotiated at Münster and the other at Osnabrück, brought an end to the Thirty Years' War. The destructive conflict began with the Holy Roman Emperor Ferdinand II's attempt to impose his will on his rebellious subjects in Bohemia, provoked a revolt among the Protestant imperial estates in what is now Germany, and drew in interventions on the anti-imperial side from Sweden, motivated to help fellow Protestants, and from France, intent on stirring up trouble for its imperial rival.

Neither rulers nor their subjects prior to that time conceived of the units they lived in as countries in the modern sense. Europe was divided between two Christian empires—the Catholic Church in the west and the Orthodox Church in the east—both nominally successors to the Roman Empire. The western empire was divided into various haphazardly arranged *regna*. These were not quite modern independent territorial states, nor were they merely provinces of an empire, as areas conquered by imperial Rome had been. They were something in between.[20] Governmental authority was divided between royal families and church authorities. Authorities overlapped between regions, particular rulers could hold multiple offices in different territories, and their holdings were often not geographically contiguous.

Alliances were often cemented through marriages within the nobility, and connections between rulers and the nationality of their subjects could be tenuous. For example, the kings and queens of England haven't really been "English" in the ethnic sense for centuries. The ruler of Denmark could be a hereditary king in one part of his realm but merely an elected duke in other parts. The king of Prussia could be both an absolute ruler of his territory and a vassal of the Holy Roman Empire. Many rulers took to adding "etc." to the end of their titles just to be sure they didn't miss anything.

What did all this mean for the lands these kings ruled and the people who lived in them? Although the seventeenth-century king of Spain was also the king of Portugal, Naples, and Sicily as well as the duke of Milan and Burgundy, this doesn't imply these territories were all one state. Travelers from Lisbon to Barcelona at that time would need a separate passport for each kingdom they passed through along the way, even though they technically never left the dominion of the king of Spain. The king himself had to contend with the influence of local nobles, who could form alliances with foreign governments or rebel against him. The historian Derek Croxton likens Europe's political arrangement at the time to the "EU in reverse": "In the EU countries share a common currency, a free trade zone, and a common immigration policy, but retain their own rules, armies and foreign policies. The Spanish monarchy was the opposite: each part had its protectionist trade policies and rules about who could serve in public offices, but they all shared a common military, foreign policy, and, of course, king."[21]

For the people who lived in these realms, the notion of nationality existed with a "fluidity which is startling to the modern mind," as C. V. Wedgwood writes. "No one thought it strange that a French soldier should command an army against the French and loyalty to a cause, to a religion, to a master, was commonly more highly esteemed than loyalty to a country."[22]

Before the seventeenth century, ordinary people in the countryside, where most people lived, generally spoke local vernacular languages, separating them from their rulers, who generally spoke Latin. Above all was a centralized church, headed by the bishop of Rome, and the emperor, who ruled over all Christendom, at least in western Europe. Political and religious authority were not sharply differentiated.

To be sure, there were emerging national identities. The English and French in particular thought of themselves as distinct from other

Europeans. But these nations weren't political constructs in the way they are today. While today, even the harshest dictatorships claim to rule at the behest—or at least with the consent—of their people, at that time, it was taken for granted that the state was the possession of its ruler.

But by the time of the Thirty Years' War, this had already been shifting for some time. This process included the emergence of independent city-states on the Italian peninsula during the Renaissance of the fourteenth and fifteenth centuries, perhaps the first entities to conduct what we might call "foreign policy" in that they formalized relations with each other by maintaining permanent ambassadors to each other's governments. Challenges to the authority of the church pushed things along further. In 1534, Henry VIII broke England away from the Catholic Church. At the same time, regna within what is now Germany were converting to Protestantism, challenging the authority of the empire and leading to several violent conflicts. By 1555, at the Peace of Augsburg, German Catholics and Protestants accepted the principle of *cujus regio, eius religio* (whose realm, his religion), allowing state governments to choose the religion to be practiced within their territory and forbidding intervention on religious grounds. The doctrine not only placed the secular government's authority above that of the church in matters of war and peace, it suggested that the religious identity of a given realm was synonymous with that of its rulers.

In the Peace of Westphalia, the empire recognized the independence of two nonmonarchial states—Switzerland and the Netherlands—and affirmed the religious liberties of the German estates. By the traditional accounting, this marked the inflection point after which nation-states became both the sole meaningful domestic power within their own territory and the most significant units in international politics.

This is a retroactive interpretation that would have surprised the authors of the Peace of Westphalia. Neither of the treaties contains the world *sovereignty,* which didn't even exist in Latin, the language in which they were written. For about 250 years after their signing, the treaties' importance was viewed mostly in terms of religious freedom. Croxton suggests that the French anarchist philosopher Pierre-Joseph Proudhon may have been the first to argue, in the 1860s, that the modern concept of sovereignty originated at Westphalia, but the idea of a "Westphalian" world didn't gain wide currency until the twentieth century. "The Peace of Westphalia did not . . . make any special point about the independence of kings and republics from Imperial authority, because it didn't need to; their independence was already assumed in both theory and practice," writes Croxton.[23] Even after Westphalia, the "Imperial Estates" of Germany remained just that, constituent parts of the empire, and the emperor continued to wield meaningful political power until 1806—even declaring war against France in 1647—though his power was never as centralized as that of modern heads of state.

By the eighteenth century, though the Holy Roman Empire would still nominally exist for another few decades, it was generally recognized that Europe was composed of sovereign independent countries, meaning they were entitled to the administration of their own territory and recognition by others. But units that we would today recognize as countries along the modern model still existed only in western Europe, comprising about 2 percent of the world's landmass.[24] Eastern Europe was still largely dominated by large multinational empires: the Austro-Hungarian, Ottoman, and Russian. While Westphalia may have developed the doctrine of sovereignty within the European context, it also reinforced the notion of the superiority of Christian civilization.[25] In the years to come, European colonialism in the Western Hemisphere, Africa, and Asia would be justified on the grounds that non-Christian peoples were unfit to exercise sovereignty.

Importantly, the countries that first developed as cohesive nation-states were those that built the most expansive global empires—Britain, France, Portugal, Spain, and the Netherlands. And it was in their colonies, inspired in part by ideas unwittingly exported by them, that the first great wave of country creation took place.

Made in America

"I've never seen the sea," Wilmer Camargo, an eighteen-year-old sailor in the Bolivian Navy, told the *Guardian* in 2008. "But when I do, I would like it to be a Bolivian sea."[26] Bolivia is landlocked: it lost its access to the Pacific Ocean in an 1879–84 war with Chile. But it maintains a navy of small patrol boats and catamarans on inland Lake Titicaca as a symbolic reminder of its desire to reacquire its coast. (In 2010, Peruvian president Alan Garcia granted the Bolivian Navy use of a dock.)[27]

Bolivia's yearning for the sea is a rare example of a desire for expansionism in a hemisphere where, in spite of no small amount of political turmoil, borders have been remarkably stable, in the geographical sense, for centuries. Since the period when Bolivia lost its coast, the map of South and North America has looked basically the same, even as the world across the Atlantic has blown itself apart and put itself together again multiple times.

What happened in North and South America between 1776 and 1825 was different than the slow process of national consolidation happening in Europe: it was the first major wave of new countries declaring their independence. For the most part, the modern nations making up the Western Hemisphere emerged in their current forms and shapes before nationalism even became a potent political force in Europe.[28]

The colonists, at least among the societal elite, didn't differ from the colonial powers in the language they spoke—English, Spanish Portuguese, or French. And most of the countries of Latin America didn't differ from each other in that regard. They certainly didn't have ancient cultural histories to draw on. Their claims to sovereignty were based on the radical new notion of "consent of the governed"; as the American Declaration of Independence puts it, "Whenever any Form of Government becomes destructive of these ends, it is the Right of the People to alter or to abolish it."

The thirteen colonies along the Eastern Seaboard of North America were first out of the gate, declaring independence from Britain in 1776, though it wasn't until the 1780s that the new country's independence was internationally recognized and its current form of government agreed upon.

Fifteen years after the U.S. declaration, inspired in part by the egalitarian rhetoric of the French Revolution, the enslaved inhabitants of the French Caribbean colony of Saint-Domingue rose up against their colonial rulers. By 1804, the movement's leaders had beaten back French attempts to retake the colony, declaring the independence of the new country of Haiti.

In South America, by the eighteenth century Spain had divided its vast territorial holdings into separate administrative units for practical purposes. These units were, counterproductively, prohibited from trading with each other. Over time, these territories, which had been formed for the purpose of exploitation by a European power, came to conceive of themselves as countries. In 1810, the colonial administration was overthrown by Simón Bolívar's revolution in Venezuela. Argentina, Colombia, Mexico, Paraguay, Chile, and Peru would quickly follow suit. Brazil was independent from Portugal by 1822.[29] The short-lived states of Gran Colombia and the Federal Republic of Central America came to an end by the mid-nineteenth century, and by that time the current borders of the Western Hemisphere were in place, with a couple of exceptions. Panama didn't become independent from Colombia until the twentieth century. Canada didn't reach its full autonomy from Great Britain until 1931. Colonialism took much longer to release its hold on the islands of the Caribbean, some of which are still under European administration today. It would also take until roughly the 1850s for the United States to encompass its current territory, extending its formal control to the Pacific.

The independence movements of South America in the nineteenth century presaged twentieth-century independence movements by their general adherence to the principle of *uti possidetis* by which each nation was to preserve the territorial status quo of 1810, the year when the movement for independence had been inaugurated.[30] Border wars were common during the nineteenth century, including a particularly devastating one between Paraguay and the triple alliance of Argentina, Brazil, and Uruguay in the 1860s, but the countries that were there at independence are still by and large the same.

Nationalism

In nineteenth-century Europe the developing norm of sovereignty—the notion that the state is the sole source of legitimate authority within a given territory—evolved into something resembling our modern conception of countries, thanks to the influence of nationalism, defined by Gellner as "a theory of political legitimacy, which requires that ethnic boundaries should not cut across political ones."[31] In other words, a people united by common culture, language, or ethnicity ought to have a territorial state of its own and its members should not be outside that territory.

The rise of nationalism can be ascribed to a number of factors, including the ideals of the French Revolution, the need for mass mobilization in response to Napoleon's revolutionary wars, the spread of literacy and a popular press that united populations under a common language and culture, the centralizing effect of industrialization, and the growth of government bureaucracies. Hannah Arendt describes this as the historical moment "when the French Revolution combined the declaration of the Rights of Man with the demand for national sovereignty."[32]

In some cases, nationalism spurred the unification of territories inhabited by culturally similar people: by the 1870s, both Italy and Germany were united under central governments. In other cases, the centralizing control of multinational empires was weakened. Greece, Romania, and Bulgaria won autonomy from the declining Ottoman Empire. Hungary and Austria became separate semiautonomous kingdoms under Habsburg rule.

The borders of Europe were in rapid flux during this time, but it was also during this era that the principles underlying the age of stasis started to develop. Nationalism builds a link between cultural identity and geographical territory—blood and soil. Nationalism gave the people of any given nation a stake in the country that existed there. As John Stuart Mill wrote in 1861: "When the sentiment of nationality exists in any force, there is a prima facie case for uniting all the members of the nationality under the same government, and a government to themselves apart. This is merely saying that the question of government ought to be decided by the governed."[33] People who believe they have a stake in who governs them are less likely to acquiesce to the land they live on being traded like poker chips among feuding nobles.

Exporting the Map

In the eighteenth and nineteenth centuries, even as they were themselves forming into something resembling the nation-states we know today, European powers continued the work of extending a system of mutually recognizing countries over the entirety of the earth's landmass, sowing the seeds of new nations that wouldn't emerge until the mid-twentieth century. European colonialists of the time certainly wouldn't have had any concept that this was what they were doing, and in fact much of the early work of colonization was done not by governments but by private entities. In 1765, the Mughal emperor Shah Alam surrendered to forces under the command of the East India Company, transferring tax-collecting power to the privately held British corporation. By the beginning of the nineteenth century, nearly all of present-day India was effectively governed from a boardroom in the city of London. The British Crown assumed direct control of the territory in 1858.[34]

Similarly, the Dutch East India Company, often considered the first multinational corporation in the world, controlled the lucrative spice trade and effectively governed present-day Indonesia throughout the seventeenth and eighteenth centuries until the Dutch Republic assumed control in 1799. While there is a great deal of discussion today about the challenge posed by the power of corporations to state sovereignty, there's little in the modern world to rival the vast territorial and political power enjoyed by these early multinationals. This sort of arrangement was much less common by the end of the nineteenth century, when direct political rule of territory in Africa and Asia from capitals in Europe was becoming the norm. (One strange and notable exception was the Congo, a free state under the despotic personal rule of Belgium's King Leopold II rather than a formal Belgian colony.)

By the nineteenth century, most of Southern and Southeast Asia was under the control of European governments ruling the territory as overseas colonies. The few countries that remained independent, notably Siam—now Thailand—did so in part by emulating the European nation-state model, building a centralized political and military bureaucracy and promoting use of a common language.[35]

The European conquest of Africa had begun in the late sixteenth century, but for centuries, European activities, mostly centered on trading slaves and commodities, were confined to small coastal outposts and a few strategically important colonies like Algeria and South Africa. As late as the 1870s, when David Livingstone made his famous journeys into central and southern Africa, only 10 percent of the continent was under direct colonial rule, and Africa's interior was considered inaccessible and unknowable by Europeans. But driven by the need for natural resources and taking advantage of greater opportunities afforded by technological and medical advances, European colonists quickly made up for lost time. By 1900, five rival nations—Germany, Italy, Portugal, France, and Britain—as well as one historically ambitious individual, King Leopold II—had colonized 90 percent of the continent, dividing among them 10 million square miles of territory, home to more than 110 million people.[36] Only the kingdom of Ethiopia and Liberia, which had been settled by African American slaves in the early nineteenth century, avoided foreign rule.

Justifying this conquest by the three Cs—Christianity, civilization, and commerce—Europeans didn't give much thought to the sovereignty of whatever governing structures were already on the ground. The legal justifications for this went back to the first age of exploration. In 1455, Pope Nicholas V had approved Portugal's claims to territory on the west coast of Africa under what came to be known as the "doctrine of discovery," the right of Europeans to claim land in the non-Christian world. The doctrine continued to be cited through the nineteenth century and has had a strange afterlife: oddly enough, it was cited in a footnote by U.S. Supreme Court justice Ruth Bader Ginsburg in a 2005 opinion pertaining to the sovereignty of land purchased by an American Indian tribe.[37]

The doctrine was never applied universally, however. European states signed treaties with non-Christian governments in both Asia and Africa, including Morocco, Zanzibar, and the Zulu Empire, though they certainly didn't apply the same rules that obtained in dealing with other European states.[38] After the Berlin Africa Conference of 1884–85, a meeting of European colonizers was convened by German chancellor Otto von Bismarck to set ground rules for the colonization of the continent, the European powers generally recognized each other's claims to territory. European-recognized political sovereignty had come to Africa.

By the end of the nineteenth century, nearly all the world was under the control of European-recognized governments. Conrad's "blank spaces" had been filled in. This is obviously a Eurocentric way of looking at the history of political geography: the history of nations as viewed from map rooms in London, Brussels, and Berlin. But it was this period of colonial expansion, and the lines that European governments drew in Asia and Africa, that formed the basis of the countries that occupy those regions today. The lines drawn in European capitals in the late nineteenth century were, in many parts of the world, the ones that stuck.

However, it was not European powers but the early twentieth century's rising superpower, the United States, that would set the next wave of country creation in motion.

The Wilsonian Dream

On January 8, 1918, less than a year after the United States entered World War I, abandoning years of official neutrality, U.S. president Woodrow Wilson spoke before a joint session of Congress to present his vision for a postwar settlement that would prevent the outbreak of another war. The fourteen points Wilson presented that day proposed a startling new vision of how states would conduct business in the postwar era.

The first four points were boilerplate, calling for diplomacy to be conducted in the open without secrecy, the assurance of freedom of navigation, the removal of barriers to trade, and a reasonable reduction of armaments. Things started to get a little more interesting around point 5, which called for: "a free, open-minded, and absolutely impartial adjustment of all colonial claims, based upon a strict observance of the principle that in determining all such questions of sovereignty the interests of the populations concerned must have equal weight with the equitable claims of the government whose title is to be determined." In points 6 through 13, Wilson got specific, proposing the evacuation of Russian territory, restoration of the nations of Belgium, Romania, Serbia, Montenegro, and the invaded portions of France, the establishment of an independent Poland, the readjustment of Italy's borders "along clearly recognizable lines of nationality," and for the various peoples of the Austro-Hungarian Empire to be "accorded the freest opportunity to autonomous development." Perhaps most consequentially for future political events, Wilson stipulated the autonomy of the non-Turkish nationalities of the Ottoman Empire—much of the Middle East at the time. In his final point, he called for the establishment of a "general association of nations . . . for the purpose of affording mutual guarantees of political independence."[39] The speech was, as Henry Kissinger has written, a message to European powers that "the international system should be based not on the balance of power but on ethnic self-determination."[40]

In December 1918, with the war won thanks in part to the contribution of U.S. military might, Wilson set sail for Paris to try to make his new vision for the world a reality. He was largely unsuccessful in his aims in 1919. While he had hoped to establish a "peace without victory," the punitive terms enforced upon Germany virtually assured future conflict. His boldest vision, the League of Nations, was crippled at birth by the fact that, thanks to a hostile U.S. Senate, the United States never joined it.

But Wilson's vision of nation-states based on ethnic self-determination had an impact far beyond what he ever intended. As historian Erez Manela writes, Wilson "launched the transformation of the norms and standards of international relations that established the self-determining nation-state as the only legitimate political form throughout the globe, as colonized and marginalized peoples demanded and eventually attained recognition as sovereign independent actors in international society."[41] The fourteen points were published throughout the world, causing a sensation in places ranging from India to Egypt to China. The president "ceased to be a common statesman; he became a messiah. Millions believed him as the bringer of untold blessings," wrote H. G. Wells in *The Shape of Things to Come*. Wilson himself was uneasy with the expectations his call for self-determination had created. "I am wondering whether you have not unconsciously spun a net for me from which there is no escape," he remarked to his propaganda chief George Creel on the way to Paris.[42]

America's twenty-eighth president was an unlikely messenger for the cause of national liberation, particularly for non-Western peoples. The southern-bred Wilson was an inveterate racist whose administration introduced segregation in government offices. For this reason, in

2015, students at his alma mater, Princeton, demonstrated to demand, unsuccessfully, that his name be removed from the Woodrow Wilson School of Public and International Affairs, one of America's top foreign-policy graduate programs.[43] The pioneering black journalist William Monroe Trotter, whom Wilson famously had removed from the White House in 1914 during a contentious meeting to discuss Jim Crow laws, tried to use Wilson's language of ethnic self-determination to win rights for African Americans. When he attempted to travel to the Paris conference to press his case, he was denied a visa by Wilson's State Department; Trotter was forced to work as a cook on board a transatlantic steamer in order to get there.

There's little evidence to suggest Wilson ever meant "consent of the governed" to apply to non-Europeans. When it came to America's own recently acquired colonial holdings in the Philippines, he argued that "the consent of the Filipinos and the 'consent' of the American colonists to government, for example, are two radically different things." He believed that the United States should follow in the tradition of British colonialism in helping "less civilized" peoples achieve the "habit of law and obedience."[44]

Wilson was also a pioneer in the controversial practice of "regime change," deploying U.S. troops to Mexico in 1914 to foment the overthrow of dictator Victoriano Huerta. He sent U.S. Marines to Haiti a year later to protect U.S. business interests, beginning a brutal two-decade occupation of the country.[45]

From the beginning, the problems with the idea of self-determination were evident. "When the president talks of 'self determination,' what unit has he in mind? Does he mean a race, a territorial area, or a community? It will raise hopes which can never be realized. It will, I fear, cost thousands of lives," vented Secretary of State Robert Lansing in frustration.[46] The main difficulty of self-determination was, as it would continue to be through the conflicts of today, the presence of minorities. With the exception of homogenous islands like Iceland or Japan, "peoples," however they define themselves, don't settle in geographically distinct units. Yes, you can draw a line around areas where one group or another predominates, but some members of some groups are always going to end up on the other side of the line, whether they're Romanians in Hungary, Serbs in Croatia, or Russians in Ukraine. And under the principle of nationalism, elevated to a universal doctrine by Wilson's fourteen points, those peoples can reasonably ask why they're not united in one state. This comes into conflict with the norm of state sovereignty, under which most national governments would do almost anything to avoid giving away territory, either to a neighboring state or a newly formed one. And that's not even addressing the problem of peoples *without* territorial states—Jews before the establishment of Israel and Kurds, for example—who in the new order found themselves alienated in a world of countries constructed on the basis of ethnic identities they could never be part of.

At the peace conference, it proved impossible to sort out nationalist claims in the Balkans and eastern Europe. Newly emergent states like Greece and Poland showed themselves adept at using the language of self-determination to expand their territorial claims as much as possible. The awarding of Turkish territory to Greece in particular would turn out to have dramatic consequences for the future of the Middle East. At the end of the conference, some 30 million people in Europe alone found themselves in countries where they were the ethnic minority by the borders drawn.[47] New creations like Czechoslovakia and Yugoslavia were, as their compound names suggest, about as artificial as could be under the criteria put forward by Wilson. The Middle Eastern territories of the Ottoman Empire were divided into spheres of influence by European powers, creating problematic borders that are still the source of instability and violence today. For all Wilson's attachment to the notion of self-determination, he was willing to allow Japan to continue occupying territory in China, a decision that would prove fateful in the lead-up to the next world war.

Wilson may have rewritten the rules of diplomacy, further making the nation-state the basic unit of international politics. But it still wasn't clear exactly what a nation or a state should look like.

The Defeat of Anarchy

World War II was the last time the world of countries faced a major threat: in the form of a Nazi empire that attempted not only to redraw the borders of Europe but to undermine the very concept of statehood, viewing it as a misguided Jewish construct preventing the German *volk* from achieving its racial destiny. "The epoch of statehood has come to an end," wrote the German legal theorist Carl Schmitt, whose work was popular among Nazi leaders. Nazi ideology disparaged "the empty concept of state territory," viewing geopolitics as a zero-sum competition between races for scarce natural resources.[48] In the process of enacting this vision, the Third Reich obliterated the countries of Czechoslovakia, Austria, Poland, and Yugoslavia and plunged the western Soviet Union into a state of anarchy. Meanwhile, the Nazi-allied empire of Japan attempted to redraw the map of Asia, occupying territory including the modern states of Indonesia, the Philippines, Malaysia, Thailand, Vietnam, and Myanmar as well as China, where it formed the puppet state Manchukuo in the northeast from 1932 until 1945.

After the Axis was defeated, the victorious powers moved aggressively to restore the map as it had existed before the war. Countries that had been annexed by Germany and its allies, including Austria,

Czechoslovakia, Poland, China, and Ethiopia, were restored to their sovereignty, with the Allies taking the position that legally speaking, these countries had never ceased to exist but had merely been occupied by a hostile power.[49] Notable exceptions were the Baltic countries, which had been independent for the twenty-two years between the two world wars but then occupied by the Soviet Union under the Molotov-Ribbentrop Pact with Nazi Germany. Though the alliance with the Nazis would be short-lived, Joseph Stalin still declined to grant the countries their independence after the war. Soviet control of the Baltics, which would continue until the early 1990s, was never legally recognized by a number of countries, including the United States and Britain.

After the war, the Munich Agreement of 1938, in which the European powers had acquiesced to Hitler's annexation of Czechoslovakia's Sudetenland, came to be viewed as the textbook example of appeasement, invoked again and again in the years to follow as a cautionary tale to deter any accommodation of authoritarian regimes. In the postwar era, global norms shifted decidedly against the redrawing of borders, norms that were reflected in the charter of the new global multilateral organization, the United Nations.

The stated purpose of the United Nations, founded in 1945, is to "develop friendly relations among nations based on respect for the principle of equal rights and self-determination of peoples." Its charter explicitly forbids "the threat or use of force against the territorial integrity or political independence of any state."[50]

In the postwar years, UN membership became a kind of gold standard for statehood, proof that one really belonged in the community of countries. At its founding, the body had fifty-one members. How it grew to nearly two hundred is the story of decolonization, the largest wave of country creation in history.[51]

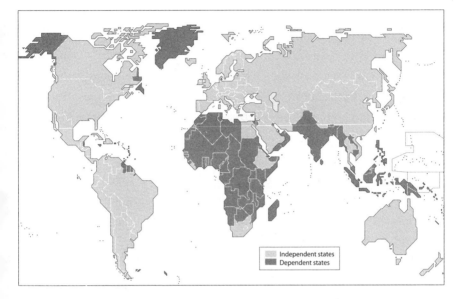

*Independent and dependent countries in 1945, based on a
United Nations map*

The Springtime of Nations

On August 17, 1945, the nationalist leader Sukarno read out a proclamation declaring the independence of Indonesia. As the proclamation's vague phrasing—"Matters relating to the transfer of power etc. will be executed carefully and as soon as possible"—indicated, it was a somewhat ad hoc affair taking advantage of a brief power vacuum following the surrender two days earlier of Japan, which had occupied the former Netherlands East Indies since 1942, and before the Dutch had a chance to try to reassert control, though Amsterdam wouldn't formally recognize the new nation's independence until 1949. It was an unlikely country, comprising more than thirteen thousand islands, over three hundred ethnic groups, seven hundred languages, and six officially recognized religions.[52]

These diverse islands have no reason to exist as one unified country except for the fact that they were all colonized by the same nation—with the exception of Portuguese East Timor, which would become problematic in the years to come. The national borders that divide the Indonesian side of the island of Papua from Papua New Guinea, and Indonesia from Malaysia and Brunei on the island of Borneo, correspond with the demarcations between Dutch and British colonial territory rather than any particular cultural difference. Indonesia is the textbook example of what Benedict Anderson called an "imagined community," a national identity forged by governing elites through the mass media, a centralizing bureaucracy, and the promotion of a national language, Bahasa Indonesia.

Indonesia wasn't the first colonial country to shake off its colonizers in the twentieth century. That was Ireland in 1939. Egypt, Jordan, Iraq, and the Philippines were nominally independent but then reoccupied during the war.[53] But the war changed everything, setting in motion the inexorable decline of Europe's empires throughout the Global South.

Sukarno's declaration was the starting gun of the process. The following month, Vietnam declared independence from France, taking advantage of a similar post-Japanese power vacuum, but the French held on longer than the Dutch, setting the stage for three decades of conflict that ended only with the last U.S. helicopters pulling out of Saigon in 1975. In 1947 and 1948, Britain's vast imperial holdings in South Asia would become the new countries of India, Pakistan, Myanmar, and Sri Lanka. In 1948, the UN voted to recognize the new state of Israel.

In Africa, the northern countries of Libya, Sudan, Morocco, and Tunisia were first out of the gate, severing their ties with Europe between 1951 and 1956. The British Gold Coast was the first sub-Saharan colony to declare independence, becoming the new country of Ghana in 1957. The year 1960 alone saw the creation of sixteen new African countries, mainly former colonies of France.

Altogether, between Sukarno's declaration and 1986, when the new countries of the Marshall Islands and Micronesia were created from former colonies of Britain and the United States respectively, ninety-four new countries were born, the vast majority of them former European colonies in Africa, Asia, the Middle East, the Caribbean, and the Pacific. The number of countries in the world had nearly tripled.[54]

The Indonesia declaration was also a precedent in that, for the most part, rather than creating entirely new territorial countries based on the cultural composition of people living there, as Wilson had proposed for Europe following World War I, the new countries of the later twentieth century were based on the borders that had formerly delineated European colonies. This was deliberate.

The decolonization wave may have created dozens of newly independent countries in what was then called the Third World, but these countries were overwhelmingly based on lines drawn up in Berlin or Paris decades earlier. These borders may have been drawn without the consultation of the people who lived within them, but from 1945 onward, the governments of what became known as the developing world have mostly demanded that they remain as they are.

The Last Countries

The end of the Cold War and the collapse of global Communism brought about the final wave of country creation. The year 1990 saw the reunification of Germany after the fall of the Berlin Wall. The Baltic countries, whose annexation by the Soviet Union during World

War II had never formally been recognized by some Western powers, took advantage of the liberalized politics of the final days of Communism to pass resolutions reasserting their sovereignty. The following year, the Soviet Union split apart into fifteen independent countries.

Meanwhile, in Yugoslavia, the multiethnic confederation held together for decades under Josip Broz Tito's rule began its bloody disintegration with the unilateral secession of Slovenia and Croatia. A brutal war in predominantly Serb areas of Croatia and ethnically mixed Bosnia followed. The bloodshed wouldn't end until the conclusion of the Kosovo War and the NATO bombing of Serbia in the late 1990s. Macedonia as well as Bosnia and Herzegovina would emerge from the war as independent countries. Montenegro and the partially recognized Kosovo would split off from Serbia later on.

In 1993, the peaceful "Velvet Divorce" resulted in the separation of Slovakia and the Czech Republic. Both Czechoslovakia and Yugoslavia were synthetic multinational constructs set up in the wake of World War I. The Soviet Union, meanwhile, was the last of the world's great territorial empires, the successor to the territory controlled by the czars, covering one-sixth of the earth's landmass.

A few more countries came along in the years that followed. After long civil wars originating in the Cold War era, Eritrea won its independence from Ethiopia in 1993, East Timor from Indonesia in 2002, and South Sudan from Sudan in 2011. The map settled into stasis.

The reasons for avoiding more adjustments to the map are understandable: borders are rarely changed without killing. But it's a raw deal for countries that missed the previous waves of country creation. The preservation of borders, whether in Iraq, Ukraine, or the Caucasus, has come to be viewed as a good in and of itself. Places like Abkhazia, without international support, will have an awfully hard time becoming anything more than breakaway pseudo-states. In short, if you hadn't created your country by the early 1990s, you were out of luck.

The Specter of Nationalism

Though war and nearly a quarter century of economic stagnation and neglect have left the Abkhaz capital, Sukhumi, the worse for wear, the city's appeal is still apparent, particularly the seafront promenade dominated by the pre-Soviet Hotel Ritsa. It's not hard to imagine the thriving seaside resort area that Abkhazia was throughout czarist and Soviet times, though there are still bombed-out structures and empty buildings everywhere. The effect is something like if the Jersey Shore were subjected to months of heavy aerial bombardment and then left to decay for twenty years, but people were still vacationing there.

Reminders of the war are everywhere. At a roadside memorial on a winding mountain, my cab driver stopped the car to drink a toast of sweet Abkhaz wine to the country's war dead, including one of his cousins, whose name was inscribed upon the statue. From the gleaming new football stadium in Sukhumi where the ConIFA World Cup took place, you could see the hulking remains of Abkhazia's Soviet parliament building, bombed by the Georgians during the war and left in ruins as a kind of national symbol. The fencing is not particularly effective, and you can wander through the building, discovering artifacts like a melted typewriter and Russian-language manuals for the masses of Soviet bureaucrats who once toiled inside.

Violence has sporadically flared up in Abkhazia since the First World War. Abkhaz elites had been pushing for independence throughout the Communist period, when the region had special and somewhat unclear administrative status within Soviet Georgia. It seems a strange setting for an ethnic conflict: Abkhazians, like Georgians, are Orthodox Christians and both have a history of grievance against Russia. But divisions between the groups grew up in the waning days of the Cold War as a newly vocal and highly nationalist Georgian government demanded independence. Already marginalized in the Soviet Union, Abkhaz leaders feared even worse treatment under an independent Georgia.

Who exactly started the war is still debated, but by the end of 1993 Abkhaz militias backed by Russia had pushed Georgian forces across the Inguri River, where I crossed twenty-four years later, and the area settled into a frozen conflict.

As the Abkhaz—as well as the Chechens, Ossetians, and others—learned, the international community's support for the peoples of the Soviet Empire throwing off the yoke of Moscow's domination had its limits. After all, supporting the sovereignty of every nationality and ethnic group from Vilnius to Vladivostok would be a recipe for endless secessionism and conflict. The world recognized the independence of the fifteen countries that had formerly been Soviet socialist republics, and that was as far as the division was allowed to go. If you found yourself on the wrong side of a previously insignificant national border, that was simply too bad. As Vladimir Putin would put it in a 2014 speech justifying the annexation of Crimea, "Millions of people went to bed in one country and awoke in different ones, overnight becoming ethnic minorities in former Union republics."[55]

The historian Charles King writes, "The post-Soviet order in the Caucasus was not the natural outcome of individual nations striving for independence but rather a reflection of the international community's capacity to tolerate one kind of secessionist but not another." Some states, such as Armenia, Azerbaijan, and Georgia, were "legitimated through international recognition and membership in multilateral organizations," whereas the unrecognized states were "viewed by outsiders as desperate attempts to rationalize the whims of separatists," even if they often functioned just as well as the recognized countries."[56] In other words, some countries are more equal than others.

The eeriest reminder of the war in Abkhazia may be the blocks and blocks of Communist-era apartment buildings that sit moldering on the outskirts of Sukhumi and particularly in the areas near the border, where the Georgian population had once been heaviest. The territory as a whole feels oddly underpopulated today, which shouldn't be a surprise. Abkhazians were a minority in their own territory: only 18 percent of the population in 1989, the result of centuries of czarist expulsions and Soviet social policies that encouraged Georgians to move to the area.[57] Human Rights Watch estimates some two hundred thousand Georgians fled Abkhazia during the war, effectively ethnically cleansing the territory.[58]

The empty buildings illustrate an uncomfortable truth about the age of stasis: its current stability is underwritten to large extent by a century of mass murder. Ethnic and religious nationalists in culturally divided countries like Iraq, or for that matter Belgium, often refer to their countries as "artificial," meaning that the borders were thrown tougher without regard to the composition of the people living within them. But this doesn't mean there's something "natural" about more ethnically homogenous countries. More than likely they got that way through a process of ethnic cleansing and genocide.

By the time Wilson put forward the notion of dividing the Ottoman and Austro-Hungarian Empires into self-determined ethnic nation-states, a long and violent process of creating those states was already under way, a process that accelerated in the years following his declaration. Some of the episodes are well known—the Armenian genocide, the Holocaust, the civil wars of the Balkans in the 1990s—but the long history of ethnic cleansing, defined by the UN in the context of Yugoslavia as "rendering an area ethnically homogenous by using force or intimidation to remove persons of given groups from the area," has been far longer and wider ranging than these examples show.[59]

This process began decades earlier. The Russian city of Sochi, just north of Abkhazia, where Vladimir Putin's government held the 2014 Olympics as a celebration of renewed Russian nationalism, was once dominated by Sunni Muslim Circassians, a group that had the unfortunate luck of living in the Caucasus between two expansionist empires, the Russians and the Ottomans. During the 1853–56 Crimean War, the British government, then allied with Turkey, encouraged the Circassians to rebel. They did so, anticipating a military intervention on their behalf that never arrived—a fate familiar to the Kurds and other more recent victims of mass atrocities. After the war, the Russian government began a process of forcibly relocating the Circassians to Turkey, destroying their villages and driving them to the coast, where they were loaded onto ships at Sochi. Around 625,000 people were killed. More than a century later the Olympics were held on the site of what some scholars argue was one of the first modern genocides.[60]

The rise of nationalism in the late nineteenth century in the Balkans saw the collapse of Ottoman rule and the creation of countries including Greece, Serbia, and Bulgaria, but also the mass expulsion of Muslim civilians as well as other minorities. The new nationalism that roiled the region was in some cases the result of racist laws during peacetime—the new Romanian state specifically excluded Jews from citizenship rights. In other cases, ethnic cleansing took place in the context of war or its immediate aftermath. The repelled Greek invasion of Anatolia following World War I led to the expulsion of thousands of

Greeks from modern-day Turkey. After World War II, 12 to 14 million ethnic Germans fled or were transferred from countries including Poland, Ukraine, and Czechoslovakia.[61]

The effects of these decades of population transfers are evident in cities like Thessaloniki, once known as Salonika. Today, it's the second-largest city in the modern nation of Greece, but it's also the hometown of the father of modern Turkey, Mustafa Kemal Atatürk, and it once boasted a large vibrant Jewish community, now almost entirely vanished. Gdansk, in Poland, was once the mainly German city of Danzig, the last days of which were recalled in Günter Grass's novel *The Tin Drum*.

The long collapse of Europe's vast multiethnic empires and the rise of ethnic nationalism, which reached its grotesque apotheosis in the 1930s, drove this process forward. But it's also an open question whether Wilson's affirmation of the self-determination of "peoples" in the fourteen points and at the Paris conference contributed to Europe's century of cleansing. There's not a huge ideological leap from "Our people deserve a state" to "Our state is only for our people." The argument that every people should have a state isn't necessarily an endorsement of ethnic cleansing, but that's often the result.

A similar process has taken place in Iraq over the past decade. Around the time of the U.S. invasion of 2003, Sunni and Shiite neighborhoods were peppered throughout Baghdad—most of the city was mixed Sunni/Shiite. With the sectarian war that kicked off in 2006 following al-Qaeda in Iraq's bombing of the Shiite al-Askari mosque in Samarra, Baghdad rapidly segregated into Sunni and Shiite areas.[62] Many analysts believe this process of segregation, not just the U.S. troop surge in 2007, was the reason the fighting abated: the rival groups were simply separated. The rise of al-Qaeda's successor ISIS has accelerated and expanded the process nationwide.

When outsiders suggest that Iraq would be better off simply separating into distinct ethnic zones, they are endorsing the result of a deliberate process of ethnic cleansing, just as Wilson did in Paris a century ago.

In a sense, the map of the world is coming to resemble Wilson's vision of self-determination: a country for every people and a people for every country. It only took a century of genocide, total war, and stifling totalitarianism to make it happen. From the Caucasus to the Middle East to Southeast Asia, the process is still ongoing.

After centuries of this progression, we've become so accustomed to territorial countries as the world's fundamental political unit that it's difficult to imagine any alternative model. But some do exist—if you know where to look for them.

Knights of the East Side

In a residential apartment building on East 47th Street in Manhattan, an outpost of a medieval European religious order poses some challenging questions about how we conceive of modern countries and the very idea of national sovereignty. There, in a suite of converted apartments, is the UN mission of the Sovereign Military Hospitaller Order of Saint John of Jerusalem of Rhodes and of Malta, better known as the Knights of Malta—a holdover from an era when sovereignty was defined a bit more fluidly than it is in the age of stasis.

According to its own account, the Order of St. John was founded in 1048 by merchants in Jerusalem as a monastic order that ran a hospital for Christian pilgrims in the Holy Land. It was later tasked by the church with responsibility for protecting Christians in the region. The knights were expelled from Jerusalem by the sultan of Egypt in 1291. They were headquartered for a time in Cyprus and then in Rhodes until 1530, when they settled on the island of Malta in the Mediterranean, where they were based for another two centuries. They participated in the battle of Lepanto against the Ottoman Empire in 1571. In 1798, Napoleon occupied the island during his Egyptian campaign, expelling the order and beginning its long period of exile.

In 1834, the order reached an agreement with the pope to set up its headquarters in Rome, where it is still based today, near the foot of the Spanish Steps. At a time before the consolidation of what is now Italy, the order was recognized as a sovereign entity, and it remains so today.[1]

The Knights of Malta have no formal connection to the Republic of Malta—a frequent source of confusion, given the name—or any official military function. It is a Catholic order that sponsors medical missions in more than 120 countries. The group boasts about thirteen thousand members worldwide, divided into mostly autonomous national chapters, as well as more than one hundred thousand employees and volunteers.

Religious orders and religious charities are hardly unusual, but what makes the Order of St. John unique is that it continues to claim sovereignty under international law. While the order has a flag and prints its own stamps, it's not quite a state under the Montevideo Convention criteria: it doesn't have any territory, except for its headquarters in Rome, or a permanent citizenry. (The knights and dames of the order are all citizens of other countries.) But it *does* have diplomatic relations with other countries—it is recognized by 106 UN member states, more than half the body's membership. And since 1994, the order has had a presence at the United Nations itself.

The UN, the main arbiter of who gets to be recognized as a country in the modern world, actually has several tiers of membership. In the top tier are the member states, all 193 of them. New member states must be approved by both the General Assembly and the Security Council. These are what we generally think of as countries, and it's a status that a number of entities, most notably Palestine in recent years, have sought to achieve. But thanks to the threat of U.S. veto, Palestine still falls into the second category: observer states, which can participate in meetings but not vote. Despite not having much more territory than the Order of St. John, the Holy See, also known as the

Vatican, is a member state. (Though Vatican City is often described as the world's smallest country, the Holy See's sovereignty is rooted not in the territory it controls but in the person of the pope himself—a technical point, but a crucial one for our purposes.)

The Order of St. John is in the third category, which has the cumbersome description of "other entities having received an invitation to participate in the work of the UN as observers." Fellow members of this hodgepodge company are the Red Cross, the International Olympic Committee, and the International Parliamentary Union. Below that are categories for nongovernmental organizations and organizations that are separate from the UN but part of the larger UN system, like UNESCO and the IMF.

So, while it doesn't enjoy the same type of membership as, say, Fiji, the Order of St. John has a higher status than most comparable organizations and higher status than a number of entities—Abkhazia, Kosovo, Taiwan—that are a lot closer to what we traditionally think of as countries. The order is a semi-country in large part because it insists on that status and guards it zealously.

In the order's mission in New York, which looks and feels very much like the luxury East Side apartment it is, its ambassador to the United Nations, the veteran Venezuelan diplomat Oscar de Rojas, explained to me his status and how it differs from the representatives of the other NGOs that also have a presence in Turtle Bay, Manhattan. "We're treated like any other diplomats. We can go into any rooms, which NGOs cannot. We can speak at formal meetings. We can distribute background documentation." The order's grand chancellor—the equivalent of a foreign minister—has been invited to address the Security Council in the past.

The order's special status at the United Nations is thanks to Francesco Paolo Fulci, a knight of the order and Italy's U.N ambassador from 1993 to 1999, who engineered its recognition. While its designation was approved without a vote, it wasn't entirely uncontroversial: four of the five permanent members of the Security Council—the United States, Britain, Russia, and China—registered objections to the order's status, worrying that it would open the floodgates to a slew of NGOs claiming sovereignty. I asked de Rojas, who was at the UN with the Venezuelan delegation at the time, if there were a large number of knights among the UN delegates. He said he couldn't be sure. There's no central membership list and knights aren't always aware of each other.

(Indeed, the criteria for membership seem a little flexible. Jazz legend Miles Davis, who was inducted into the knights in 1988, wrote in his autobiography that he didn't "know what all those words in the order's name actually mean, but I'm told that as a member I can get into thirty or forty countries without a visa. I was also told that I was chosen for this honor because I have class, because I'm a genius.")[2]

The order's anomalous status in international relations and the secrecy of its membership list both contribute to the suspicion some have of the Knights of Malta. De Rojas alluded to the order's reputation as an elitist club of European aristocrats who might do a little social work, but that image is benign compared to some of the things that have been said about the order. Past members are rumored to have included CIA directors William Casey and John McCone and secretary of state Alexander Haig.[3] The order's secrecy and rituals—its leader, referred to as the "prince and grand master," is elected in a secret conclave and must be approved by the pope—have made it a frequent target of conspiracy theorists. In one of the less convincing scoops of his illustrious career, the veteran investigative journalist Seymour Hersh claimed in a 2011 speech that U.S. special operations commanders Stanley McChrystal and William McRaven had infiltrated the U.S. military on behalf of the Knights of Malta as part of a holy mission to convert Muslims into Christians.[4] "The worse thing is that they call us crusaders," de Rojas told me, claiming that the order has not had any military function for centuries.

Its specific charitable and religious role aside, the order's sovereign status makes it a throwback to an earlier, more fluid era of international politics when sovereignty was tied more closely to ruling families or dynasties than to fixed territories. Today, for instance, the historic kingdom of Burgundy is associated with the central French region of that name. But in his book *Vanished Kingdoms,* the British historian Norman Davies identifies fifteen historic kingdoms of Burgundy dating back to 410 and occupying locations from the west bank of the Rhine to what is now Switzerland to the Netherlands. Describing the disintegration of Burgundy in the thirteenth century, Davies writes, "The typical Burgundian count was no longer the ruler of one straightforward fief dependent on one overlord. More often he was head of a complex clutch of lands, titles, and claims assembled over the generations by the combined efforts of his family's knights, wives, children and lawyers."[5]

Some scholars have asked whether it might be possible to return to this more fluid version of statehood. In an influential 1998 article, Wharton School professor Stephen Kobrin suggested that the current world order, characterized by spatially defined countries and "the division of the globe's surface into fixed, mutually exclusive, geographically defined jurisdictions enclosed by discrete and meaningful borders . . . may well be unique, a product of a very specific historical context." In an age when geopolitics is becoming ever more complex and rivals to the authority of the nation-state are emerging, Kobrin suggested that we could be entering a "neomedieval" period in which political power is organized along lines closer to those observed in Europe during the

Middle Ages, when "overlapping and competing political authorities were the norm rather than the exception."[6] If this really is the case, it's worth looking at the order as a rare survivor of this earlier fluid era, when political power had less of a one-size-fits-all definition and different types of sovereign entities were tolerated. Could this throwback in fact be a sign of things to come?

For now, that seems a long way off, and the order will remain a curiosity in international relations rather than a model for countries of the future. De Rojas said there are some members who would like to see the order's status upgraded even further, to full UN member state, but he cautioned, "You have to be extremely careful. It would be very uphill. People would say, 'This is not a country, they're fine where they are.' It's better we stay where we are for the time being. It's taken us nine hundred years to get here."

I spoke with the ambassador in the summer of 2016. By January 2017, the order was facing one of the toughest challenges of this nine-hundred-year fight for survival and independence—a fight that put its special political status and development work at odds with the Catholic Church's views on sex and reproduction. In December 2016, Grand Master Matthew Festing attempted to remove Grand Chancellor Albrecht von Boeselager from his position over revelations that projects run by the order in Myanmar had, under his watch, distributed condoms to sex workers in contravention of Catholic teachings on contraception. Boeselager fought back, appealing directly to the pope, arguing that his removal was illegal. The controversy divided the order along ideological lines. In late January 2017, Pope Francis, who has urged members of the church to avoid getting dragged into controversial "culture wars," demanded and received Festing's ouster and took charge of the order until a suitable replacement could be found. Although the knights had always in some sense deferred to the church, the Vatican had generally respected the order's independence, so this was a major break in precedent.[7]

The Vatican, as noted above, is barely more of a country than the Knights of Malta by the traditional criteria of nationhood. It has no permanent citizenry, only about one hundred acres of land area, and technically, it derives its sovereignty not from this piece of land but from the person of the pope himself. But since signing a treaty with Benito Mussolini's government in 1929, the Vatican has been formally recognized as a sovereign state, one *more* sovereign than the Order of St. John.

Throughout the showdown with the Holy See, the order continued to insist on its sovereignty, but it was hard to avoid the impression that something had changed irrevocably. One legal expert wrote, "In terms of international law, the Holy See just annexed another sovereign entity." An anonymous source close to the order told the *Spectator,* "It's like an invasion. Nine hundred years of sovereignty wiped out overnight."[8]

The dust from that controversy has now settled somewhat, and both the order and Pope Francis have affirmed that the order is still considered a sovereign entity—but it's also clear that anomalies will be tolerated only to a limited extent in the age of stasis.

2

A Nation between Countries

"Sir, can you take your hands out of your pockets, please?"

I complied, sitting uncomfortably on a metal bench as a customs and border patrol agent flipped through the pages of my passport. This was the second time in less than twelve hours I had been asked to get out of my car and submit to additional questioning. The first time was the night before, when I was crossing the U.S.-Canadian border north into the city of Cornwall, Ontario, where I had decided to spend the night. Coming back into the United States the next day, it was the same thing. Both times my car was searched, I was questioned about whom I was meeting in the area, queried about the topic of my research (this book), quizzed about the other stamps in my passport and asked—several times—whether the tape recorder I had brought to do interviews was turned on.

I had expected my visit to Akwesasne to be the low-stress portion of my travel. After all, I was in a place where everyone spoke English and there was no war or terrorist activity to worry about. I needed no visas. I was driving a rental car and staying at a Best Western. During the course of my research for this book, I would go to three places where the U.S. State Department specifically advises Americans *not* to go, two of which—Iraq and Somalia—are prime destinations for jihadist recruits. (This was still in the closing months of the Obama administration, before the issue of travel from those countries became even more fraught.) But by far the most contentious border-crossing experience, and the only one in which I felt like I was being viewed with genuine suspicion, was between the United States and Canada. But then again, I wasn't quite crossing between those countries, or not *just* between them. In Akwesasne, things are a little more complicated than that.

During two visits to Akwesasne, I officially crossed the U.S.-Canadian border eight times. Unofficially, it was dozens, including a few I probably wasn't even aware of. This Mohawk community of around thirteen thousand people (three hours' drive northeast of Syracuse or two hours' travel southwest from Montreal) sits astride the world's longest border, not quite a part of either country, but not quite independent either. It's a place where the border, in some respects, doesn't really exist, even while it is also a constant presence in people's daily lives. Akwesasne may be the most geopolitically absurd town in North America.

"Our culture is so intertwined with space and a specific geographic area," reflected Doug George-Kanentiio. We were sitting on his front porch near Oneida, New York, and the author, journalist, and activist was reflecting on geography. "People don't understand how the Iroquois got to be as powerful as we once were. A lot of it was rooted in our philosophy and our military abilities, our fighting capacity. But it couldn't always be that because we only had a few thousand people capable of doing that and we controlled an area that was 26 million acres: from Lake Champlain to Lake Ontario, from central Pennsylvania all the way to Montreal. How do you oversee that?"

Doug George-Kanentiio talked for a few minutes about the history of Iroquois trade and commerce and about lost opportunities. Then he paused, looking out at the busy road running by his house. "You know, over here there used to be the main road," he said. "We used to have a species of animal—it's now extinct—called woodland buffalo. They were smaller than the plains buffalo. If we were sitting here in the old days, we'd watch herds of buffalo go through here to western Massachusetts. It was a natural flow."

George-Kanentiio lives in Oneida now, but he comes from Akwesasne, about four hours' drive north. Akwesasne is a town that's also a nation. It's a place that serves as a reminder that political entities governing territory did not come into being with the modern nation-state and that even in the current age of stasis, the lines that divide the world into countries are not as cut and dried as we like to think.

Mohawks had been living in the area long before Europeans arrived, but the permanent settlement on the St. Lawrence River dates back to the 1700s, when it was established by a group fleeing the larger community at Kahnawake, just south of Montreal, during the French and Indian War. The border between the United States and what was then British Canada was drawn following the American Revolution, a conflict in which Mohawks fought on both sides. British settlers nibbled away at Mohawk lands on the north side of the river, forming what is now the city of Cornwall, Ontario, leaving Akwesasne just a handful of islands and a strip of land on the south bank of the river.

Driving east into Akwesasne along New York State Route 37, you'll pass a turn to the left that takes you into Canada via Cornwall Island and the respectfully named Three Nations Bridge. This is the only official border crossing in the area. Keep going straight and you'll pass into the American portion of the reservation. Even if you missed the sign, you'd still know pretty quickly that you weren't *quite* in New York State anymore by the unusually high number of tobacco stores and gas stations along the side of the highway, beneficiaries of the reservation's exemption from state taxes. A few miles further up the

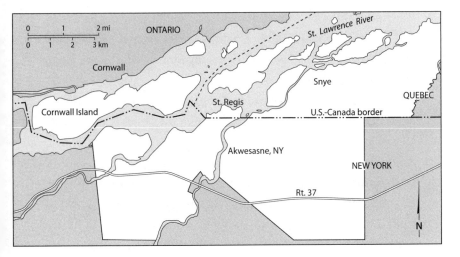

Akwesasne

road and you get to the sprawling Akwesasne Casino. Indian reservations in the United States have been taking advantage of their political
sovereignty to host lucrative casinos since the late 1980s. Opinions are
divided on whether the facilities have generally been a net positive or
negative for the communities that host them. In Akwesasne, opponents and supporters waged a bitter and at times violent confrontation prior to the casino's construction in 1990. Several people I met,
particularly followers of traditional Mohawk religious beliefs, were
adamant that they had never set foot in the place and never would.
From what I saw one afternoon when I dipped into the casino's dim
interior, packed mainly with Quebecois retirees, and rapidly fed (and
rapidly lost) $20 in tokens into a slot machine, the locals aren't miss-
ing much.

From Route 37 you can turn left onto Cook Road, which takes
you into the rural area of Snye, partially in Quebec. In Snye you can

drive along the aptly named Border Road, with Canada on your left and the United States on your right. The only way to tell the two countries apart is the color of the fire hydrants: red in the United States, yellow in Canada.

Turn left on St. Regis Road and you'll find yourself in the village of St. Regis, a quieter part of the reservation that is home to the Mohawk Council and one of the oldest Catholic churches in North America. The names around here are a bit confusing. Cornwall Island, on the reservation, is distinct from Cornwall, Ontario. The American portion of the reservation is sometimes referred to as Hogansburg, the name of the adjoining town in New York. All of the reservation was once known as St. Regis, and the government on the American side is still called the St. Regis Mohawk Council. However, the village of St. Regis is in Canada.

Confusion about where exactly we meant when we were talking about St. Regis was what got me the extra attention from the border guards. I meant to say I had been only on the U.S. side of the border before crossing into Canada, but by saying I had been in St. Regis, I accidentally copped to an illegal border crossing.

All this was pretty amusing to Grand Chief Abram Benedict of the Mohawk Council of Akwesasne, chief executive of the Canadian portion of the reservation. "We need to check this guy's papers!" he said to his staff as we walked out of his office in St. Regis after our interview.

Akwesasne's situation is complicated by the fact that the U.S.-Canadian border in this spot follows the 45th parallel rather than the St. Lawrence River, as it does to the territory's west, meaning that traveling between the Canadian portions of the reservation requires crossing through the United States. It gets stranger: the Canadian border post used to be located on Cornwall Island, roughly where the actual border is. But as part of an effort to beef up security on the border after 9/11, the Canadian government wanted to arm its border guards. Locals objected to armed Canadian officers in their territory, so in 2009, the border post was moved north to the city of Cornwall.[1] While the change was an important political victory, it complicated the commutes of people like Grand Chief Benedict, who lives on the island but works in St. Regis. When he heads home from work at night, he has to drive north to Cornwall, check in at the border post, then make a U-turn back across the bridge to the island. Failure to check in is grounds for car seizure: and dozens of cars are seized every year. A number of residents of the town have adapted to this situation by keeping two cars: one for each country.

The border issue has clearly changed over a short period of time. "It's increasingly gotten more difficult," said Benedict. "Prior to [9/11], anybody could cross the border. We didn't have wait times; identification wasn't required. The Canadian government's move to provide their officers with firearms caused some real concern in the community. That's clearly from 9/11. Everybody's more concerned about the border of a sovereign nation."

Benedict sketched out some of the other complications of governing a town in two countries at once. "Here in St. Regis, it's difficult to get services and provide general repair services because they have to come out of Cornwall, transit through the United States, and come up here. If you're the repairman or the photocopy guy and you're trying to get into Snye and you have a criminal record or you don't have proper documentation, they're not going to let you into the United States to get there. Trying to operate an ambulance service in three jurisdictions is challenging. They have to be licensed in Quebec, New York, Ontario. Cops can't come over here and arrest someone because they're in another country."

The border going through Akwesasne has created a jurisdictional nightmare. The town has three different governments: one elected council recognized by Canada, one by the United States, and a traditional government affiliated with the Iroquois Confederacy. All told, including the United States, Canada, the state of New York, and the provinces of Quebec and Ontario, there are eight governments with some level of jurisdiction over a territory with an area of less than forty square miles.

Akwesasne's unique status makes it a curiosity, though not a particularly amusing one to the residents, who feel their right to free movement is violated on a daily basis by a border they don't recognize. It's also a perfect place to explore how modern bordered countries came to replace older forms of political organization, how those borders thickened and hardened over time to disrupt the lives of those who live on either side of them, and how political entities that *aren't* countries, as we typically define them, are fighting to reclaim their sovereignty and independence.

On Indian Land

In the opening scene of the 1969 documentary film *You Are on Indian Land,* passionate young activist Mike Mitchell addresses a packed public meeting. "We don't want to be Canadian citizens. We don't want to be American citizens. They told us a long time ago that we were North American Indians, and today we feel this way too. We feel this way because we believe that this reservation is ours. It does not belong to the white man. It's the only part we have left."[2]

The film, produced by the National Film Board of Canada, documents a confrontation between the residents of Akwesasne—then known as St. Regis—and the Cornwall police after a group of Mohawks blocked the road crossing the border to protest the duty charged on groceries brought across the border. After a tense and chaotic standoff in a freezing winter blizzard, many of the demonstrators were arrested, including Mitchell. The demonstration took place during a high point of indigenous activism in the United States, shortly after the American Indian Movement's occupation of Alcatraz Island, in which Mitchell, then a film student, had also taken part. In the film we see the demonstrators, reflecting the spirit of the times, singing "We Shall Overcome" as they are crammed into the back of police cars.

The film ends with Mitchell, who also narrates the film and was one of its producers, back in the conference room, discussing the Jay Treaty, the urtext of the Mohawk border struggle, with a local Canadian government representative. The 1795 treaty between Britain and the United States, which addressed unresolved issues from the American Revolution, specifies border-crossing rights for American Indians between the United States and what was then British territory in Canada. Mohawks maintain that their rights under the treaty have been repeatedly violated by government measures, from the duties during the 1960s to the stringent border-crossing requirements today.

The treaty, Mitchell says in the film, "stated in there that the Indians were obliged to cease making wars on the white man. When that treaty was broken, that means that we must again be at war with the white man, because when you break a treaty this is what it signifies. We are still at peace. We didn't go to war . . . yet," he says as the frame freezes portentously and the credits roll.

Mitchell never went to war. He went into politics. Surprisingly, he did so via the reservation's Canadian government–recognized band council, portrayed in the film as an ineffectual puppet of Ottawa. He served in government for three decades, from 1982 to 2015, including two stints as grand chief.[3] When we met for breakfast at the Twin Leaf

Diner on Route 37, he looked remarkably unchanged from the young man in the film of nearly fifty years ago.

Mitchell pointedly refers to his political project as "nation-building." "There's a colonial mindset," he said. "They mentally put into our head that we're no longer a nation. They're using this psychology to make us belittle ourselves, and we came to accept that. But when we signed treaties with outside powers, it was always as a nation."

Mitchell was the first grand chief of Akwesasne who followed traditional Mohawk religious beliefs rather than Christianity. He recalls that just after his election, someone on the council joked, "Not to worry. We're going to string him up in a couple of months anyway. We've never had a pagan for chief."

Under Mitchell, Akwesasne dropped the name St. Regis and the council stopped referring to itself as a "band council," the term used under Canada's Indian Act. Reflecting on the changes during his tenure, Mitchell said, "The most important aren't physical things. It's how people think of themselves. Young people aren't ashamed to be native anymore."

Early in his tenure as grand chief, he put a coffee cup in the center of the council's meeting table in which employees had to drop in 25¢ toward the office's coffee fund every time they used the words *band* or *reservation*. "We had a lot of money for coffee in those early months," he remembers.

The words are also indicative of the differences between the status of indigenous government in the United States and Canada. The disparity is likewise the main reason why Akwesasne has three governments rather than one, which would seem far more logical; a single government would require the United States and Canada to harmonize their approaches.

In Canada, "First Nations," as they've been known for the last few decades, are still governed under the Indian Act of 1867, which aimed to "do away with the tribal system and assimilate the Indian people in all respects with the other inhabitants of the Dominion as speedily as they are fit to change."[4] Some of the more controversial aspects of that act, such as prohibiting the speaking of native languages and forcing indigenous children into assimilationist residential schools, have been eliminated over time, but the law remains the primary basis under which the Canadian government interacts with native governments. Most critically, the Indian Act means that the land on which First Nations live is not considered their sovereign territory. "The land that is still occupied under the Indian Act—we no longer own it. It's just there for our benefit," Mitchell said.

Under the U.S. Constitution, three kinds of governments possess sovereignty: the U.S. federal government; the state governments, which reserve all rights not held by the federal government; and Native American governments, which are semi-sovereign nations. This means that American Indians are citizens of three polities: their tribal nation, the United States, and the state they live in.[5] In the United States, American Indian tribes are considered "domestic dependent natives," a status upheld by several U.S. Supreme Court decisions. They are, as the landmark 1832 case *Worcester v. Georgia* put it, "distinct independent political communities retaining their original natural rights as the undisputed possessors of the soil from time immemorial."[6] This means that relations between the U.S. federal government and Indian governments are conducted on the basis of treaty law rather than domestic law. As former president George W. Bush put it, "My administration is committed to continuing to work with federally-recognized tribal governments on a government-to-government basis and strongly supports and respects tribal sovereignty and self-determination for tribal governments within the United States."[7]

This is not to say that the rights of Indian governments to the lands under their nominal control, or their sovereignty within those lands, have always been respected by the U.S. federal government. They have certainly not been. But it's still a legal approach that's somewhat more open to the goals of nationalist-minded leaders like Mitchell than Canada's. This is also not to say that the American government is particularly well liked by Mohawk nationalists either. As Doug George-Kanentiio put it in an interview with me: "What the Americans have done is poured a lot of money into the community, which creates dependency. And they filter that money through the colonial governments, and they still oppose the rise of the Mohawk Nation. And I can see why, from their perspective. It's a dangerous thing to unleash that kind of emotion in any colonial people. The British should have learned that in Africa in the 1960s and '70s, as did the French in Vietnam. That thing was always there, amongst the Mohawks, the desire to be one single community."

Whatever hostility tribal nations have faced, their political status has transformed in significant ways in recent decades. The story of the building of modern Indian nations began in the late 1960s and 1970s, during the era of the Alcatraz occupation and the standoff at Wounded Knee between the American Indian Movement and U.S. marshals. In 1975, Congress passed the Indian Self-Determination Act, which began the process of transferring the administration of reservations from the Bureau of Indian Affairs to local governments. This was a reversal of the assimilationist "termination policy" in place since the end of World War II, which sought to gradually eliminate the separate sovereignty of Indian nations. As author Charles Wilkinson has summarized, the decades since then have seen an unprecedented effort to "reverse the termination

policy; break the [Bureau of Indian Affairs'] paternalistic hold and reestablish tribes as sovereign governments within reservation territory; enforce treaty rights to land, water, and hunting and fishing, and at once
achieve economic progress and preserve ancient traditions in a technological age."[8] To varying extents, many of these goals have been achieved.
Some tribal nations, such as the Iroquois, the Mississippi Choctaw, and
the Navajo, have established a remarkable degree of political sovereignty,
with independent courts and law enforcement bodies, education systems, and governments ranging in form from elective councils to religious theocracies.

The revolution in Indian sovereignty also coincided with the emergence of casino gambling as a source of revenue for tribal governments,
though many of these political developments were already under way by
the time reservation casinos were legalized by a 1987 Supreme Court decision. Economic conditions vary widely between reservations—Buffalo
County, South Dakota, home of the Crow Creek Sioux Tribe, is the
poorest county in the United States—but politically the transformation
has been remarkable.[9] In his book *Blood Struggle*, Wilkinson argues that
"the Indian revival of the second half of the twentieth century deserves to
be recognized as a major episode in American history."[10]

It should also be seen as a major development in international
relations. With 314 reservations and trust lands in the United States
encompassing 100 million acres—56 million in the lower forty-eight
states—Indian America is roughly the size of Iceland or South
Korea.[11] With approximately 2.5 million people, it's more populous
than Qatar or Latvia. Yes, these are just fractions of the lands and
peoples who lived in what is now the continental United States prior
to colonization, but together they are also an emerging nation rarely
considered by either the United States or the international community in discussions of sovereignty, borders, and nationalism.

Periodically, there have been attempts to make the independence of Indian nations more formal. In 2007, Lakota activist Russell Means, a key player in the Wounded Knee standoff, visited the State Department in Washington to announce that the Lakota Nation was unilaterally withdrawing from treaties signed with the United States in the nineteenth century, effectively declaring independence in territory comprising parts of North Dakota, South Dakota, Nebraska, and Montana, including the city of Omaha and Mount Rushmore. "We are now a free country and independent of the United States of America," Means told South Dakota's *Rapid City Journal.* "This is all completely legal." He said that anyone would be allowed to live in the territory as long as he or she renounced U.S. citizenship.[12]

Means's move, based on the Vienna Convention on the Law of Treaties, was never recognized by the United States or by the elected Lakota governments, which preferred to work to gain more autonomy within the U.S. political system. But it was nonetheless an example of tribes beginning to conceive of themselves as nations, rather than ethnic groups or cultural minorities, a concept that some members of the Iroquois Confederacy, including the Mohawk, have always embraced fully.

According to tradition, the Iroquois emerged in the twelfth century as an alliance among five formerly warring tribes spearheaded by a figure known as the Peacemaker. (I'm using the term *Iroquois* for its familiarity, though members of the tribes generally prefer to be called Haudenosaunee, meaning "They built the house." The word *Iroquois* comes from Basque slang *hirokoa,* or "killer people." It's pronounced *Iri-koy* in the United States and the more French *Iri-kwa* in Canada.) These tribes, listed from west to east, are the Seneca, the Cayuga, the Onondaga, the Oneida, and the Mohawk. The Tuscarora of North

Carolina were adopted into the league in the eighteenth century. The confederacy structure was established by the sixteenth century.[13] The Great Law, passed down from the time of the Peacemaker, requires consensual decision-making among representatives and unanimity between the nations in decisions made as a league. The semi-democratic political structure was studied by Ben Franklin, and some argue that it influenced the framers of the U.S. Constitution.

The arrival of Europeans in what is now the northeastern United States and Canada disrupted Iroquois life through new competition for resources and the introduction of diseases hitherto unknown—in 1634, the Mohawk population dropped from 7,740 to 2,830 in a matter of months—though trade also provided a new source of wealth. In 1613, the confederacy reached a noninterference agreement with the Dutch government in what is now New York State that has become known as the "two-row wampum agreement." Wampum are shells or beads traditionally used as currency that can be woven into symbolic belts. The two rows on this wampum belt symbolize two canoes traveling side by side. Iroquois view the two-row wampum as the basis for all subsequent agreements with European and North American governments.[14]

Geography and nationhood are intimately bound together in the Iroquois political system, an arrangement that long predates the modern organization of geographically bounded countries. The central feature of political life among Iroquois nations is the longhouse, a wooden structure where people once lived that is still used for important meetings today. According to tradition, the five nations of the league are arranged as a metaphorical longhouse: the Mohawk guarding the eastern door, the Seneca at the western door, and the Onondaga keeping the fire in the middle.[15]

But the Iroquois were never a country in the modern sense, nor even an empire in the premodern sense, with defined territory surrounded by borders. This would increasingly become an issue as European countries and later North American ones consolidated territory around them, chipping away at their territory and dividing loyalties.

The American Revolution was catastrophic for the league, with loyalties divided between the British and the colonists. The Mohawk, the Seneca, the Onondaga, and the Cayuga were generally pro-English, while the Oneida and Tuscarora were generally pro-American. The fire at the Iroquois Confederacy longhouse at Onondaga was covered in 1777, symbolically ending the league's work. While the league was later revived, it never wielded the same power as a real governing political unit.[16]

By the mid-nineteenth century, New York State had gobbled away most of what remained of Iroquois land. Akwesasne was established in 1796 when New York State and the Mohawk reached an agreement in which the latter surrendered claims in the United States beyond Akwesasne itself and a few other small parcels in return for an annual payment.

Predating the founding of either the United States or Canada, and living on either side of the border between them, the Iroquois have always been insistent on their own nationhood and sovereignty, particularly when it comes to the right to travel freely over the U.S.-Canadian border. Mohawks have traditionally taken jobs in metalworking, traveling back and forth across the border during the mid-century building boom. A 1929 article in the *New Yorker* by the social critic Edmund Wilson described the Mohawks of the St. Lawrence River region as "the most footloose Indians in North America." Interestingly, Wilson also alluded to the "emerging Iroquois nationalism" of the time.[17]

One of the most significant events in the emergence of that nationalism occurred in 1923, when Deskaheh, a Cayuga chief from the

Six Nation territory in Ontario, traveled to Geneva to present a complaint against Canada to the recently founded League of Nations. Before 1914, the Canadian government had accorded the Iroquois the status of separate nation, allowing them free movement across the border. When he was young, Deskaheh, born Levi General, had taken advantage of this, like many other Cayugas, working as a lumberjack in the Allegheny Mountains. In 1914, needing troops, the Canadian government began an effort to assimilate Indian populations. After the war, Deskaheh traveled to Britain, on a passport issued by the Iroquois Nation, to petition King George V to confirm Iroquois rights under the Jay Treaty. He was rebuffed by the British on the grounds that they would not weigh in on a Canadian domestic dispute.

And so he traveled to Geneva, hoping that the League of Nations, founded on the basis of Woodrow Wilson's rhetoric of self-determination, might recognize that the Iroquois were not merely a racial group but a nation with treaty rights under international law. Though he received a fair amount of sympathetic press and enthusiastic audiences at several speeches, he was mainly met with indifference by the foreign governments. Never permitted to address the League of Nations assembly, he left disappointed in 1924.[18]

Deskaheh died in Rochester a few months later. But his notion that the Iroquois should think of themselves as a sovereign nation rather than a cultural group was to prove influential and shape future Iroquois challenges to the status quo on both sides of the border.

In 1924, the U.S. government passed the Indian Citizenship Act, making all American Indians U.S. citizens. The Iroquois rejected citizenship: "We were not United States citizens, no matter what the government said. We were Six Nations citizens," said the prominent Tuscarora chief Clinton Rickard years later.[19]

The following year, Paul Diabo, a Mohawk ironworker from Kahnewake, just south of Montreal, was arrested in Montreal as an illegal alien, based on the Immigration Act of 1924, which had been passed mainly to keep Asians out of the United States. Diabo contended that he had the right to cross the border under the Jay Treaty. He eventually won his case in the U.S. courts, which ruled that Mohawks had the right to cross into the United States. (Getting back into Canada is a little more complicated.)[20]

The Mohawks are not the only indigenous people in North America to face this issue. In the short story "Borders," American-Canadian author Thomas King imagines a Blackfoot family's dialogue with a border guard while attempting to cross from Canada into the United States:

"Morning, ma'am."
"Good morning."
"Any firearms or tobacco?"
"No."
"Citizenship?"
"Blackfoot."

He told us to sit in the car and wait, and we did. In about five minutes, another guard came out with the first man. They were talking as they came, both men swaying back and forth like two cowboys headed for a bar or a gunfight.

"Morning, ma'am."
"Good morning."
"Cecil tells me you and the boy are Blackfoot."
That's right."
"Now I know that we got Blackfeet on the American side and the Canadians got Blackfeet on their side. Just so we can keep our records straight, what side do you come from?"

I knew exactly what my mother was going to say, and I could have told them if they had asked me.

"Canadian side or American side?" asked the guard.

"Blackfoot side," she said.

It didn't take them long to lose their sense of humor, I can tell you that.[21]

To this day, many Iroquois, like Deskaheh before them, travel internationally using Iroquois Confederacy passports printed by the Onondaga Nation—or they attempt to, anyway. In 2010, this practice caused an international incident when the twenty-three players of the Iroquois national lacrosse team were denied entry into Britain because they intended to travel with Iroquois Confederacy passports. Despite being granted a waiver by then U.S. secretary of state Hillary Clinton, the team lost its appeal to the British government and was unable to compete internationally in the sport that Iroquois people invented.[22]

In 2011, Joyce King, the director of justice for the Mohawk Council of Akwesasne, had her Iroquois Confederacy passport seized when traveling from her home in the Quebec portion of the reservation to Cornwall. "They called it a 'fantasy document,' but that's my identity," she told Canada's *National Post* of the passport, which she says had been previously accepted at the Montreal airport. "If it's a fantasy document, does that make me a fantasy person living in a fantasy country?"[23] (Many people in Akwesasne do, for practicality's sake, have a U.S. or Canadian passport that they use to cross the border, even if they would prefer not to identify as either U.S. or Canadian citizens.)

The issue came up again in 2015 when a delegation from the Six Nations traveled to Bolivia to take part in a climate change conference sponsored by President Evo Morales. A planned ten-day trip turned into a twenty-nine-day ordeal, much of it spent in El Salvador, where the members of the delegation had planned to catch a connection but were prevented from boarding a plane. They refused to accept emergency temporary passports from the Canadian government. Eventually a U.S. official intervened and the delegation was able to fly into the United States through Miami to make its way back home.

That delegation included Howard Thompson, an elder with the Mohawk Nation Council of Chiefs, Akwesasne's traditional government, whom I met with on my visit to the nation. Sitting alone with Thompson in the traditional longhouse, dark and quiet on a wet, gray day, I asked him why Iroquois people in particular were so insistent on national sovereignty compared to other Indian tribes. "The assimilation process had more effect in other parts of the United States," he told me. "Whole tribes and whole nations consider themselves U.S. citizens. It's hard to push for your own nationhood if a majority of the people in the United States already consider themselves U.S. citizens."

While Thompson defends the role of Akwesasne's traditional government, he concedes that the federally recognized elected governments in town are the ones with legal power. "Our biggest role is in the spirituality of the people, trying to get them to understand their culture and their heritage and what they believe in," he said of the Mohawk Nation, which is affiliated with the Iroquois Confederacy. "We should be involved in the federal government responsibilities, but we're not. The elected governments just recognize us as the historic government. But that's a name. That's not a responsibility."

The divisions in Akwesasne aren't just national. In the early 1990s, a conflict between supporters of casino gambling (including the militant Akwesasne Mohawk Warrior Society) and opponents, who see gambling as antithetical to traditional values, turned violent. Two men were killed in the clashes and the offices of Doug George-Kanentiio's newspaper, *Akwesasne Notes,* were firebombed by supporters of the casino. In his 1996 book on the Iroquois, Penn State anthropologist Dean Snow describes Akwesasne as a community that "persists as a longhouse divided against itself," beset with "conditions that encourage smuggling and unusually complex political factionalism."[24]

But Thompson sees the divisions beginning to fade away. "The borders used to be really prominent fifty years ago," he said. "People from Cornwall were Canadians. People from Hogansburg were Americans. That border that runs through our communities, we put it through ourselves. It didn't belong there but we put it in there. The improvement now is the lack of division. More people see Akwesasne as one community."

While the community's worst days may be behind it, there are still deep divisions about how exactly Akwesasne should be governed and how it should interact with the two nations on either side of it.

Benedict, the current grand chief on the Canadian side, has taken a pragmatic approach to territory, entering into a partnership with the neighboring city of Cornwall, Ontario, to co-develop a waterfront port. Benedict, who notes that "regionally we've seen a loss of a number of good jobs in the surrounding area," sees the port project as an economic opportunity for Akwesasne and a way for the community to regain at least partial control over an area that locals believe was unjustly separated from the community. He argues that the partnership agreement could be "a model for other indigenous and nonindigenous communities to strive towards."

But the project is controversial, with some in town arguing that co-ownership undermines Akwesasne's land claims, and that the Mohawk Council, one of three governments in the community, shouldn't have the right to enter into the partnership on its own. Benedict makes the case that Cornwall isn't exactly going anywhere, and that Akwesasne ought to at least be benefiting from its own waterfront. The logic is hard to argue with.

"The port offers an opportunity. If you could establish a port of entry there run by Mohawk people, you could have orders coming in from across the world," said Doug George-Kanentiio, who nonetheless feels the deal should have been negotiated through the Mohawk Nation Council.

Black Hole

In his 2005 book *Illicit,* an investigation of how globalization has driven an explosion of black market and criminal activity, the columnist and former Venezuelan government minister Moises Naim (whom I worked for when he was editor of *Foreign Policy* magazine) discusses what he calls "geopolitical black holes." Just as "black holes are regions in the universe where the traditional—Newtonian—laws of physics do not apply," geopolitical black holes are places where the "traditional ways of thinking about world politics and international relations do not apply either." Because legal jurisdiction in these areas tends to be contested or uncertain, they are places where, Naim writes, "trafficking networks live and thrive."[25]

Akwesasne is a textbook example of such a place, and it's acquired a reputation in Canada as a hub of illegal activity. The most common practice is the smuggling of cigarettes, known as "buttlegging," which became a major source of income for many people on the reservation during the 1990s. Cigarettes would be purchased for export in Canada, brought into the United States, then brought back into Canada without permit to be sold tax-free. Driving across the border with a trunk full of smokes was an easy—if risky—way to make a few bucks. Nowadays, locals say the fines have become so exorbitant that only major smugglers bringing large hauls across still do it—there have been reports in the Canadian media that major organized crime rings, even the Russian mafia, have been involved in cigarette smuggling through Akwesasne, often on boats crossing the St. Lawrence around the islands that obscure both sightlines and legal jurisdictions. "It built a lot of houses and bought a lot of cars here, but now it's mostly people from out of Akwesasne" who participate, said Margie Skidders, editor of the local newspaper *Indian Time.*

Police have also alleged that the area is a popular conduit for smuggling hard drugs and firearms between the two countries.[26] According to Canada's 2010 drug threat assessment report, as much as 20 percent of the high-potency marijuana grown in Canada each year at that time was smuggled through Akwesasne.[27]

(Akwesasne has a counterpart at the U.S.-Mexican border, the Tohono O'odham territory straddling the border between Arizona and Mexico, which for similar reasons has been targeted by people smugglers and drug cartels. As of this writing, the Tohono O'odham Nation is fighting to prevent Donald Trump's proposed border wall being built through the center of the territory, a problem with which, thankfully, Akwesasne has not yet had to contend.)[28]

Since 9/11, U.S. authorities have also raised concerns about terrorists crossing the U.S.-Canadian border. Though there's no truth to the oddly persistent belief, repeated by a number of American politicians including then senator Hillary Clinton, that the 9/11 hijackers entered the United States through Canada, a Government Accountability Office report in 2010 did argue that the U.S.-Canadian border is a larger potential terrorism concern than the southern U.S. border with Mexico.[29]

The site is also a potentially attractive crossing point for refugees and migrants trying to enter the United States. In 2015, two men from India drowned and a third plus a smuggler were taken into custody after attempting to cross the St. Lawrence by boat at Akwesasne.[30] "They're not bad people, just people looking for a better life trying to get into the States," said Mike Mitchell of the migrants attempting to cross through his community. "Once it becomes known as a complicated jurisdiction you see a lot of people trying to pass through."

"Complicated jurisdictions" are always attractive to those attempting to break national laws, whether they are simply seeking a better life for themselves and their families or whether they have more nefarious purposes. Another complicating factor in Akwesasne is that for many, the most benign form of smuggling, buttlegging, is not generally considered nefarious. The Iroquois, after all, have been trading tobacco since long before either the United States or Canada existed, and why should they be bound by the laws of countries they don't recognize? Smuggling can be viewed as an assertion of sovereignty, albeit one that just happens to be personally lucrative.

Skidders said she and the staff of her newspaper *Indian Time* debated whether to even continue printing the Royal Canadian Mounted Police's press releases on the issue. "We don't view it as smuggling. We view it as trade," she said. "But in the end we decided we would continue" publishing the notices "because [the issue is] still there, it's what we deal with every day of our lives."

The main strip of slightly seedy tobacco stores aside, Akwesasne does not feel much like the anarchic smuggler's paradise often portrayed in the Canadian press. The "Indian revival" of the last four decades is very much in evidence in the community. For one thing, the community is making an effort to promote the use of the Mohawk language. The Mohawk Council of Akwesasne, the government on the Canadian side, now runs a Mohawk immersion school for kindergarten through sixth grade. (No public equivalent exists on the American side, though a private initiative to teach children the language has been set up.) Teaching in a language with no textbooks presents some special challenges for educators. "We can't just go to a store and buy materials for the program. Everything has to be created from scratch," said Donna Wahienha:wi Lahache, director of education for the Mohawk Council. The school administrators take English-language Canadian books and paste translated captions over them. For some subjects, particularly science, they've been in the unique position of inventing new words for concepts like photosynthesis.

"It's kind of rare to find speakers," acknowledges principal Alice King. "I guess it all goes back to the residential school time, when [Mohawk] language was forbidden. Even in my day, it wasn't outright punishment happening, but there was encouragement to speak French, because Mohawk wasn't going to get you anywhere. There wasn't that vision of helping your community." She said that few people under the age of sixty speak the language anymore. "We're losing the language. It was taken. And when something's taken from you, you want to get it back."

In addition to the school, the community is taking other steps to promote the Mohawk language, including traffic signs written in Mohawk and community outreach urging people to use Mohawk in the name of cultural survival.

At the time I visited, Akwesasne was enjoying a rare stretch of good publicity thanks to the Mohawk Council's establishment of the first indigenous legal system in Canada that operates outside the country's federal system.[31] The community will enforce thirty-two laws pertaining to civic matters like traffic violations, property disputes, and wildlife preservation in a court that mixes Canadian judicial norms with traditional Mohawk customs. The court emphasizes restorative justice over punishment in dealing with minor crimes.

"If there's a person who's a very good lacrosse player, and they spray graffiti on the school, and they take responsibility, the justice can say, 'Not only will you clean up that graffiti, you're going to teach the children lacrosse.' So he uses his positive skills and develops a relationship with those children," Joyce King, the director of justice for Akwesasne, told me. "We call those skills the gift the creator has given them."

Prosecutor Bonnie Cole pointed to a difference in mindset that underlies how the court is set up. "We're not just looking at them as an offender. I don't even like using that word," she said. "These are our people. These are our neighbors. You have a frame of reference. There's not this great fog you have when you go into most courtrooms. Most courts, the judge knows absolutely nothing about the person in front of them. They say that's a good thing, but I don't know if that is."

This, like many of my conversations in Akwesasne, brings us back to the border. The issue is always there. "Whether crossing the border or traveling outside," said Cole, "there's always this assumption of criminality hanging over anyone from Akwesasne. Whereas in our court, we all know each other and there's none of those presumptions. We see each other as people. When we go outside, even me as a lawyer, last week when I was in Cornwall, they looked at me like I didn't have the right to be there."

Not having to explain oneself on a daily basis to representatives of law enforcement in a setting where criminality, if not presumed, is at least suspected, is a privilege not to be taken for granted. Daily life in Akwesasne brought to mind African American communities in the United States where "stop-and-frisk" policing methods have been implemented. Even if nine times out of ten, the interactions at the border are businesslike and perfunctory, the possibility that it could go bad adds an extra element of tension to daily life.

Skidders said she was once brought in for secondary questioning simply for suggesting to border guards that they open up an extra lane to accommodate the traffic flowing through the checkpoint. "I have to go through the border three times a day, and I live here," said Skidders, who lives on the U.S. side. "I have a passport but why would I use a passport to enter from one part of my land to another part? You're not going to use a passport to go from Albany to New York City, are you?"

On the other hand, there are a few advantages to Akwesasne's location, particularly for a news organization. The building containing the offices of Skidders's newspaper *Indian Time* and the unlicensed radio station CKON (the word *she:kon* is Mohawk for "hello") sits literally on the U.S.-Canadian border. "No one can sue us," Skidders said. "We're on sovereign land. What court would that even go to? We haven't really stretched that and used that. We've been threatened with lawsuits twice. So maybe we're doing something right."

Of the dozens of smoke stores and head shops dotted along Route 37, one looks a little different—emblazoned with a red flag featuring the head of a Mohawk warrior. A metal monument in the parking lot serves as a makeshift memorial for Mohawk metalworkers. The store is owned by metalworker Bill Sears, formerly a resident of Brooklyn, who helped build the original World Trade Center. "9/11 felt like a personal attack on me," Sears told me as we sat outside his store. Some, particularly in the Canadian government, would find Sears's denunciation of terrorism a little ironic. Sears is a war chief in the Mohawk Warrior Society, a group advocating active—at times violent—resistance in support of Mohawk sovereignty.

In 1990, Sears took part in an infamous standoff between Mohawk activists and Canadian troops and Mounties in Oka, Quebec, over the planned expansion of a local golf course onto what had traditionally been Mohawk land near the town of Kanehsatake. The standoff led to a shootout in which one Quebec provincial police officer was killed—responsibility for the death was never determined. The golf course expansion was eventually cancelled but the territorial dispute over the land remains unresolved.[32] The Warrior Society was listed as a terrorist organization in Canadian military training materials for several years, which the government eventually apologized for in 2010.[33]

The Oka crisis briefly made the Mohawk's grievances a cause célèbre in the Canadian and international media, much to the frustration of nonviolent activists like Doug George-Kanentiio. "Oka was a big lie," he said, arguing that the perpetrators were involved in criminal activity and that the violence of the incident set back the Mohawk cause.

I asked Sears if he saw Oka as a watershed moment in the movement for Mohawk political independence. "It was a watershed to assimilation," he told me. "It didn't give us what we were fighting for, which was sovereignty." Nowadays, the Warrior Society isn't quite what it once was. "We're not as volatile as we were in the '80s or the '90s. Our goal is the land. To keep our heritage and keep our land."

The symbol of the Warrior Society is pretty visible around town, but Sears sees this as more of a radical chic affectation than anything else. "Everyone wants a warrior shirt and a warrior patch, but what are you going to do with it?" he asks. (Nonetheless, he's happy to sell both at his store.)

As for what he's up to these days, Sears said, "We just watch what's going on. We watch to make sure that the other governments don't give away too much." And, he added, "I lift weights every day. I've got one more fight left in me."

Off the Grid

The anthropologist James Scott has argued that one of the main projects of modern states is to make society "legible," scientifically and rationally ordered so that it can be controlled by a centralized bureaucracy without reliance on local knowledge. A modern state prefers its people stationary and accounted for, its systems orderly and uniform. Scott is a philosophical anarchist whose writing celebrates nomadic cultures that defy state legibility by adhering to premodern, mobile lifestyles.[34]

The existence of modern Indian nations is a challenge to the legibility of citizenship and territory. The United States and Canada have both sought in the past to assimilate their native populations as citizens, but as a result of a decades-long campaign of resistance and the assertion of native sovereignty, both countries have come to accept indigenous political difference to a limited extent. In the United States, courts have upheld that Native Americans are citizens of their own nations as well as of the United States, though many of them choose not to recognize the latter. Canada has been slower to come around to this view but seems to be heading that way as well. Likewise, Indian land is both *in* one of these countries and at the same time separate. In a world divided neatly into nonoverlapping sovereign countries, places like this shouldn't exist, yet they do. Indigenous people defy the dominant system by insisting on their right to cross borders freely and refusing citizenship in any recognized country.

As the Mohawk anthropologist Audra Simpson writes, "The Mohawks . . . are nationals of a pre-contact Indigenous polity that simply refuse to stop being themselves. In other words, they insist on being and acting as peoples who belong to a nation other than the United States or Canada." Simpson argues that this is a challenge to the recognized authority of the countries that the Mohawks live within. "As indigenous nations are enframed by settler states that call themselves nations and appear to have a monopoly on institutional and military power, this is a significant assertion. There is more than one political show in town," she writes. She discusses Indian nations as a form of "nested sovereignty" that "has implications for the sturdiness of nation-states."[35]

The challenge is only more profound in an era of cartographical stasis, in which claims to nationhood are premised on the notion that certain national boundaries are more "natural" than others. Spend any time in Akwesasne and you quickly realize just how arbitrary the lines on the map really are.

During my time in Akwesasne, I asked the same question to several of the people I met: What if representatives of the U.S. and Canadian governments were to come to the community one day and say, "Look, we all know this is a mess. We're just going to redraw the border so that this town is either entirely within the United States or entirely within Canada, but you get to choose." Which would they prefer? Most people I spoke to rejected the premise of the question. As Skidders put it, "I think the people would say, let us just be here. Let us just be the Akwesasne nation. We'll figure the rest out."

For all the progress that Indian nations have made in gaining increased recognition and sovereignty in recent decades, there's also an argument that this recognition implies acceptance of a nation-state system that the indigenous people of North America never chose. Taiaiake Alfred, a professor of indigenous governance at the University of Victoria and a Mohawk from Kahnewake, argues that the modern Indian political movement's emphasis on sovereignty is misguided. "One of the inherent parts of sovereignty is recognition by other sovereigns," he told me in a phone interview. "So in the recognition that we see on a global scale, there are conditions that are put in place in terms of institutional structure, legal interface, and the restructuring of your polity in order to mesh with the system that you're aspiring to be part of." Alfred argues that "the form of governance that characterizes indigenous governance doesn't interface with contemporary forms of neoliberal government and the state system. So you have to sacrifice part of what you are to be recognized." In particular, he suggests that "the idea of the government having authority that's separate from the people is foreign to indigenous people." Modern nationhood as defined by "bounded territory, monopoly on the use of force: every one of those principles is abhorrent to an indigenous philosophy and worldview." More fundamentally, he believes, "We already are sovereign in the philosophical sense, so to reorient ourselves in order to enter a form of relationship with a state, we have to sacrifice part of who we are."

Alfred made clear he's not against Indian nations using treaty rights to demand government recognition as a means to achieve more independence, but he feels these should be secondary to the goal of preserving indigenous culture and reestablishing a relationship with the natural environment. "There's no proof that political autonomy has any real positive effect on alleviating the problems that come from being colonized," he told me. "People define their goals in terms of these types of things instead of looking at the root cause of the problems. Problems in native communities have nothing to do with money. They have to do with the psychophysical effects of colonization on our communities."

All well and good, but it's hard to conceptualize exactly what a world in which Alfred's "anarcho-indigenism" would look like put into practice. In his book *Wasase: Indigenous Pathways of Action and Freedom,* Alfred writes, "Settlers must come to accept Onkwehonwe [indigenous people] existence as autonomous nations and, with this, recognize the need for a fundamental reshaping of their countries."[36]

He acknowledged in our interview that this is a different notion of decolonization than that practiced by the new independent countries that came into existence in the twentieth century, most of which were outside of Europe but fought for recognition as European-style nation-states. "The only model there for them to conceive of themselves as an autonomous political community was the state system," he said.

Alfred's argument, therefore, is that rather than fighting for a space on the map to call their own, indigenous Americans should work to define themselves politically without concern with whether other nations recognize them. That this notion is such a tricky mental leap both for indigenous people themselves and for the governments they are trying to gain autonomy from is an indication of just how thoroughly people have internalized countryhood as the basic definition of political independence. You're either a "tribe"—an anthropological definition—or a nation/state/country—a political definition. The current international political system doesn't accommodate alternative arrangements.

During my second visit to Akwesasne, in the fall of 2016, issues of indigenous sovereignty were enjoying a rare moment in the public spotlight thanks to the ongoing protests at the Standing Rock Reservation in North Dakota. Standing Rock, a Sioux community long at the forefront of the sovereignty movement, was protesting a plan to run the Dakota Access Pipeline, carrying oil from the Bakken shale fields of North Dakota, just half a mile north of the reservation, crossing land containing sacred sites and burial places that the Lakota argue were unjustly taken from them during the nineteenth century. There were also concerns that the pipeline would threaten the community's water supply.

The protests against the pipeline became a major international story during the closing months of the Obama administration, attracting environmental activists motivated by concerns about climate change as well as environmental racism: the decision to run the pipeline near Standing Rock was made after a previous route near the predominantly white city of Bismarck was rejected. Advocates also hoped that Standing Rock could be a turning point for Indian sovereignty in the way that Alcatraz and Wounded Knee were for a previous generation—an instance in which increasingly influential and sovereign indigenous governments demanded the recognition they are entitled to under U.S. treaties, court decisions, and federal law. The protests attracted activists from tribes throughout the United States, including some Mohawks.

The Standing Rock movement eventually failed, as the Trump administration reversed an earlier Obama decision and ordered the pipeline built. The protest camp was eventually demolished. But the dispute pushed the issue of tribal sovereignty into the mainstream. As German Lopez wrote for *Vox,* the dispute was "intrinsically linked to Supreme Court cases from 200 years ago" and the "legal idea that Native American tribes aren't formally part of the states they reside in, but rather semi-autonomous nations with rights to self-governance that stop states and, in some cases, even the federal government from interfering with tribal issues."[37]

These nations continue to push for these rights on a number of fronts, including the courtroom. In 2016, a 4–4 split in the U.S. Supreme Court left in place the authority of tribal courts to hear suits against nontribal businesses. This authority is being used most notably in an ongoing suit by the Pawnee against several oil companies in the tribal court system over earthquake damage caused by hydraulic fracking. "We are a sovereign nation and we have the rule of law here,"

Andrew Knife Chief, the Pawnee Nation's executive director, told the Associated Press. "We're using our tribal laws, our tribal processes, to hold these guys accountable."[38] The case could turn out to be a landmark decision upholding tribal nations' ability to enforce their own laws and protect their own natural territory. It's also a textbook example of the kind of "nested sovereignty" Simpson discusses, and if the massive militarized response to the Standing Rock protests is any indication, U.S. federal authorities may push back against it.

Americans tend to think of border and territorial disputes as something that happens in the Middle East or eastern Europe, but North America itself was contested land—both among European powers and between settlers and indigenous people—not so long ago. And for all the United States fixates on its external borders, particularly under the current administration, it still has unfinished business with the territorial challenges from within.

On the other hand, this discussion assumes that being a country requires physical space in the world at all.

Virtual Countries, Real Borders

On an unseasonably warm April day, I hurriedly made my way up Embassy Row in Washington, DC, my documents clutched in my hand. As I sweated through the suit I rarely wear to work, the eagle on the cover of my passport seemed to be looking up at me accusingly. More than eighty years ago, my grandfather left his home in eastern Europe to move to America. Now I was about to take a journey in the opposite direction. I double-checked that all my papers were in order as I rang the bell at the embassy door. I was about to apply for residency in Estonia. Well, not really.

In October 2014, Estonia announced that it would be the first country to offer "e-residency" to foreign nationals, allowing them to take advantage of the same digital services as Estonian citizens.[1] The status was initially offered to foreigners living in the country. The following year, it became available to people outside Estonia's physical borders.

It's not surprising that the first country to offer this would be the Baltic republic that likes to tout itself as "E-stonia." The government has embraced information technology, and the nation's healthy startup scene birthed Skype. But much of the early news coverage of the announcement questioned what exactly one could do with e-residency. Was it a pyramid scheme? Or the state-run equivalent of one of those companies that "sells" you property on the moon? Or was it a prescient glimpse of a world in which new communications technologies will render physical borders obsolete? To find out, I decided I would have to become an E-stonian myself.

Perhaps appropriately for such an experiment like this, I have never been to the physical country of Estonia. While I like to think I have basic knowledge of the country's politics and history, the fact is I don't know too much about it. Until applying for e-residency, the only Estonians I had much knowledge of were Jaan Tallinn, the post-humanist apocalypse-predicting Skype co-founder; Toomas Hendrik Ilves, the country's acerbic, bow-tied former president, who's a must-follow on Twitter; and the monkish, minimalist composer Arvo Pärt, who's created some of my favorite chilled-out work music. But it's a stable and democratic country, and one I certainly don't mind being associated with, particularly as the obligations associated with e-residency are pretty minimal: I don't have to pay taxes or serve in the country's military, after all.

My lack of any connection to real-world Estonia didn't seem to be much of a problem when I arrived at the embassy for an appointment with the exceedingly friendly political affairs secretary who took my paperwork, telling me I was the first one to apply there. (At the time I applied, prospective e-residents had to file paperwork in person at an Estonian embassy or consulate, but it's now possible to apply online.) I turned over an 80 euro application fee, my passport (the secretary either didn't notice or didn't care about the rather ostentatious Russian visa sticker from a previous reporting trip), and a personal statement about why I was interested in e-residency. I was up-front about the fact that I was a journalist interested in learning more about e-residency, despite having little to no connection to Estonia. I expressed a vague but sincere desire to someday visit the physical country, e-residency card in hand.

The whole process at the embassy took about ten minutes, which is not long for an immigration procedure but is kind of a lot to sign up for an online membership program. When I stepped back into the sunlight of Massachusetts Avenue, I still wasn't sure quite what I had signed up for.

E-residency gives holders the ability to digitally sign documents and contracts, register companies in Estonia ("within a day," according to the website), file Estonian taxes online, encrypt documents, and conduct e-banking. As of 2017, there were nearly eighteen thousand e-residents from 137 countries. The highest number come from neighboring Finland and Russia, followed by the United States.

Katre Kasmel, communications director for the e-residency program, told me by email, "The persons who have signed up for e-Residency have been mostly entrepreneurs who have businesses in Estonia. With e-Residency they can manage their company online without the need to come to Estonia to sign contracts and other documents." Others, he told me, are people "who live in Estonia, like foreign specialists, students, teachers, spouses of diplomats, etc."

The very first e-resident, the *Economist* correspondent Edward Lucas, who lived in Estonia for a number of years, told the *Atlantic* that he likes "having a digital signature valid anywhere in the EU, or in any other country which uses electronic authentication."[2] Charles Brett of the British tech site the *Register,* who currently lives in the real Estonia in addition to being a recent e-resident, is also a fan: "As an e-Resident you can do everything legally required for a business by electronic means from afar, including setting up a company, signing contracts, opening bank accounts, making and receiving payments and paying all taxes."[3]

Given that I didn't pretend to have any intention of doing any of those things, I was still not quite sure they would actually let me become an e-resident. But sure enough, about one month later, I received an email saying my e-residency card had been shipped from Tallinn and was ready for pickup. After one more trip to the embassy, this time to have my fingerprints scanned, I was officially a proud E-stonian.

I was issued a packet containing an ID card embedded with an EMV chip like those in credit and debit cards. I also received a personal code like those held by real Estonians, a chip reader to plug into my USB port, and a document of pin codes needed to access e-residency services. I excitedly installed the necessary software (ignoring my skeptical coworkers' warnings that I was likely exposing myself to a Russian botnet attack) and plugged my card into the reader. After a couple of tries, I was able to access the e-residency site—and quickly found there was nothing really for me to do.

I'm not planning on registering a business in Estonia and I don't really have any documents needing a digital signature. The kind of journalism I do doesn't exactly require Edward Snowden–level crypto, but even if it did, I'm not sure I would trust encryption software provided by a government, even one as tech-friendly as Estonia's.

But perhaps there are more ineffable benefits. I don't feel any particular stirrings listening to my adoptive digital homeland's national anthem. But I will now happily root for the white, black, and blue as my second-favorite team at the next Olympics. I probably wouldn't recommend e-residency to anyone not planning on taking up real residency in Estonia, and I'm still not exactly certain that it will ever appeal much beyond that group. But it's early days. E-residency is still evolving. This may be the first time I've been an early adopter of anything, and I'm happy that it coincides with the struggle to define what nationality means on the Internet.

In its early days, the Internet was supposed to pose a mortal threat to the authority of nation-states. At Davos in 1996, John Perry Barlow, former Grateful Dead lyricist turned Internet rights activist, penned the document he called the "Declaration of the Independence of Cyberspace." "Governments of the Industrial World, you weary giants of flesh and steel," he wrote, "I come from Cyberspace, the new home of Mind. On behalf of the future, I ask you of the past to leave us alone. You are not welcome among us. You have no sovereignty where we gather."[4]

Barlow, who went on to found the influential NGO Electronic Frontier Foundation, was not alone in his predictions. Despite the Internet's origins in research funded by the U.S. Defense Department's DARPA agency, Internet culture has always had a libertarian edge, skeptical of control by state agencies and, more than previous communications technologies, able to operate largely outside the control over governments.

Even those who don't share Barlow's libertarian worldview regarded the Internet as antithetical to government control. In 2000, President Bill Clinton dismissed China's efforts to censor the Internet as "trying to nail jello to the wall."[5] The years since have not been kind to Clinton's formulation—the Chinese government has gotten quite adept at nailing jello—but events since then, including the Iranian election protests of 2009, the 2011 upheavals in the Arab world, and the more modest impact made by the Occupy Wall Street movement, have generated a new round of excitement about the power of social media to turn the tables and give activists an advantage against powerful governments.

The cryptocurrency Bitcoin, digitally distributed and backed by no government, is meant to be a challenge to government control of the global monetary supply. Before founding WikiLeaks, Julian Assange waxed hopeful in published manifestos about the power of new technologies to disrupt "important communication between authoritarian conspirators, foment strong resistance to authoritarian planning and create powerful incentives for more humane forms of governance."[6]

These days, such notions look out of date, as countries have moved aggressively to impose authority and territoriality over the Internet. This was demonstrated by a recent American court decision ruling that the U.S. government could not compel Microsoft to turn over customer emails stored on servers in Ireland, or for that matter anywhere outside the borders of the United States.[7] While many data privacy advocates celebrated the decision, it sets an odd precedent: the notion that governments have physical jurisdiction over data stored within their borders, no matter the nationality or location of the person sending or receiving that data. It could give ammunition to a number of countries, many of them authoritarian regimes with a track record of stamping out speech and dissent online, that have embraced the idea of "Internet sovereignty," the notion that national governance should exercise control over Internet activity within their borders.

One of the many things Donald Trump and Vladimir Putin agree on is that the Internet *belongs* to America. Trump suggested during his campaign that a good response to groups like ISIS using the Internet would be to ask Bill Gates, for unclear reasons, to "clos[e] that Internet up" in "certain areas." His logic: "It was our idea. . . . I don't want them using our Internet."[8] (Thankfully, he doesn't appear to have acted on this notion since coming to office.)

Putin sees it the same way, arguing at a forum in St. Petersburg in 2014 that the Internet is a "CIA project" and "is still developing as such."[9] Putin is not totally wrong; the Internet does trace its origins back to data-sharing systems developed by U.S. intelligence in the 1980s. But the implications of his remarks were ominous. They came just a few days after Russia's parliament passed a bill that required foreign Internet companies, including Google, Facebook, and Microsoft, to store Russian customer data in servers on Russian soil, widely seen as a way for the government to strengthen its control over its citizens' Internet use.

China, which has developed one of the world's most advanced and wide-ranging Web censorship systems, nicknamed the "Great Firewall," is also enthusiastic about Internet sovereignty. Iran has for years promoted a "national Internet" project aimed at protecting its citizens from unwelcome outside influences.[10] The idea is not attractive only to dictatorships. As more information about American Web surveillance has come to light, many democracies have also been asking why they can't have more control over their own data. In the wake of Edward Snowden's revelations that the U.S. National Security Agency had intercepted the communications of Brazil's then president Dilma Rousseff, her government supported, though eventually abandoned, a data storage law similar to Russia's.[11]

The Internet is clearly not destined to be the utopian realm free from state control that many hoped in its early years. To some extent, the speech, commerce, and political activity that takes place online within a particular country will be subject to that country's laws, even if the technology needed to enforce those laws often lags behind.

The territoriality of the real world exists online in more subtle ways as well. The google.so page that my browser opened up when I was in Somaliland was a reminder of the fact that according to the rest of the world, I was in Somalia. Similarly, google.iq reminded me I was technically in Iraq when I was in Kurdistan, and google.ge placed me in Georgia when I was in Abkhazia. The Kurdish government did register the .krd domain name in 2016, but as a "generic" name rather than a country code. Nonetheless, it was seen as a nationalist gesture. "Those who imprisoned us within these geographical boundaries do not have the same leverage in cyberspace," Hiwa Afandi, head of the Department of Information Technology for the Kurdish Regional

Government, told Reuters. "In the internet we choose our own borders. We would rather live in a country called Kurdistan, be it physical or in cyberspace."[12]

Controversies have periodically erupted over the designation of disputed regions on Google Maps. The company has sidestepped this problem by simply displaying the local politically correct designations for the country in which you access the site. So, fire up Google Maps in Russia and you will see Crimea as part of Russia. Check in Ukraine and it's still part of Ukraine.[13] Anywhere else you get a dotted line letting you know the status is disputed. The lines that divide the earth's landmass in the age of stasis divide cyberspace as well.

Estonia proposes a different, more open model of nationality on the Internet, one not limited to citizens of the physical country it's connected to, and one that suggests a compromise between the post-national aspirations of the early cyberutopians and the realities of operating in a world of countries. I'm still not quite sure what it means, but for now, I'm happy to live online in E-stonia.

3

The Invisible Country

It was near midnight on the side of a dark desert road, miles from the nearest town, with only the light of our cell phones to help my traveling companions change a flat tire, around the time when the *second* spare we tried failed to align with the wheel, that I began to contemplate the phrase "middle of nowhere."

It was my last day in Somaliland, an independent but unrecognized country in the Horn of Africa, officially considered by the rest of the world to be the northern section of Somalia. I had reserved the last day for sightseeing with some members of the Somaliland national football team whom I had met on my trip to Abkhazia. As a foreigner in Somaliland, I was required to hire an armed government minder when leaving the capital, a bored but affable security guard in full uniform carrying an AK-47 who didn't say too much but was a good sport about posing with us for selfies. After lunching on fried fish in what felt like blast-furnace heat in the port city of Berbera—currently in the midst of a Dubai-funded renovation—we had driven up narrow winding paths into the mountains and made a sundown visit to a beach on the Gulf of Aden.

Now, however, we were stuck on the side of the road, not in any particular danger—I did, after all, have a large man with a gun in charge of keeping me safe—but certainly in the kind of situation that makes a traveler take stock of his location on the globe.

Once upon a time, the world was big enough that its full vastness was unknowable to any particular person in any particular location. To Europeans, central Africa was a mystery. To ancient Polynesians, who traveled almost unthinkable distances across the Pacific, acquiring detailed knowledge of geography, tides, and weather conditions, the topography of Belgium or Boston would have been equally mysterious.

Today, when one can access a satellite image of almost any point on the globe—from the rain forests of Borneo to Rio de Janeiro's favelas—with a flick of a finger on Google Earth, the middle of nowhere doesn't mean quite the same thing. But the strange geopolitical twilight realm that Somaliland has inhabited for the past twenty-six years suggests that today being in the middle of nowhere has less to do with physical distance or the difficulty of travel to a given place (I had reached Somaliland on a normal commercial flight from Dubai, the busiest international airport on earth) than perception. Somaliland is somewhere, but also nowhere, mainly because most of the rest of the world is either unaware of it or has opted to deny that it exists.

When you're in Somaliland, there's never any question that you're in Somali*land*. The place has all the trappings of countryhood. At the airport, over which flies the Somaliland flag, a customs officer in a Somaliland uniform checked my Somaliland visa issued by the Somaliland consulate in Washington, DC. During my visit, I paid Somaliland shillings to drivers of cabs with Somaliland plates who took me to the offices of ministers of the Somaliland government. But according to the U.S. State Department, the United Nations, the African Union, and every other government on earth, I was not in Somaliland, a poor but stable and mostly functional country on the Horn of Africa. I was in Somalia, global shorthand for violent anarchy and state failure.

Somaliland is a special case, even among unrecognized states—both completely, unambiguously independent and entirely isolated politically. Unlike South Sudan before its independence, Somaliland's claim for statehood is based not on a redrawing of colonial borders but an attempt to reestablish them. Unlike Abkhazia, it doesn't have a powerful state backer. Unlike Taiwan, it's shackled not to a richer, more powerful country but a poorer, weaker one. Unlike Palestine, its quest for independence is not a popular cause for activists around the world. Not that Somaliland really has any enemies, other than Somalia. To the degree that foreign officials acknowledge it at all, they're generally sympathetic to its history and admiring of its recent accomplishments.

Somaliland's main obstacle is not the world's animosity but its indifference. Its current predicament answers the question What would happen if you created a new country, and no one noticed?

The journalist Graeme Wood has described places like Somaliland and Abkhazia as the "limbo world": entities that "start by acting like real countries, and then hope to become them."[1]

As I wrote earlier, what separates "real" from "self-proclaimed" countries is simply the recognition of other countries. There's no ultimate legal authority in international relations that decides what is or isn't a real country, and differences of opinion on that question are common. What separates the Somalilands of the world from, say, Sweden is that Sweden is recognized by its peers. Recognition is a political rather than a legal act. Twenty-five countries currently don't formally recognize Israel.[2] Palestine is generally not recognized as an independent state by a number of countries in Europe and North America but is by 135 countries overall.[3] Russia and its ideological allies recognize the breakaway Georgian regions of Abkhazia and South

Ossetia, but these countries generally don't recognize the independence of Kosovo. The Pacific islands of Nauru, Vanuatu, and Tuvalu have taken a mercenary approach to recognition disputes, trading recognition or nonrecognition of controversial would-be countries like Abkhazia and Taiwan in exchange for favorable relations with Russia and China.[4]

Recognizing a country is not the same thing as having diplomatic relations with a country. The United States may view Kim Jong-un's government in North Korea as illegitimate, but it doesn't deny that North Korea is a country or the fact that Kim is the ruler of it.[5] There's a separate question of the recognition of governments as opposed to states. The general policy of the United States has been to recognize whatever government has de facto control of a country, regardless of the circumstances in which it came to power. This tradition dates back to the (at the time) controversial decision to recognize the government that took power in France after the revolution in 1792.[6] The United States has deviated from this principle a number of times, particularly in Latin America where nonrecognition was used as a political weapon to punish governments the United States viewed as illegitimate, generally those that came to power after revolutions or coups. The Obama administration also muddied the already murky waters by deciding to, as Secretary of State Hillary Clinton put it, recognize the anti-Qaddafi Transitional National Council "as the legitimate governing authority for Libya." Obama also announced in late 2012 that Syria's "opposition Coalition is now inclusive enough, is reflective and representative enough of the Syrian population that we consider them the legitimate representative of the Syrian people in opposition to the Assad regime."[7] As Assad's ouster came to look less likely and the administration negotiated a deal to remove the regime's nuclear weapons, the United States backed off its nonrecognition stance.

But even this form of nonrecognition doesn't imply that the United States didn't view Libya or Syria as real, existing countries. Sometimes the line between those concepts is blurry. From the end of World War II until 1971, the United States didn't recognize the People's Republic of China, conferring recognition instead on the Republic of China government based in Taiwan. This was a means of denying legitimacy to the "red" Chinese government, but in a legal sense was essentially a denial of the existence of the world's largest country.

Since the establishment of the United Nations in 1945, membership in that body has become the gold standard of international legitimacy. UN membership requires approval by two-thirds of the General Assembly and, more critically, a reference from the Security Council. Until the United States changes its stance, Palestinian efforts to gain full membership will be for naught. Ditto for Kosovo, because of Russia, and for Taiwan—which has applied for full membership every year since 1993—because of China.[8]

Statehood may be a legal concept, but achieving it is an entirely political process. Any attempt to pin down universal laws that are always enforced regarding who's in and who's out will be fruitless.

Acting Like a Country

Compared to Abkhazia, Somaliland is pretty easy to get to. There are regular flights to Hargeisa from Dubai and Addis Ababa. Americans can fairly easily obtain a visa from Somaliland's unofficial "consulate" in Washington, DC, which, as far as I could tell, consisted of one guy, whom I never actually met, working out of a coworking space near Farragut Square.

From the plane, approaching Hargeisa's Egal International Airport, Somaliland looks uninhabited, if not uninhabitable. The arid scrub

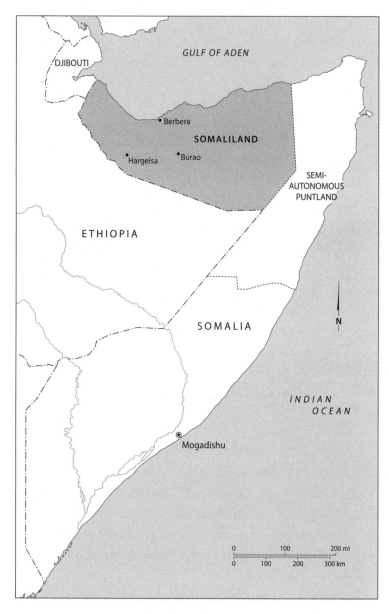

Somaliland

brush and jagged mountains that stretch for miles around the capital city don't look like the most inviting spot for human settlement.

Hargeisa, nestled in a pleasantly cool, hilly region that looks almost Californian if you squint a little bit, is a scruffy, sprawling town of cinderblock houses and potholed roads. The city feels coated in a fine film of desert dust and it's extraordinarily dry, though periodic violent downpours in the rainy season leave the mostly unpaved streets damp and soggy. Driving in Hargeisa, which I attempted only once, can be harrowing, not least because Somalilanders, for unclear reasons, drive on the right side of the road but also mostly drive British-style right-hand-drive cars, making passing the car ahead of you an act of faith as much as skill.

Camels are the traditional livelihood, food source, and currency of Somali herders, and even in the big city, it's not unusual to see them loping through busy downtown traffic. Sidewalk-stall restaurants crank out steaming, heaping plates of chewy camel meat (not bad) and thick, frothy camel milk (nauseating—to me, anyway). Camel liver, another specialty, is usually only eaten at breakfast.

From street-side stands, money changers dispense grimy, faded bricks of shilling banknotes held together by rubber bands. When I was visiting, the shilling was trading at about seven thousand to the dollar. Given that you can't exchange Somaliland shillings anywhere outside Somaliland, I don't exactly understand how this exchange rate is set. When paying for anything in a store with shillings, unless you know what you're doing, it's generally best to just hand over one of these bricks to the clerk and let him take out what he needs. Nowadays, most people are more likely to pay for basic goods and services by transferring cell phone credit.

Somaliland society is generally pretty freewheeling. Libertarians curious about what a basically functional society would look like with a bare minimum of both services and regulations from a barely funded government should check it out.

Try to book a hotel in Somaliland online and you're likely to be referred to a travel advisory stating, "The U.S. Department of State warns U.S. citizens to avoid travel to Somalia because of continuous threats by the al-Qaeda affiliated terrorist group, al-Shabaab."[9] But once you're there you quickly realize that such warnings are unnecessary. Hargeisa is one of the safest large cities in Africa, and aside from the pollution and the traffic, there's not too much to be concerned about when you're walking around, though foreigners traveling outside the capital have been required to hire an armed guard since the killing of four foreign aid workers by bandits in 2004.[10] There's been almost no terrorist activity in Somaliland since 2008, when suicide bombers attacked the presidential palace and Ethiopian consulate.[11] In contrast to the south, there's no pirate activity along Somaliland's shores, though pirates caught by international naval forces have been sent to Hargeisa for imprisonment.[12]

The population of Somaliland is nearly 100 percent Muslim, though locals will tell you that levels of observance vary. Nearly all women wear hijabs, and in recent years, the full-face-covering niqab has become more common under the influence of Saudi-funded religious schools. There's no alcohol for sale, at least officially. I did spend a slightly harrowing night with some local acquaintances cruising downtown Hargeisa in search of black-market alcohol. We purchased a plastic water bottle full of vodka, mixed it with Coke, and consumed it in our car in a restaurant parking lot, bringing back memories of illicit high school parties.

Somaliland's narcotic of choice is *qat,* the mildly stimulating leaves chewed for hours on end daily by a remarkably high percentage of men in the Horn of Africa and Yemen, from laborers to senior government ministers. Qat, mostly trucked in from Ethiopia, is sold in bushels of branches, whose leaves are plucked off one by one for chewing. Qat is chewed almost exclusively by men and packed and sold almost exclusively by women. Around 3 p.m. or so every day, most formal businesses in Hargeisa shut down as the chewing sessions begin in private homes and offices throughout the city. People will tell you that this isn't wasted time, that a lot of important business and negotiations are conducted in these sessions, and this may be true, though it's not hard to imagine other, more productive uses for the massive amount of money and time spent each day getting the men of Somaliland their fix.

Hargeisa's main work of public art is a war memorial consisting of a stubby MiG fighter plane—a real one—shot down in 1988 and now mounted on a pedestal along the city's main thoroughfare. Hargeisans will tell you, with some ironic pride, that their city is one of the few places in the world that was bombed by planes that took off *from that same city.* The event is part of a long chain of events, most of them tragic, leading up to the country's strange current predicament.

As the names of their countries suggest, there's little ethnic or linguistic difference between the people of Somalia and Somaliland. Both are descendants of the earliest Somali-speakers in the region, who arrived from Ethiopia around 500 BCE—camel-keeping herders migrating in response to environmental pressure in search of better grazing land.[13] In contrast to the situation in other parts of Africa, where diverse ethnic and linguistic groups were lumped together in modern states created within colonial boundaries, Somalis are a large and linguistically homogenous group *separated* by colonial boundaries. The five points of the white star on the Republic of Somalia's flag represent the five divisions of what was once optimistically referred to as "Greater Somalia." During the colonial era, the region was divided into British Somaliland (now Somaliland), Italian Somaliland (now

Somalia), and French Somaliland (now Djibouti.) The other two points on the star represent the heavily Somali regions of northern Kenya and the Ogaden region of eastern Ethiopia.

The entity that today calls itself the Republic of Somaliland owes its existence to two factors: its proximity to Yemen and its abundance of sheep. In the late nineteenth century, Britain, with the support of Italy, and France, with the support of Russia, were locked in a multi-decade struggle for control of the Nile. As a means of both countering French influence and ensuring a regular supply of mutton for its garrison at Aden, Britain signed a series of agreements with tribes in northern Somalia. For seventy-six years Britain ruled Somaliland, what historian Ioan Lewis characterizes as "in relation to its size and significance . . . undoubtedly . . . one of Britain's least rewarding possessions."[14]

There's a good case to be made that its marginal status as a colony benefited the country in the long run. Whereas Somaliland had been considered a backwater by the British and therefore left mostly to govern itself through existing clan structure, Italy considered Somalia an integral part of its short-lived ambitions to build a North African empire that also included modern-day Libya and parts of Egypt. Italy poured resources into building infrastructure in Mogadishu, educating civil servants and setting up the rudiments of a centralized state.[15]

It shouldn't be surprising that today the territory where the colonizing power had more ambitious state-building goals is the more unstable. There's fairly convincing evidence from studies of regions of India and other parts of Africa to support the notion that postcolonial countries where colonizers had a lighter touch turned out better in the long term.[16]

As Somalilanders will often remind you, they were, in the past, an independent country, fully recognized by the international community, including the United Nations. But this halcyon period lasted less than a week. On June 26, 1960, the former Protectorate of Somaliland became fully independent from British rule, its independence recognized by thirty-five countries around the world including the United States. The next day, its new legislature passed a law approving a union with the south. On July 1, Somalia became independent from Italy, and the two were joined together—a decision Somaliland has regretted almost ever since.[17] Difficulties emerged almost immediately over harmonizing the two territories' political systems, and just a year after independence, voters in the north rejected a new constitution. The marriage was off to a rocky start. Things would go from bad to worse in 1969 when an officers' coup brought Siad Barre to power.

Somali clan structure is the critical underlying factor behind almost all politics in both countries. There are six main Somali clans, which are broken into dozens of subclans. The vast majority of those living in what is now Somaliland come from various branches of the Isaaq clan. The south is more heterogeneous, which is almost certainly one factor contributing to its greater instability. Somalilanders generally point to this difference to explain why their claim for nationhood is based on more than just reestablishing a colonial boundary between Somalis: the differences between the two are cultural as well.[18]

"It's not a new country. When we joined the Somalia Republic, we had our own culture. We are a completely different Somali," Mohammed Ahmed Mohamoud, aka Barwani, a civil society activist and director of the Somaliland Nonstate Actors Forum, told me in an interview in the lobby of the swanky Maan Soor hotel. Sitting with us was Mohamed Omar Hagi, a Britain-based Somali activist visiting the country, who also objected to the idea that Somalis are somehow obligated by ethnicity to join together in one country. "Yes, we speak the same language, same religion, same color," he said. "But the Arab world has fifteen different countries with the same language and same religion. If they have fifteen different states, why not us?"

The tensions within Somaliland society only got worse as Barre's long reign continued. Since independence, Somalia's and Somaliland's leaders have tended to favor members of their own clans and subclans with patronage. Barre may have espoused a doctrine of "scientific socialism," a fusion of terrible governance ideas imported from China, North Korea, and Nasserite Egypt, but he was not above ethnic nationalism, privileging his own Darod clan, which added to the resentment of the northern Isaaqs.

Things began to take a turn for the disastrous when Barre launched an invasion of Ethiopia on behalf of Somali separatists in the Ogaden region. The Soviet Union, previously a backer of Barre's scientific socialism, switched to support the Ethiopians, and the Somalis were routed. The war, combined with a crippling drought, led hundreds of thousands of Ogaden refugees to stream into unprepared Somalia—by 1980, one out of four people in the country was a refugee, and support for Barre and his harsh military regime began to erode.

During the 1980s, a primarily Isaaq northern rebel group known, somewhat misleadingly, as the Somali National Movement (SNM) emerged to challenge Mogadishu's rule, prompting harsh crackdowns and adding to the perception that the north was a region under occupation. This culminated in an all-out civil war between the SNM and the central government in the late 1980s—including the infamous bombing of Hargeisa, commemorated by the jet fighter propped up in the center of town—during which thousands were killed and millions fled. Just as thousands had streamed in from Ethiopia a decade earlier, now the tide of humanity flowed in the opposite direction. From Ethiopia and Djibouti, there was a Somali diaspora; Somalis fled throughout the world.

On May 18, 1991, the SNM proclaimed that the region was reestablishing its independence, severing its ties to the south, and would now be known as the Republic of Somaliland. The world, for the most part, shrugged. The slow and steady process of state formation in the north would be almost entirely overshadowed in the international media by the chaos engulfing the south, particularly after an international intervention led to the killing of nineteen American troops in the infamous Black Hawk Down incident during the battle of Mogadishu two years later.

So why has Somaliland been more successful and stable than its southern neighbor, even with virtually no assistance from the international community? Being for the most part populated by only one clan no doubt helped it avoid the tribal conflicts that have troubled its southern neighbors, though divisions between subclans of the Isaaq are still stark, and in Hargeisa often determine where in town people choose to live.

Most Somalilanders also point to the role of clan elders, who in Somaliland are integrated into the country's governance. In 1993, two years after declaring independence, the government of Somaliland, with no assistance from the United Nations, which was still formally committed to a unified Somalia, organized a conference of elders, or *gurti,* to reach consensus on pressing issues and establish a structure for the new government.[19] In addition to a president and a traditional elected parliament, Somaliland has an unelected upper house of gurti, somewhat similar to Britain's House of Lords, which has a consultative role on certain legislation and is entrusted with settling disputes between the country's subclans. "It's the elders who really made this peace," Hagi said. "The social contract between the tribes of Somaliland is made by the elders, not the government or the international community."

Structural factors aside, it is also clear that Somaliland has been lucky to benefit from the leadership of a few individuals, people like Edna Adan.

The runner Mo Farah, a member of the Isaaq clan whose family lives in Gabiley, about an hour and a half west of Hargeisa, is arguably the world's most famous Somalilander. But he was born in Mogadishu, trains in the United States, and runs for Britain so, as with many Somalis, his national identity is a little fluid.

The most famous person *in* Somaliland, and the country's most prominent global advocate, is undoubtedly Edna Adan, generally just referred to in Somaliland as Edna. "We don't have a George Clooney," one local journalist told me, referring to the Hollywood star's advocacy on behalf of South Sudan's independence. "All we've got is Edna."

When I met Adan at the maternity hospital and midwifery school she runs in Hargeisa, which everyone just calls Edna Hospital, she handed me her business card, which on the back features the caption "Where is Somaliland?" with an arrow pointing to the country's location on a map of the Horn of Africa. Job one for Adan, who's traveled throughout the world, is simply telling people what and where her country is. "I can't get anyone to come here," she sighs. "The teachers and doctors cannot come to us because their governments tell them not to. I don't know how you slipped through the net."

It was Bastille Day, and the hospital, which receives some French funding, was somewhat incongruously decked out in the *tricolore*. As we spoke, we were interrupted by doctors wanting a go-ahead to provide certain procedures, students with questions about the courses, staff wondering what to do with the leftovers from the Bastille Day party. It was clear that not a lot happened around this place without Edna's approval.

Her office was decorated with photos of dignitaries she's met, from Hillary Clinton to Kofi Annan to the journalists Nicholas Kristof and Sheryl WuDunn, who profiled her in their book *Half the Sky.*[20] A centerpiece of the office was a striking photo of a very young Edna with her late husband, Mohamed Ibrahim Egal, at the White House with Lyndon Johnson in 1968 when Egal was prime minister of Somalia.

She was Somalia's first qualified nurse-midwife and the first woman to drive. She spent years as a UN and WHO official before returning to Somaliland to build the hospital with her own savings; the hospital, for all the limitations on personnel and equipment that Adan gripes about, is one of the premier facilities in the Horn of Africa, attracting patients from throughout Somaliland as well as neighboring countries. She's been called the Muslim Mother Teresa for her work in promoting women's health and campaigning against female genital mutilation.[21] She also served for several years as Somaliland's foreign minister, continuing to deliver babies while on the job.

Though her political activities get less attention than her public health work, Adan is also a tireless advocate for Somaliland's independence. "For twenty-five years I've been waiting for the world to see how stable, peaceful, and governable we are," she told me, decrying what she called the "world conspiracy against Somaliland's recognition." Adan sees Somaliland's unrecognized status as the main reason for its lack of economic progress over the past quarter century. "I've got brilliant kids here—and plenty of rubbish—but some absolutely brilliant kids. They don't have opportunities. They are denied the right to be taught by people who are qualified to teach, because those people's governments forbid them from coming here," she said. "Nobody should be denied access to health, human rights, and development because of the name of their country,"

Nonrecognition by Western powers is having an impact on the status of women as well, she argued, saying that Western countries' lack of engagement was opening the door to the influence of fundamentalists from the Gulf. She pointed to an old photo of herself as first lady in a chic cocktail dress: "You see my pictures! We never used to cover ourselves from head to toe," she said. "We had necks, we had hair, we were people. Others are getting into Somaliland faster than the West. And if that keeps on like this, heaven help us."

She echoed a theme I heard a lot in Somaliland, that the country is a rare beacon of stability in a very dangerous neighborhood. "You have Eritrea, which is a mess, you have Somalia, which doesn't exist, you have Yemen, which has collapsed, you have Djibouti with all your military power there but it still has political turbulence, and then you've got Somaliland, which is stable. Somaliland should be in the ranks of the law-abiding countries. If Somaliland goes the other way, Djibouti and Ethiopia are going to fall. We are the lifejacket."

Somaliland is indeed stable by local standards, but it's not exactly prospering. Reliable statistics are hard to come by, but in 2012 the World Bank estimated its GDP per capita at just $348, which would make it the fourth-poorest country in the world.[22] Its main industry is livestock export, which accounts for about 70 percent of jobs. The main customers are in the Middle East, and business picks up during the annual Hajj in Mecca. With few opportunities at home, it's not surprising that an estimated 44 percent of unemployed youth have stated their intention to migrate.[23]

A large number of people are also dependent on $500 million per year in remittances from the roughly million-strong Somaliland diaspora living for the most part in Britain, the United States, Scandinavia, and elsewhere in Africa.[24] This isn't unusual for developing countries, though in Somaliland's case, the country's ambiguous status seems to make the divide between homeland and diaspora even more porous than normal. Many of the senior government ministers are returnees from careers in America or Europe. In the summer months, Hargeisa is flooded with diaspora youth visiting relatives, including several of the players on the Somaliland national football team, to the point that Western-style restaurants have emerged almost exclusively to provide European and North American kids with a taste of their adopted homelands.

But officials are understandably worried that this flow of cash from abroad is a finite resource. Most members of the diaspora are refugees who left the country during the violence of the 1980s and their children. *Their* children are less likely to feel the need to support aunts and uncles they barely know. "These offspring are now basically Americans or British or French or whatever," Energy Minister Hussein Abdi Dualeh told me. "They don't have the same attachment to the country." With remittances likely to dry up in the coming years and livestock an unreliable resource—Saudi Arabia banned Somaliland imports for ten years until 2009 because of concerns about the mosquito-borne virus Rift Valley fever—the government is looking for other sources of investment, but Somaliland is a place with an image problem.[25]

"The name always scares people," said Dualeh. "Anything that starts with 'Somali-,' no matter how it ends, is a red flag for a lot of people. But companies who are here realize it's a very benign, very safe environment." The twin hopes for the Somali economy right now are oil exploration—currently by a handful of hardier energy firms off the coast—and a plan by Dubai Ports World to develop the Red Sea port of Berbera, which could conceivably be an alternative means of bringing goods by sea into landlocked Ethiopia, but it's hard to imagine that plan taking off without a serious improvement in roads and infrastructure. For that, international investment is probably necessary.

And for that, once again, it would be helpful for other countries to know that Somaliland exists and isn't the same thing as Somalia.

Nonrecognition is also a problem for Somalilanders who try to travel abroad. The country's status means that few countries accept its passport as a valid travel document. Only Djibouti, Ethiopia, Kenya, South Africa, and South Sudan are open to Somaliland passport holders, though the *Somaliland Sun* reported in 2015 that talks were ongoing with the United Arab Emirates.[26] The players on the Somaliland national team who traveled via Moscow to Abkhazia for the World Football Cup had to get special permission from the Russian government to allow them to travel to the event, a predicament not all that unlike that faced by the Mohawk lacrosse team.

There's a tragic irony to Somaliland's predicament: traditionally nomadic people, who still pride themselves on being prodigious travelers who have settled around the globe, are being isolated from the rest of the world. "You're locked up and can't go anywhere," said Abdire Zaki Aalen, a Hargeisa-based journalist. "Before the Europeans came to Africa, people used to cross borders, there weren't any borders. Since the borders were established they've extinguished that."

But another unique feature of the country's situation is that it's not actually looking to challenge the much-maligned borders drawn by Europeans across the African continent—it's looking to restore them. "The international community said we seceded from Somalia. We did not. We already had our own nation," said Barwani. "Our borders were established through an agreement between the Italian government and the British," said Foreign Minister Saad Ali Shire. "It's an internationally determined boundary."

Although Somaliland voluntarily erased the border with Somalia in 1960, Somalilanders don't consider that decision irreversible. As Somalilanders often point out, theirs wouldn't be the first country to back out of a postcolonial merger. Senegal and the Gambia, a narrow strip of a country located completely within Senegal's territory, were joined together as the confederation of Senegambia from 1982 to 1989. Egypt and Syria were briefly joined together as the United Arab Republic from 1958 to 1961 until Syria seceded. If these countries couldn't make their marriages work, why, Somalilanders ask, should Somaliland be stuck in a loveless alliance? Or as Edna Adan more colorfully puts it, Somaliland is "like a widow who is being asked to produce a divorce certificate signed by their spouse. We've been separated for thirty-six years. We don't know each other. People are pushing us toward reuniting with a putrefied cadaver."

"We think we have a better case than Eritrea and South Sudan and East Timor, other countries that are recognized around the world," said Shire. "We have a better case than most of the new countries that have been recognized." There's little attachment to the idea of "Greater Somalia" today, and Somalilanders balk at the idea that they ought to be part of the same country as their southern neighbor just because they're all Somalis.

These arguments were hard to refute in Hargeisa. But in the outside world, they're unlikely to be particularly persuasive. The frustrating reality Somaliland finds itself up against is that the world map is preserved in place less by international law or even custom than by path dependence. Countries tend to stay the way they are and people, with some justification, believe it would be awfully difficult and dangerous to change them.

Why Stasis?

The last major wave of country creation took place in the early 1990s as the end of the Cold War hastened the breakup of the Soviet Union and the explosion of Yugoslavia. Since then, only a handful of new countries have joined the club.

In 1999, Indonesia gave up control of East Timor. It was formally admitted to the United Nations in 2002, becoming the first new universally recognized country of the twenty-first century. The eastern half of the island of Timor had been a Portuguese colony until 1975, when it achieved independence but was then promptly annexed by Indonesia, leading to a decades-long war for independence.[27]

Kosovo's parliament formally declared independence in 2008 after a NATO air campaign forced Serbia to withdraw its troops from the majority ethnic Albanian region.[28]

Another former portion of Serbia, Montenegro, became independent after a referendum held in 2006. Unlike Kosovo, viewed by Serbs as a historic and contiguous part of the country's territory, Montenegro, which had been independent as recently as the early twentieth century, had coexisted with Serbia in a loose federation since the breakup of Yugoslavia, making it easier for the Serbian government and its Russian ally to accept the result of the referendum. Montenegro was admitted to the United Nations that same year.[29]

In 2011, South Sudan, with the backing of the United States after a two-decade civil war, declared its independence, becoming the 193rd and most recent UN member state.[30] Palestine is widely recognized as independent outside of Europe and North America, but it is still occupied by Israel and has been shut out of full membership in the United Nations by the threat of U.S. veto.

In short, it's very hard to get recognized as a new country these days, a fact that the few places that have managed to do it don't really disprove. Montenegro and Kosovo can be viewed as the unfinished business of the early 1990s, the last pieces to break off of the desiccated shell of Yugoslavia. (And even so, Kosovo has still fallen short of full international recognition.) East Timor's independence was an adjustment back to colonial borders. It was never part of the Dutch colonial empire that formed most of what is now Indonesia. South Sudan was a genuine exception to the rule, and one that six years later has come to be seen as a cautionary tale about recognizing new countries that aren't yet ready to stand on their own.

So why is it that the wave of border readjustment stopped in the early 1990s? What caused the age of stasis?

The first factor is that the low-hanging fruit for potential countries has been exhausted. The contiguous multinational empires that once played such a major role in world politics shuffled off into the dustbin of history in the twentieth century and were divided into independent countries. The Ottoman and Austro-Hungarian Empires were dissolved after World War I. The Soviet Union lurched on in ever more zombified form until it finally broke up in the 1990s.

The Western Hemisphere was composed almost entirely of independent countries by the early nineteenth century. The post–World War II wave of decolonization that kicked off with Indonesia's declaration of independence in 1945 mostly came to an end in the 1970s and 1980s. There simply weren't that many colonies left to free. Djibouti, which achieved independence from France in 1977, was the last European colonial possession on the continent of Africa, not counting some tiny Spanish enclaves in Morocco. Brunei was the last in Asia.[31] The UN today has only seventeen entries on its list of "non-self-governing territories," nearly all of them islands in the Caribbean or Pacific, with the exception of Moroccan-controlled Western Sahara.[32] The ongoing controversies over the status of Puerto Rico, Gibraltar, and the Falkland/Malvina Islands notwithstanding, the sun has effectively set on the world's great territorial empires.

These empires, the old-fashioned kind involving the formal control of overseas territory, have decidedly gone out of fashion. Without downplaying the tragedy of millions killed in anticolonial struggles throughout the world over the course of the twentieth century in places like Algeria, Angola, and Vietnam, we can say that the breakup of these empires into independent states seems, from today's vantage point, like a historically inevitable process. These empires had become both economically impractical in an era of free trade and economic globalization and morally indefensible as self-determination movements grew within the colonies and paternalist racial attitudes ever so slowly dissolved in the West. The idea that it was natural or justified for Belgium to rule over the Congo or Britain to rule India was once commonplace but today is expressed only by atavistic colonial nostalgists and racists.

After the empires left the stage, any future redrawing of borders would require existing countries to give up territory—not possessions thousands of miles away populated primarily by people of a different cultural or racial group, but areas within their own borders. This is a much tougher sell.

The disintegration of empires over the course of the twentieth century that divided the world's landmass into roughly two hundred sovereign countries fixed one problem but left another: many of the people within those countries didn't particularly want to be part of them. This problem was particularly acute in the Middle East and Africa, where the borders of new states had often been determined more by late nineteenth- or early twentieth-century European power politics than by any connection to ethnic reality in those territories themselves.

But rather than committing to a Wilsonian quest for maximum self-determination around the world—a state for every people, a people for every state—the governments of both the former colonizers and the formerly colonized almost invariably preferred to keep current borders as they were. The new United Nations included language specifically nodding to self-determination in its charter, but this language referred to "territories whose peoples have not yet attained a full measure of self-government," which was generally interpreted to refer to existing territorial units rather than the claims of people who might not be satisfied with the shape of those units.[33] In other words, colonized countries should be independent, but once independent, further adjustments should be avoided.

This stance was made more explicit in UN Resolution 1514, adopted by the General Assembly in 1960, which formally declared colonialism to be a "denial of fundamental human rights" and stated that "all peoples have the right to self-determination." The resolution was a milestone in the era of decolonization, opposed by most of the colonial powers at the time. The framers of the resolution anticipated future complications involving the shape of the new states by including language stating that "any attempt aimed at the partial or total disruption of the national unity and the territorial integrity of a country is incompatible with the purposes and principles of the Charter of the United Nations."[34]

Secretary-General U Thant stated this principle explicitly in 1970: "The United Nations' attitude is unequivocal. As an international organization, the United Nations has never accepted and does not accept and I do not believe it will ever accept the principle of secession of a part of its member states."[35] The UN is, after all, a club of member states. It shouldn't be surprising that it would frown on the breakup of one of its members, which could be used as a precedent for future adjustments.

Other multilateral organizations have followed suit. The Organisation for African Unity (OAU), established in 1963 to support decolonization and bolster the newly independent states on the continent, declared in its charter that it is "determined to safeguard and consolidate the hard-won independence as well as the sovereignty and territorial integrity of our states, and to fight against neocolonialism in all its forms."[36] Preserving territorial integrity is presented as part and parcel of the anticolonial struggle even if the actual territories being defended are themselves the products of colonialism. The charter of the African Union, the OAU's successor organization, made this principle even more explicit in 2000 with a charter pleading with members to "respect . . . [the] borders existing on achievement of independence."[37]

Uti possidetis, the principle that newly sovereign states should maintain the borders of the entity that preceded them, was still the general operating procedure, as it had been when the countries of the Americas became independent in the nineteenth century.[38] As Yuval Shany, a professor of international law at Hebrew University, has written, during this time "a no-secession rule emerged, limiting the application of self-determination to exceptional cases involving colonialism, foreign occupation, racial exclusion from government, and disintegration of existing states."[39]

Another factor contributing to the age of stasis is surely the decline in interstate war. For most of human history, rulers and governments have gone to war over territory, and the ceding or exchange of land was a common feature of conflict resolution. Today, countries very rarely go to war with each other. The first decade of the twenty-first century saw an average of fewer than one interstate armed conflict per year, down from around three during the 1980s. Most of those were small, such as the brief 2011 border skirmish between Thailand and Cambodia. Prior to the current ongoing conflict in Ukraine, the last time two governments fought a major high-casualty war over territory was the Ethiopia-Eritrea war that ended in 2000.[40]

Harvard psychologist Steven Pinker argued in his controversial 2011 book *The Better Angels of Our Nature* that this trend is part of a larger decline in human violence that has been going on since the Middle Ages, with the bloody world wars of the twentieth century as a major anomaly.[41] The decline in violence thesis advanced by Pinker and others has been looking shakier lately, thanks largely to the Syrian civil war, which can arguably be described as a Middle East world war and has pushed the number of global battlefield deaths back up to levels not seen in decades.

A more cynical explanation than Pinker's for the reasons behind the decline in violence is simply that the immense firepower developed during the twentieth century, nuclear weapons in particular, has simply made the costs of interstate war too high. Two major industrialized powers have not fought directly on the battlefield since the Korean War.

Another reason war over territory is less popular than ever is that the people who live in any given territory now expect to have a say in what country they live in. Military historian Martin Van Creveld believes the turning point came in 1871 when Germany, having won a war against France, demanded payment in the form of real estate, as countless conquerors had done since time immemorial, only to find, despite the fact that the French government agreed to a transfer, that the people of the conquered provinces of Alsace and Lorraine refused to accept that they were now Germans. A change had occurred since the rise of nationalism in the mid-nineteenth century. Land was no longer simply real estate to be traded between rulers. It was an integral part of the notion of "country" with which the people who lived there identified strongly. Germany's first chancellor, Otto von Bismarck, came to view the annexation of Alsace-Lorraine as the worst mistake of his career. As Van Creveld writes, "From now on, every other state that nursed a grudge against Germany could invariably count on French support."[42] Alsace-Lorraine became a flash point and was ceded back to France in the Treaty of Versailles. Whatever the reason, this is a major change. For most of human history, the primary reason that countries have gone to war with each other is to control territory. Today, that almost never happens.

More common today are *intra*state conflicts, fought within countries between governments and nonstate armed groups. These wars can be deadly and destabilizing, but they don't typically result in the reapportionment of territory when they conclude.

Interestingly, respect for territorial integrity during this period has not been quite the same as respect for territorial sovereignty, which is under assault more than ever. The United States and other industrialized powers have repeatedly launched military interventions in the developing world, from Vietnam to Haiti to Iraq to Rwanda to Syria, justifying them under international law as necessary for the maintenance of global security or the prevention of atrocities. However, when industrialized powers have launched military interventions overseas, such as the U.S. invasions of Iraq and Afghanistan or France's interventions in Mali and the Central African Republic, they've left existing borders in place.

Major powers have also fought wars in the modern era aimed at maintaining rather than redrawing existing borders. Putting aside world oil markets, the First Gulf War was launched by the United States and its allies to maintain the global norm of territorial integrity, which Saddam Hussein had violated with his invasion of Kuwait— the first time since the Korean War that there had been an attempt to occupy a sovereign country and wipe it off the map entirely. The recent U.S.-led military intervention in Iraq and Syria could also be viewed as a war to maintain the geographical status quo, in this case from the threat posed by the self-declared Islamic State.

All these factors—the emerging political norms of territorial integrity, the role of the United States as backer of the geographical status quo, and the decline of interstate war—have helped create the age of stasis. If not for the unavoidable declines of both the European colonial empires and Soviet Communism, the era would probably have begun much earlier.

The response by the United States in particular to the threat of international terrorism in the years following 9/11, especially the Obama and Trump administrations' reliance on drones and Special Forces operators to fight al-Qaeda affiliates and ISIS, has blurred the line between wartime and peacetime and created a norm in which the United States can carry out combat in multiple countries for an undefined period of time under a broad mandate to fight terrorism. The United States may have no desire to wipe Pakistan off the map as a political and geographical entity, but it is more than willing to ignore Pakistan's sovereignty over its own territory when the opportunity arises to kill the world's most wanted terrorist leader. As recently as the 2008 U.S. election, Senator John McCain called it evidence of political naïveté that Obama was willing to "bomb a country that is a sovereign nation"—Pakistan—in response to actionable intelligence about terrorist targets.[43] This seems downright quaint today after a decade of covert drone strikes, not to mention the raid that killed Osama bin Laden.

We live in a world where Weber's famous definition of the state— the entity that has a monopoly on the use of violence in a given territory—no longer holds for many of the recognized states in the world, both because of violent nonstate actors and the impingements by the world's largest militaries on the sovereignty of both allies and enemies. These are discussed in terms of "failed states," the preferred term for those governments that fail to meet the basic requirements of statehood. Yet that these countries should continue to exist in their current shape is rarely questioned. We may doubt the statehood of places like Somalia, Afghanistan, and Syria, but we do not question their countryhood.

Some might also argue simply that the character of countries that recently successfully became states demonstrates why creating new nations is such a bad idea. No place bolsters this view more than South Sudan, a precedent that backers of Somaliland are obligated to grapple with.

There was some thought at the time of South Sudan's independence in 2011 that it would set a precedent for a redrawing of the map of Africa, or even a new age of global independence movements. International relations theorist Parag Khanna predicted a "wave of self-determination" sweeping the globe.[44]

But South Sudan now looks less like a harbinger of an age of geographical readjustment than an outlier. A big part of what made its independence possible was the rare support of the United States for an independence movement. The role of the United States was critical. When the new nation finally raised its flag in the capital, Juba, in 2011, the *New York Times* reported that spectators waved signs reading, "Thank you George Bush."[45] Independence came six years after the conclusion of a twenty-two-year civil war, one of the longest in history, and more than a million deaths. The conflict is often characterized as one between the Christian or animist African southerners and the dominant Arab, Muslim north. As is normally the case with civil conflicts in Africa, the situation is a little more complicated than that, but the narrative certainly helped the south win Western support in the years following the 9/11 attacks. Sudanese president Omar al-Bashir certainly didn't help his own cause with the United States by embracing ultra-conservative Islam and, for a time, providing refuge to Osama bin Laden.

The United States helped negotiate a peace agreement that brought an end to the conflict in 2005, giving the south political autonomy and a share of oil revenues for a six-year period, after which it could decide if it wanted full independence. During that time global outrage against the Sudanese government grew as a result of the Darfur conflict, for which Bashir was charged with genocide in 2010. South Sudan was a separate issue, but many of those who had campaigned for action on Darfur also took up its cause. In the United States, the South Sudanese cause brought together an unlikely coalition of high-profile backers including liberal movie star George Clooney and the right-wing evangelist Franklin Graham. The region also had a prominent backer in the White House with George W. Bush, who was so concerned with the region that one official later joked to *Foreign Policy* that he "could have been the desk officer." South Sudanese leader Salva Kiir made three different visits to the White House under Bush, remarkable for any African leader, not to mention one who did not technically have his own country yet.[46]

Barack Obama's administration, although not nearly as engaged with the issue, was hardly about to discourage the birth of a new nation after a long struggle against a government led by a genocidal, fundamentalist war criminal, and the president granted recognition to South Sudan immediately after it formally seceded. Despite some unease from China, a major purchaser of Sudanese oil, the UN Security Council voted unanimously to recognize the country and it became the UN's 193rd member on July 14, 2011.

Since then, things have taken a dark turn. A political feud between Kiir and his vice president exposed an ethnic rift between the Dinka and the Nuer, the country's two largest ethnic groups, that spiraled into civil war in late 2013 and has killed tens of thousands of people and displaced nearly 2 million.[47]

In retrospect, with one of the world's poorest and least educated populations, an unsettled oil-rich border with Sudan, virtually no existing civil institutions, and a total of thirty-five miles of paved roads in a country the size of France, South Sudan presented an almost complete checklist of the warning signs for state failure. Even South Sudan's most enthusiastic backers acknowledged from the beginning that the new country would be heavily dependent on foreign aid for the foreseeable future, but its collapse has in many ways exposed the limits of that aid. Foreign NGOs can do a great job solving straightforward technical problems (building roads or immunizing children, for instance) but are generally not cut out for building governing institutions from scratch.

Some might take South Sudan's experience as an argument for stasis and a demonstration of the folly of meddling by Western do-gooders. ("Why Is Sudan a Hellhole? Blame George Clooney," one flippant *Gawker* headline read in 2015.)[48] That's not quite fair. South Sudan was hardly peaceful and prosperous under Bashir's rule. But the country is also a clear cautionary tale for those who might argue that simply redrawing the lines in Africa or the Middle East could resolve long-simmering conflicts. The creation of new states can ignite new conflicts as previous allies fight over the spoils of the new national economy. This danger is especially serious if, like South Sudan, the country wasn't ready for statehood to begin with.

The South Sudanese example isn't exactly helpful for somewhere like Somaliland, which is asking the international community to take a gamble on another poor northeast African nation with aspirations of statehood. When South Sudan celebrated its independence in 2011, a delegation from Somaliland traveled to Juba wearing shirts reading, "Somaliland next."[49] Today, that feels like a warning.

But, as Shire, the foreign minister, points out, Somaliland *does* exist already, and it's long past time for the international community to recognize that. "Somaliland fulfills all the conditions for an independent state. Of course, we are aware of the Montevideo Agreement, which says that a state will be recognized as a state if it fulfills four conditions: permanent population, defined boundaries, government authority, and the ability to enter into agreements with other international institutions," he said. "I think everyone sympathizes with the Somaliland case. Even when we are not recognized de jure, we are recognized de facto. When I travel I am treated like a foreign minister. We deal with the UN and the international community as an independent country. We are treated as de facto independent, it is only the de jure recognition of sovereignty [we lack]."

Could Somaliland's recognition destabilize the region? "There's no Pandora's box here," Shire says. "From the security perspective alone, Somaliland should be recognized. Extremist organizations and destabilizing elements take advantage of administrative gaps where you don't have a government."

The argument against Somaliland's independence rests largely on factors beyond the country's control. Somaliland officials are used to hearing that if their independence were recognized, it would set off a domino effect for nationalist movements, destabilizing the continent. If Somaliland were independent, what would stop other regions from trying the same thing? Neighboring Puntland, another autonomous region of Somalia, isn't yet pushing for full statehood, but that could change. The secessionist state of Biafra, which fought a devastating civil war against Nigeria in the 1960s and where nationalist sentiment still exists, might try its luck again. Nearby Kenya has an active secessionist movement in its Indian Ocean coast region as well. In short, a sign from the international community that the postcolonial boundaries of Africa were back under discussion could be a green light to nationalist movements throughout the continent, leading to a new wave of civil wars.

International organizations like the African Union and the Arab League are hostile to the idea of recognizing further territorial divisions, and Somaliland's argument that's it's merely *restoring* a border that should never have been drawn in the first place doesn't carry much weight. Countries wary of their own separatist movements don't want to establish any sort of precedent. The United Nations, which has invested enormous resources in promoting stability and unity in Somalia as a whole views Somaliland as a hindrance to those goals rather than any sort of beacon of stability. Somaliland's neighbor Ethiopia mostly supports it—someone has to buy all that qat—but given Addis Ababa's wariness about its own Somali separatists, it likely prefers the status quo, a weak and divided Somalia, rather than a strong independent Somali state on its borders. The two most recent instances of country creation in Africa—autocratic, impoverished Eritrea and anarchic, violent South Sudan—have not bolstered Somaliland's argument that its recognition would be a boon to regional and global stability.

Western observers, both governmental and nongovernmental, have generally been kinder. Noting that Somaliland, unlike most of its neighbors, has had several contested elections and peaceful transfers of power since independence, the U.S. NGO Freedom House classified it as an "emerging democracy," and it is the only country in its region considered at least "partly free" or higher on the group's annual rankings.[50]

As far back as 2003, the International Crisis Group argued that the choice facing the international community was to "develop pragmatic responses to Somaliland's demand for self-determination or continue to insist upon the increasingly abstract notion of the unity and territorial integrity of the Somali Republic."[51] In 2007, a U.S. defense official described Somaliland to the *Washington Post* as "an entity that works" and said that in the Pentagon's view "Somaliland should be independent."[52]

But even if non-African governments are, on the whole, generally sympathetic to Somaliland, it's not enough of a priority to upset the status quo. Somalilanders like to joke mischievously that they've been *too* well behaved. After all, the other countries that have gained recognition in recent years have done so after wars and genocides. The world isn't necessarily hostile to Somaliland, but given how quiet things are there, there's not really any reason for the world to pay attention to it. "Being a peaceful, democratic, and developing state isn't helping Somaliland gain international recognition," said Hagi. "Somaliland is very quiet. It's a peaceful place. The international community doesn't really care about a peaceful place. When there is a problem in a country, the international community is always there—Somalia, Iraq, Syria, Libya. When there's no problem there, there's no point in coming to build a state."

Or, as Edna Adan more succinctly puts it, "At seventy-eight, I don't want to face the possibility that everything I've been taught about democracy and human rights is wrong. Maybe I should just go join the Taliban."

I should stress again that they are joking, but absent some major turning point or dramatic shift in global priorities, it's hard to see Somaliland winning recognition. The world will continue to defend an abstract principle of territorial integrity in the face of the clear will of the people of Somaliland and their demonstrated success at building a state.

Separatists within Separatists

This is not to say that the Somaliland idea is flawless or that its separation would be entirely peaceful.

Remarkably, the separatist enclave has its own separatist enclave. The self-proclaimed state of Khatumo, formed in 2012 out of three provinces in the east of Somaliland, is inhabited primarily by the Dhulbahante, a subclan of the Darod, separate from the Isaaq, who predominate in most of Somaliland. The Dhulbahante feel marginalized by the Isaaq-dominated government just as the Isaaq once felt marginalized as part of Somalia. The leaders of the Khatumo state want to join Puntland, a semi-autonomous region bordering Somaliland. Unlike their counterparts in Hargeisa, the leaders of both Puntland and Khatumo want to be part of Somalia under a federal structure. This has led to periodic violent border clashes between Puntland and Somaliland as well as violence between subclans in the region.

I met with Omar Mohamed Ali, a *garaad,* or traditional tribal leader, in a secluded booth at a popular Hargeisa restaurant to discuss the Dhulbahante's grievances against the Somaliland state. He argued that in the former government, intellectuals and professionals from all of Somalia's clans were represented, but after the formation of Somaliland, they were pushed out in favor of the Isaaq. "In the constitution it was written that all the clans would be treated equally. This never happened."

Throughout my visit, I had been hearing Somalilanders contrast their stable safe country with the chaos and violence of Somalia, so I asked Ali why, whatever grievances he might have, he would want to be part of an entity as dysfunctional as Somalia. "For us, there's not [any] difference," he told me. "We're not impressed by Somaliland. We don't have any peace. The peace you're talking about in Somaliland and war in Somalia—for us they are the same."

Officials in Hargeisa dispute that the Dhulbahante are actually that marginalized, and during the time I was visiting, the president and several of his ministers were conducting a voter registration drive in their region. They would also argue, once again, that it wasn't the Isaaq who drew the borders; it was an agreement between Britain and Italy.

But my conversation with Ali hammered home one of the main themes I encountered again and again in my research for this book: that there are almost no "natural" borders—people don't divide themselves neatly, and whenever you try to draw lines between groups of people, someone is going to end up on the wrong side.

For all its many serious problems, it is hard to argue with Somaliland's relative success. Perhaps this is the bigotry of low expectations, but whatever negatives you can say about the place, it's not Somalia. Over the course of my short visit to the country, I started to wonder if the lack of recognition might have been a blessing in disguise. With little help from the outside, Somaliland has had to do an awful lot on its own, and arguably done it better than many of its recognized counterparts.

"In many African countries that have been recognized, they are still struggling," said Barwani. "So sometimes we say that maybe being a de facto state is better. Because many recognized states in Africa failed, and they became a one-party system of a dictatorship with no free media and no space for citizen participation. For us, we have so many things. No limitations, no restrictions. Even our neighbor countries, the situation is completely different but they have recognized governments."

Looking at the decades of support given by the United States to dictators like Mobutu Sese Seko or considering the destabilizing role of Western oil companies in countries like Nigeria, there's a case to be made that if that's what engagement with the outside world means for fragile African states, maybe Somaliland has been better off without it. If at some point in the future the world does decide to recognize its independence, bringing with it the attendant investment and diplomatic engagement, Somaliland will be in a stronger and more stable position to handle it. Shire remains optimistic that this day will come. "We've waited twenty-five years already. We don't mind waiting another twenty-five."

Several months after that interview, Donald Trump issued an executive order temporarily banning travel to the United States from citizens of seven (six in the later amended version) majority-Muslim countries, including Somalia. As the United States still does not recognize Somaliland as an independent country, that means Somalilanders would be banned as well.

Shire gave an interview to NPR in which, in characteristic Somaliland fashion, he took issue not with the intent of the ban itself but with Somaliland once again being punished for Somalia's bad behavior. "Immigration policies directed at Somalia must not be applied to our country," he said. "I think we should be judged on our own merits. Have we controlled terrorism? Have we controlled our borders? I think the answer is yes. Do we pose a risk? No."[53]

Somaliland is used to being ignored because of its nonrecognition. With Trump ascendant and Western governments taking a harder line on countries deemed to be terrorist threats, it could now become more dangerous for Somaliland to be lumped in with its neighbor. Somaliland may no longer be able to afford the patient approach.

As the night wore on, I was starting to get a little concerned about our predicament on the side of the road. The spare tire in the trunk of our rented car hadn't fit on the wheel. We were riding in two different cars, so we tried the spare from the other one: no luck. It was then that midfielder Mohamed Khader, the driver of our car, hit upon a solution. He removed one of the tires from the other car, replacing it with the spare. He then tried to put the tire he had removed on our car. Using the last of our cell phone batteries to light his work and whispering bismillahs under our breath, we watched as Mohamed slid the tire onto the posts. It fit. Within a few minutes we were back on the road to Hargeisa, where just a few hours later I was due at the airport for a flight to Dubai, then a connection to Kurdistan.

Like his country, Mohamed was operating without the basics he should have been able to expect—in his case, a spare tire that fit on the car he was driving, in his country's case, a normal political and economic relationship with the outside world. But he had cobbled together a solution with what limited means were available to him, there in the middle of nowhere. It was a very Somaliland moment.

Land of the Free

It was January 20, 2017. I was just off the Washington Mall, where throngs of people in Make America Great Again hats were gathering to watch Donald J. Trump be sworn in as the forty-fifth president of the United States. But I was there to meet a different president. Vit Jedlicka of the Free Republic of Liberland, due to meet me at the Federal Center metro station, was running late.

I wrote in the first chapter that the world's landmass, at least since a deal was reached over Svalbard in 1920, is now entirely claimed by one country or another, but that isn't entirely true. There are still a couple of unclaimed patches of terra nullius here and there if you know where to find them. Jedlicka had found one.

In April 2015, he proclaimed a new nation on a 2.7-square-mile territory on a riverbank between Croatia and Serbia.[1] It would be the third-smallest country in the world, after Vatican City and Monaco. The land is subject to dispute but, unusually, the dispute is that *neither* country wants it. It is under Croatian control but the Croatian government wants to cede it in exchange for other parcels of land controlled by Serbia, so its status remains unresolved.

Jedlicka is a member of the Czech Republic's libertarian, Euro-skeptic Party of Free Citizens. In 2016, speaking to me via Skype from the roof of his "embassy" in Prague, he told me, "I used to want to just make changes in Czech politics. I worked for five years to bring about

Liberland

more freedom, less regulation. Then it appeared to me one day that it would be easier to find a new state than to change anything in Czech politics."

The Free Republic of Liberland, he suggested, "might be ideologically the strongest nation in the world. We all believe in freedom, that the government should be minimal, that taxes should be voluntary. It's a very strong idea." You can apply for citizenship online. Over four hundred thousand people have so far, and Jedlicka estimates that around one hundred thousand of them are serious about it. (My own application for citizenship seems to be languishing in the queue, perhaps because I've been ignoring the emails suggesting that I donate to the project in order to gain "merits" toward citizenship. I'm not actually a libertarian and besides, I already electronically reside in Estonia.)

Liberland, I say with all respect to Jedlicka and his officials, is not quite in the same category as places like Somaliland, Abkhazia, or Akweasasne that people have fought and died for. But the questions the project raises are valid ones: if people from ostensibly democratic countries decide the laws of those countries aren't working for them and are willing to go through the time and effort of setting up a new political unit, why shouldn't they be able to create a country of their own? Is the answer just that there isn't room for anymore countries? What if they manage to find some?

One small problem with the Liberland project is that at the moment Croatia is preventing anyone from entering the territory. Jedlicka is undaunted by this hiccup. "They are actually affirming our claim by setting up very strong borders and saying that if you're going there you're illegally leaving Croatia," he said. Liberlanders have been approaching the territory by boat.

In September 2017, Liberland signed a memorandum of understanding with Somaliland of all places, but it has yet to gain recognition from any widely recognized country, which Jedlicka said does not concern him. "Recognition is not that important for us at this stage. First we have to become a recognizable entity." The Liberland government does claim to be in contact with Beppe Grillo of the opposition Five Star Movement in Italy and is optimistic that it can build ties to Donald Trump's administration. "He's an entrepreneur and we're going to be entrepreneur-friendly," Jedlicka told me on the Mall as we made our way through the gates toward our assigned section. "I think he will understand how we strive to get rid of regulations. Maybe he will move the United States a little bit more toward Liberland." He also hoped he could leverage the Trump children's

Czech heritage to Liberland's advantage. He said he was in communication with the offices of several elected officials in DC but declined to name any he might be meeting with.

Also on hand was Liberland's just appointed vice president, Bogie Wozniak, a mustachioed Chicago retiree originally from Poland. An enthusiastic Trump supporter, Wozniak had helped coordinate the publication of a Polish translation of the president's 2015 book *Crippled America* (Polish title: *Donald Trump: Prezydent Biznesmen*). He didn't see a contradiction in backing both the America-first president and the nation-building project in the Balkans. "First we make America great again. Then Liberland."

Along with the crowd, we were funneled onto a knoll southwest of the Capitol steps that afforded a partially obstructed view of the Jumbotron. "I thought we'd be a bit closer," mumbled one member of the Liberland delegation. For much of the ceremony, Jedlicka struggled to get a strong enough cell signal to live-stream a message to people attending the opening of a new libertarian think tank in the Czech Republic. The man in a suit and tie speaking Czech into his phone got a few quizzical looks from the Trump supporters in the crowd around us.

As Trump began railing against trade deals and the loss of American jobs overseas, Jedlicka winced a bit. "I'm not sure about this protectionism. That's probably where we differ," he said of his fellow head of state.

The Liberlanders aren't the only people to have the idea of starting a new country on terra nullius. There is also small patch in the desert between Egypt and Sudan that is claimed by neither country. In 2014, Virginia man Jeremiah Heaton gained media attention for traveling to the territory and proclaiming it the Kingdom of North Sudan. The coverage focused on the parenting aspect of Heaton traveling halfway across the world so that his daughter could be a princess—Disney bought the film rights to the story—but Heaton claimed he had larger goals, telling me in an interview for *Slate* in 2015 that he aimed to create "a city in the desert that maximizes the use of space and maximizes energy efficiency," providing a "home for people who have a love for this Earth that want to work to help advance this science."[2]

The monopoly that countries have on the world's landmass is a problem for nationalist entrepreneurs. Except for these small patches, at least one government claims a monopoly on the use of force on every square inch of land in the world and they tend not to give them up without a fight. Sure, my neighbors and I can proclaim our block to be an independent country, but the U.S. government isn't going to take well to it if we decide we don't have to pay taxes or follow the same laws they follow one block over.

This has led some dreamers to devise creative solutions to the territory problem. One of the more celebrated examples of an unrecognized country is the case of the Principality of Sealand, a micro-nation established on a disused ten-thousand-square-foot British artillery platform in the North Sea by pirate radio DJ Paddy Roy Bates in 1967.[3] Sealand has a football team that participates in ConIFA and has played exhibition games against Somaliland in Britain. The country even experienced a brief military conflict in 1968 when Bates fired shots at a British boat. He was tried but acquitted on the grounds that he was outside British jurisdiction. The project was more durable than most micro-states: Bates ruled it until his death in 2012. It still exists under the rule of his son but is a lot less active these days.

Taking a page from Sealand's book, the Seasteading Institute founded by Patri Friedman—grandson of free-market economist Milton Friedman—is dedicated to building new political entities floating in the open ocean. It's still theoretical at this point but in

2016, the institute signed a memorandum of understanding with French Polynesia that could pave the way for an actual seasted to be built in the territory's waters.[4] As is true of the membership of most projects of this type, Seasteaders are mostly political libertarians, but they suggest such new entities could have any political orientation, as long as membership is voluntary.

Jedlicka takes a similar let-a-thousand-nations-bloom attitude. "It would be very nice to have more Liberlands around the world," he said. Could small autonomous voluntary communities, not unlike the "burbclaves" of Neal Stephenson's *Snow Crash,* be our political future? For now, the odds are stacked against these projects and for now it's something of a fringe movement, but it's certainly not impossible and, as Jedlicka points out, not really any stranger than the countries we have today. "It's funny because they say Liberland is a virtual country, but so are all the other ones," he said. "It's nothing but the imagination of people that creates a country."

4

The Dream of Independence

"First of all, this is Kurdistan, it is our land," Mahmoud Arif Sarokhar told me. It was a blazing hot afternoon in July 2016, and we were standing on the dusty main thoroughfare of the Kowergosk refugee camp, about thirty minutes from Erbil, the capital of the Kurdish region of Iraq. Home to over ten thousand Syrian refugees, nearly all of them Kurdish, the camp, which was founded in 2013, had begun to feel a little more like a permanent settlement, with a bustling shopping street running through the tents where locals hawked food, drinks, clothing, and mobile phones.

Sarokhar, a sixty-two-year-old father of thirteen, was explaining to me why, when he left Syria in 2013, he chose to come to northern Iraq, where he was living in a tent at Kowergosk. "Secondly, it's safe and it's governed by [President Masoud] Barzani. And it's governed by the United States. All these made me choose this piece of the world."

I asked if he planned to return home now that an autonomous Kurdish government had been formed in the region of eastern Syria that Kurds call Rojava, which means "west," as in the western portion of greater Kurdistan. "Of course I will go back to Rojava. Now it has a new administration supported by the Americans. Wherever Americans support is safe." We laughed for a while, as he continued to thank the United States and profusely praise the leadership of Barack Obama, but the exchange couldn't help but make me think of George

H. W. Bush, Henry Kissinger, even Woodrow Wilson, and all the promises that America has made to the Kurds over the past century.

There's a saying in Kurdistan that the Kurds' only friends are the mountains, meaning that when things get bad, their best option has traditionally been to head for the intimidating hills where they've enjoyed a tactical advantage over adversaries for centuries. It's not entirely true: the United States has been a friend to Kurdistan for a long time—but that friendship has limits.

For the past century, and particularly over the past quarter century, as it has become the world's preeminent superpower, the United States has also acted as the world's primary guarantor of stasis. Even as it has intervened militarily throughout the world, it has nearly always preferred to leave existing national borders in place. Nowhere is the difficulty of this approach—attempting to transform countries internally while preserving their external form—exemplified better than in Iraq, the country that America has now been locked in a violent and tragic relationship with for decades. And nowhere is the contradiction between the Wilsonian ideal of self-determination and the realist desire to preserve stasis exemplified better than in the case of the Kurds.

"If you talk about a state, you need a people, you need a government," said Fuad Hussein, chief of staff to the president of the Kurdish Regional Government (KRG), as we talked in his office in downtown Erbil. "Let's have a look: we have our territory, we have our people, we have our culture, we have our history, we have our government, we have our army. So in fact, we have everything that a state has got. But it's not recognized."

Of all the would-be countries of the world in the second decade of the twenty-first century, Kurdistan—Iraqi Kurdistan at least—is probably the closest to achieving its long-sought goal of fully recognized independence. Or at least it appeared that way at the time I visited in 2016. A year later, things would look very different.

Iraqi Kurdistan has been de facto autonomous for twenty-five years, thanks to both its own perseverance and a couple of crucial military interventions led by the United States. And while ISIS's rampage through Iraq beginning in 2014 was a political and humanitarian catastrophe, it also allowed Kurdish Peshmerga forces, one of the most effective anti-ISIS forces on the ground, to expand the KRG's de facto territory and consolidate political control. More than ever, the case for an independent country for the Kurds seemed both politically logical and morally unassailable. But, as always in this part of the world, the reality was a little more complicated.

There are between 25 million and 40 million Kurds living in the Middle East, mainly in a region that includes southeastern Turkey, northeastern Syria, northern Iraq, and northwestern Iran. They are predominantly Sunni Muslims, though significant minorities are Shiites, Yazidis, and Christians. The Kurdish language is divided into two dialects: Kurmanji, spoken mainly in Turkey, Iraq, and Syria, and Sorani, spoken in Iran and parts of Iraq. Kurds frequently claim, reasonably, to be the largest "people" in the world without a state of their own. (More people in the world speak Kurmanji Kurdish, the language's more popular dialect, than Greek or Swedish.) So why didn't the Kurds end up with their own country when the Middle East was being carved up after the collapse of the Ottoman Empire following World War I? They very nearly did.

The Treaty of Sèvres, signed in 1920 in a porcelain factory in a suburb of Paris, began the process of dividing up formerly Ottoman territory, including Kurdish lands, into European spheres of influence. Though it gets much less attention than the Sykes-Picot agreement

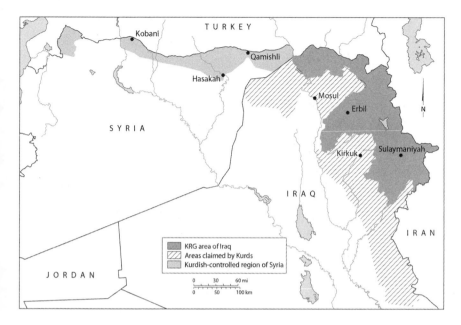

Kurdish regions of Iraq and Syria

signed between Britain and France four years earlier, the treaty was much more consequential for the future politics and political geography of the Middle East.[1]

Istanbul and the Bosphorus were to be internationalized, and the rest of the seven-hundred-year-old empire, with the exception of a much-diminished Turkish state in central Anatolia, would be divided among the Greeks, the Armenians, the French, the British, the Italians . . . and the Kurds. In his book on modern Kurdistan, *The Invisible Nation,* journalist Quil Lawrence describes the 1920 Treaty of Sèvres as "something like a Dead Sea scroll for Kurdish nationalists."[2] Indeed, the treaty is prominently displayed in Kurdish government buildings today, including in the waiting room of the Kurdish Regional Government's representative office and de facto embassy in Washington. The treaty specified that a commission would be formed to create "a scheme of local autonomy for the predominantly Kurdish areas lying east of the Euphrates, south of the southern boundary of Armenia as it may be hereafter determined, and north of the frontier of Turkey with Syria and Mesopotamia." It also made provisions for full Kurdish independence within a year if it was shown "that a majority of the population of these areas desires independence from Turkey." This provision was very much in the spirit of Wilson's fourteen points, promising that the "nationalities which are now under Turkish rule should be assured an undoubted security of life and an absolutely unmolested opportunity of autonomous development."[3]

It never happened. Turkish nationalists, led by Mustafa Kemal Atatürk, fought back against the foreign plot to divide the country up, consolidating their territory into the Turkish state we know today, formally recognized in the 1923 Treaty of Lausanne. The new nationalist, secularist Turkey denied the very existence of Kurds for decades, referring to residents of the southeast as "mountain Turks." International plans to set up a Kurdish state were put on the back burner as their territory was divided between the Middle East's newly established countries.

For Kurds, the treaty represents one of a series of betrayals by the West that have defined their modern nationalist movement. Kurds continued to fight for independence, often invoking the promises made to them. Mahmud Barzanji, who led an uprising against British rule in the newly established protectorate of Iraq, could reportedly quote Wilson's fourteen points verbatim and wore a Kurdish copy of the Treaty of Sèvres wrapped around his arm.[4] The British used aerial bombardment to put down a Kurdish rebellion in northern Iraq, a grim precursor of what was to come under Saddam Hussein. It was shortly after this time that Mustafa Barzani, the metaphorical father of Kurdish nationalism and literal father of former KRG president Masoud Barzani, began his decades-long guerrilla campaign to push back against domination from Baghdad and establish an autonomous Kurdistan.

Though it's little remembered today, Kurds did at one point succeed in forming a fully autonomous state, not in Iraq but in Iran. During World War II, Britain and the Soviet Union occupied western Iran to secure oil fields from the country's ruler, Reza Shah Pahlavi, who was believed to be sympathetic to the Nazis. The Soviets promoted Kurdish nationalism in their territory, allowing safe passage to Barzani. The independent Republic of Mahabad was proclaimed in January 1946, but by the summer, the Soviets withdrew their troops from western Iran and the republic was consumed by infighting between Barzani and the territory's Iranian Kurdish president, Qazi Muhammad. By the end of the year, Iranian forces had reentered the area and resumed control. Barzani and his forces returned to Iraq to continue the fight there. The Kurds' first, and thus far only, independent state lasted a little less than a year.[5]

After World War II, the United States replaced Britain as the foreign power most critical to the Kurdish cause. Iraqi Kurds attach great importance today to maintaining the support of the U.S. government, but are also understandably wary that this support could disappear very quickly when American foreign-policy priorities shift. Henry Kissinger is widely despised in Kurdistan to this day for what's seen as a double-cross in the 1970s: the Nixon administration had helped facilitate Iranian aid to Kurdish rebels fighting Saddam Hussein's socialist government and continued to encourage the rebels even as the United States knew that the shah was in the process of making peace with Saddam. When the two governments struck an agreement in 1975 and Iran cut off aid to the Kurdish rebels, the Peshmerga were left with no aid, and years of killings, ethnic cleansing, and torture of Kurds under Saddam ensued. This dark period culminated in the Anfal campaign, the mass murder of over one hundred thousand Kurdish civilians, and the gas attack on the city of Halabja—acts of genocide under nearly any definition. "Some people in their history, they have been a victim of genocide, but it became history for them. My generation, I have seen it three or four times," said Fuad Hussein. "Every ten years we are a victim of genocide."

The Kurds' fortunes shifted yet again in 1990 when Saddam's government invaded Kuwait, prompting the U.S.-led Operation Desert Storm. On February 16, 1991, as coalition forces were crushing the Iraqi military in a relentless onslaught, President George H. W. Bush said, "There's another way for the bloodshed to stop, and that is for the Iraqi military and the Iraqi people to take matters into their own hands and force Saddam Hussein, the dictator, to step aside."[6]

Kurds, along with Iraqi Shiites, did rise up, but despite the U.S. president's offhand remark, the United States had no plans of openly supporting the uprising or—to the consternation of the increasingly influential neoconservatives in Washington—actually overthrowing Saddam Hussein. As historian David McDowall writes, "There were practical reasons why the Coalition was unwilling openly to support the [rebellion]. It feared the break up of Iraq, and the unleashing of both internal and external forces that might try to seize parts of the country. Within Iraq there was the fear that Kurds and Shiites might shake off Iraqi sovereignty in their respective lands. Externally, there was the danger that Turkey and Iran would intervene in the event of internal collapse."[7] The concern mirrors the Bush administration's similar reluctance to back the breakup of the Soviet Union or of Yugoslavia until they were very nearly complete.

As Bush's son's administration would prove a decade later, there was good reason to be cautious about the prospect of setting off a sectarian scramble for control of Iraq, but from the Kurds' perspective, the elder Bush followed Nixon and Wilson on the list of American presidents whose words they had made the mistake of taking literally. Saddam was able to keep his military helicopters as part of the terms of his surrender and within weeks was attacking Kurdish villages, sending thousands of refugees streaming toward the Turkish border.

With scenes of the devastation and chaos broadcast around the world, the Bush administration was under heavy criticism for betraying the Iraqi uprising and—with a presidential election year looming— losing the political triumph it had won with the easy military victory over Saddam. In April, the United States and the other Gulf War coalition nations launched Operation Provide Comfort, clearing the Iraqi military from the Kurdish areas in the north and enforcing a no-fly zone over the area. It was a humanitarian mission, undertaken reluctantly, that was supposed to last only a few weeks. But Provide Comfort and its successor Northern Watch would last for twelve years, giving Kurdish national aspirations an unprecedented period of protection. As Quil Lawrence writes, "Washington unwittingly had become the midwife to a de facto Kurdish state, something it certainly never desired."[8]

The Kurds have a fair claim to being the main winners of the mostly disastrous 2003 invasion of Iraq, though not to the extent they might have hoped. After the overthrow of Saddam Hussein, Iraq's new constitution granted Kurds significant guarantees of political autonomy and cultural rights, and a Kurd, Jalal Talabani, became Iraq's first non-Arab president in 2005. Even as insurgency wracked the rest of the country, Kurdistan remained an island of stability.

"When Saddam collapsed in 2003 and Iraq was liberated, we were thinking that it was finished and now we could have some rest," said

Hussein. "Not only we—we were thinking about our fathers and grand-fathers. But after two or three years, threats started from Baghdad."

Relations between Erbil and Baghdad deteriorated under Prime Minister Nouri al-Maliki, with disputes over the status of the mixed city of Kirkuk and over oil revenues. As Maliki gradually consolidated power over the Iraqi judiciary and security services, he was accused of blatantly sectarian policies benefiting the Shia at the expense of Iraq's other main groups, the Sunnis and the Kurds. In the meantime, the KRG cultivated closer ties with Turkey and sought to convince the United States to deliver it weapons directly, rather than diverting them through Baghdad. While some American politicians, notably then senator Joe Biden in a widely criticized 2006 *New York Times* op-ed, suggested that the breakup of Iraq ethnic regions was inevitable and that federalization should be encouraged. Washington's default position under both the Bush and Obama administrations was that Iraq should remain as one country.[9]

America the Enforcer

Kurdistan has had the misfortune of seeking independence in an era when the United States was the world's preeminent political and military superpower. While America has reserved for itself the right to intervene militarily in other countries, it has, in contrast to its imperial predecessors, held existing borders sacrosanct. This has been a matter of bipartisan consensus, even in cases where Americans have vehemently disagreed.

For example, consider President Barack Obama's words in defense of the invasion of the Iraq, an action undertaken by his predecessor that he had vigorously—and famously—opposed throughout his rise to the presidency. His speech in Brussels on March 26, 2014, a day of meetings with NATO and European Union allies, was meant to address the annexation of Crimea by Russia, which had been ratified by Russia's federal assembly just a few days earlier. Russian president Vladimir Putin had brushed aside U.S. objections to the annexation as hypocrisy, given America's own invasion of Iraq, and Obama clearly bristled at the comparison:

> Russia has pointed to America's decision to go into Iraq as an example of Western hypocrisy. Now, it is true that the Iraq war was a subject of vigorous debate, not just around the world but in the United States, as well. I participated in that debate, and I opposed our military intervention there.
>
> But even in Iraq, America sought to work within the international system. We did not claim or annex Iraq's territory. We did not grab its resources for our own gain. Instead, we ended our war and left Iraq to its people in a fully sovereign Iraqi state that can make decisions about its own future.[10]

Liberal American critics, many of whom had supported the president in large part because his early opposition to "dumb" wars like Iraq distinguished him from pro-war Democrats like Hillary Clinton, were dumbfounded by the argument that the Bush administration had worked "within the international system" in the lead-up to the Iraq war, but Obama was making a distinction more fundamental than partisan debates over any particular foreign-policy action. Obama may have objected to the invasion of Iraq, but he wanted to make clear that redrawing borders was another thing entirely.

Secretary of State John Kerry described the Crimea annexation as "19th century behavior."[11] As a modern power, America, by contrast, likes to project its political and economic power throughout the world, but it prefers the map of that world, divided into 193 or so sovereign states, to remain unchanged. Changing them by force is a "red line" that will prompt the strongest possible U.S. response, including military force in some cases. The distinction is fundamental to America's self-image as a postcolonial world power.

As an emerging global superpower, the United States may have set off a wave of self-determination with Wilson's stance at the Paris Peace Conference in 1919, but in the years since, America has more often acted as a deterrent to the creation of new nations, supporting them only after reality on the ground makes a change in position unavoidable. As Secretary of State John Foster Dulles put it in 1957, explaining U.S. reluctance to recognize the Communist government of the People's Republic of China, "No government has a right to have recognition. It is a privilege that is accorded and we accord it when we think it will fit in with our national interest, and if it doesn't, we don't accord it."[12]

More often than not, it has not been considered in the U.S. interest to recognize new states. "The breakup of a state into its ethnic components, it was feared, could increase the risk of armed conflict and destabilize other multiethnic states," suggested a 1992 report from the Carnegie Endowment for International Peace. The report continued: "Not only did the United States favor the preservation of existing states, it also favored the integration of a number of states into multilateral groupings" such as the European Union.[13] This attitude continued up through the Obama and Trump administrations' hostility to Scottish and Catalan independence.

During the Cold War, this tendency resulted in formal U.S. neutrality during the wars of independence in Biafra (1967–70) and Bangladesh (1971). Despite media-fueled outrage over the grisly suffering inflicted on civilians in both these conflicts and public pressure to support the rebels, the United States was reluctant to abandon staunch Cold War allies: Nigeria and Pakistan, respectively.

U.S. reluctance to see the world map redrawn was evident in the end of the Cold War itself. There's a tendency among American conservative Reagan nostalgists as well as Putin-era Russian revisionists to hold the United States somehow responsible for the end of the Soviet Union. In fact, as historian Serhii Plokhy recounts in his book *The Last Empire,* while Washington was certainly happy to see a transition away from Communism in the Soviet Union, the prospect of the union itself fracturing terrified U.S. policy makers. Secretary of State James Baker, in particular, worried about the "prospect of violence and bloodshed as well as the possibility of nuclear proliferation" if the union began to split apart, calling the situation a potential "Yugoslavia with nukes."[14]

On August 1, 1991, a few months before a planned independence referendum, President George H. W. Bush visited Ukraine to warn the nascent country's citizens, "Freedom is not the same as independence" and "Americans will not support those who seek independence in order to replace a far-off tyranny with a local despotism." Ukrainian nationalists and American conservatives were livid and the *New York Times'* William Safire dubbed it the "Chicken Kiev" speech.[15]

Baker's fears of chaos and ethnic bloodshed weren't entirely unfounded, as Georgia's and Abkhazia's experiences demonstrate. But the results of the Soviet Union's collapse also weren't nearly as dire as many predicted, and other than Vladimir Putin and his supporters, few would argue today that the world would be better off if Bush and Baker had gotten their wish and a vast Eurasian empire were still ruled from Moscow today.

The United States was similarly reluctant to see the breakup of Yugoslavia. A U.S. State Department dispatch on May 24, 1991, shortly after Croatia held a referendum for independence, declared that the United States remained committed to the "territorial integrity of

Yugoslavia within its present borders." This stance didn't stop, or even slow, the breakup of Yugoslavia, though some critics have charged it emboldened Slobodan Milošević's Serbian government to "believe that it had a free hand to do whatever was necessary to keep Yugoslavia together or, at a minimum, create a Greater Serbia."[16]

Sometimes American hostility to separatism has gotten a little over the top. During a 1996 visit to Russia, Bill Clinton defended the country's brutal and repressive war in Chechnya by comparing President Boris Yeltsin to Abraham Lincoln, who, Clinton said, "gave his life for [the proposition] that no state had a right to withdraw from our union." A charitable interpretation of this would be that America's own history of civil war has given secession a bad rap among Americans. But even Clinton realized soon after that "I really painted a bull's-eye on my butt with that Lincoln line."[17]

Foreign-policy debates in the United States tend to be simplified into the distinction between interventionism (in both its liberal and neoconservative varieties) and realism. The realist stance has traditionally been more attached to the preservation of the map. The foreign policy designed by arch-realist Henry Kissinger was responsible for U.S. opposition to the separatism of Biafra and Bangladesh during the 1970s. In the 1990s, the realist-leaning George H. W. Bush administration led to the launch of the First Gulf War in order to preserve the sovereignty of Kuwait. In keeping with its interventionist, neoconservative impulses, the administration of George W. Bush made a bit of a break with this tradition in its support for Kosovo and South Sudan, but this break had its limits. The George W. Bush administration remained fully committed to preserving the unity and sovereignty of Iraq, and that stance remained in place throughout the Obama administration, despite the lip service paid to Kurdish national aspirations.

The problem was that even as Washington remained committed to the cartographical status quo, the region was coming apart at the seams.

Nations on the Move

Zahra Waly thought she'd be back home in her village north of Mosul in a day or two. "I remember the day when people in the town starting telling each other that Mosul had fallen to Daesh," she remembered, using the locally preferred derogatory nickname for ISIS. "At the time we were confused, we hoped they were lying, and we didn't expect that our situation would be like it is now. We didn't think about where we were going. But we found that there was one solution and that was Kurdistan."

Forty-seven-year-old Waly and her family of seven, members of the Shabak religious minority, left Mosul in the summer of 2014. In 2016, they were living in ramshackle lodgings in the Harsham displaced persons camp on the outskirts of Erbil.

In 2014, ISIS invaded Iraq, pledging to establish a caliphate cleansed of Shiites, Christians, and other religious minorities. By 2018, ISIS had lost nearly all its territory in Iraq and Syria and been pushed out of all the major cities it had once controlled, including its former capital, Raqqa. But after years of war, genocide, and mass displacement, many are unsure if Iraq, as a country, is still worth fighting to preserve.

Though less than a two-hour drive from then ISIS-held Mosul, Erbil certainly didn't feel like a city at war. The most visible signs of the conflict were the camps that had sprouted around the city and throughout Kurdistan to accommodate the massive influx of civilians fleeing the conflict. At the time I visited, the Kurdistan region, with a population of around 5.5 million, had taken in around 1.8 million displaced people and refugees.

"Noah's ship saved humanity from the deluge. What's happening in the Middle East now is like the deluge. Kurdistan is like the ship. Many people—Christians, IDPs [internally displaced people], refugees—are in the ship," said fifty-three-year-old Mohammad Saifaddin, a refugee from Syria running a small shoe store from his tent in the Kawragosk refugee camp, about forty-five minutes west of Erbil. A Syrian Kurd from the eastern city of Qamishli on the Turkish border, he fled in 2013 when jihadist groups including the al-Qaeda–linked Al-Nusra Front came into his area, filling the vacuum left by retreating regime forces. One of his sons, a soldier in Assad's military, had deserted and fled. "I had never imagined that I would live in a tent one day," he said. "It's a horrible experience. I can't describe it in words."

Saifaddin opposed the current government in Kurdish Syria— Rojava—which he saw as insufficiently committed to Kurdish nationalism and which he accused of collusion with Assad's regime. He preferred the more overtly nationalistic leadership of Iraqi Kurdistan. "President [Masoud] Barzani and the brave Peshmerga are fighting against ISIS and are destroying the wall which was built by Sykes-Picot. Unfortunately, some Kurdish parties are rebuilding this wall."

NGOs and the UN distinguish between refugees, who flee to other countries, and internally displaced people, who flee within their own country's borders. But in Kurdistan, the categories were a little misleading. The refugees admitted from Syria were nearly all Syrian Kurds, whereas most of the Iraqis IDPs were Arabs or members of ethnic groups who may have felt far more out of place.

The refugees I spoke with nearly all said they preferred to identify as Kurds rather than Syrians. Before the war, Syrian Kurds faced widespread discrimination from Bashar al-Assad's government and were barred from speaking their language in official settings, giving their children Kurdish names, and, in many cases, registering as citizens.

"The word *Syrian* for us is not a good word. It doesn't make sense for us," said Hevin, twenty-nine, who, like many, preferred not to give her full name. "I'm yearning to go to Rojava. Here is part of Kurdistan as well, but that's our home. Things are so expensive and unavailable there and things are still violent and blockaded. I talk to my parents every day and they say things are still not good there."

Hevin, a mother of four, said she was "told that there are many jobs here and many opportunities for my husband," but they found few. After a long economic boom following the U.S. occupation of Iraq in 2003, Iraqi Kurdistan was in the midst of a financial crisis exacerbated by the ISIS war and the plummeting price of oil, the region's economic lifeblood. Many complained of failing to find work in cities, forcing them to remain in the camps. Dilgesh Sweish, thirty-four, who had worked as a cook in Damascus and participated in the early demonstrations against Assad's regime in 2003, said he found jobs in several restaurants in Erbil but was taken advantage of as a refugee. "I worked in many companies and many restaurants and they didn't give me my salary. All my rights are ignored. I'm disappointed. There is no humanity in this country. Syrian refugees are very poorly treated. They don't consider us Kurds here." Sweish ran a vegetable stand in the Dasharkan refugee camp but, he said, "My dream is to go to Europe."

Rizgar Hisem Saleh, a former employee at an oil refinery in Qamishli and a resident of Dasharkan for three months, also wanted to move abroad—he had relatives in Australia who were helping him and his wife file for asylum—but he was rapidly losing hope. "I submitted my papers, but I'm not optimistic. No countries are taking in Syrians these days. I'm looking for a job here but I'm not finding anything. I may just go back to Rojava. At least there I have a job."

Saleh preferred to say he was from "Greater Kurdistan" rather than Syria, but he wasn't optimistic that redrawing the borders of the region would change anything. "Even if there are new borders, if there's the same mentality here, it will be useless," he said.

While there's fierce disagreement over method and timing, the Iraqi Kurdish officials I spoke with nearly all supported eventual independence from Baghdad. The arrival of ISIS and the U.S.-backed Iraqi government's collapse in the face of it seemed to have boosted the chance of this happening in the near future. But the arrival of a million and a half Iraqis from other regions of the country, many of them Sunni Arabs, was a complicating factor. Kurds are particularly wary of this, given the history of "Arabization"—the forced displacement of Kurds from areas that were then repopulated with Arabs—under Saddam Hussein's regime.

"We cannot close the door," said Hussein, the KRG chief of staff. "But we were also victims of Arabization. This is part of our culture and history. Most of those who are here are Arabs from Ramadi. We hope that now that Ramadi has been liberated and Fallujah has been liberated, they can go back. That's our hope. We're not going to force them, but one day they must go back."

This was a particularly fraught issue around Kirkuk, a formerly Kurdish city Arabized under Saddam and taken over by Kurdish forces from ISIS after the collapse of the Iraqi military in 2014. In 2016, Kirkuk was believed to be majority Kurdish with significant populations of Arabs and Turkmen. When I met with then governor Najmiddin Karim, he suspected a deliberate policy to tip the city's demographic balance in Baghdad's favor. "We have half a million IDPs. In six months people from Fallujah who are in Kirkuk will be eligible to become citizens of Kirkuk. By July of next year, Kurds could become a minority. That's a red flag for us," he said.

As it turned out later, the refugee issue was the least of the problems facing the Kurdish statehood effort. But the demographic anxiety suggested that for all of Kurdistan's democratic, secular bona fides, it wasn't immune from the classic dilemma of nationalists: what to do with people within the borders of your new country that never wanted to be there.

Most Arabs in Kurdistan, of course, say they came out of desperation, not any political agenda. "We came here because it was the only door open," said Mohammad Ramadan, sixty-one, a married father of twelve from south of Mosul who arrived about a month ago to the Dibaga IDP camp. "Two years we were under the rule of Daesh. We were like prisoners. We couldn't move freely. Starvation, hunger, exhaustion, fear, tyranny. No food, no air, no bread. We were just suffering." His town had been liberated a month before we spoke, and he was waiting for the all clear to go back home.

The Arab IDPs I spoke to had mixed feelings on dividing Iraq. "We are against the separation of Iraq. We want it to be one country," said fifteen-year-old Basim from Mosul, who recounted the horrific story of his cousin, a government employee, who was executed by being thrown from a tall building by ISIS.

Ahmed Hassan Ahmed, a twenty-four-year-old student from Mosul, said dividing Iraq into three regions would be the best solution. "We will never accept each other. It's better to have three regions or three states. We'll be good neighbors, but as long as we're all together, there will be confusion. We want other parts of Iraq to be like [Kurdistan.]"

"There is no more Iraq now," said Khidir, twenty-seven, a former member of the Iraqi Special Forces selling candies in the bazaar in Kirkuk. "If people ask where I'm from, I will say from the Sunni region. If the situation continues like this, with no borders, there will just be confusion."

Hindi Saleh from Makhmour, a town roughly halfway between Mosul and Erbil, was more skeptical. "If we stay united in one country, we will fight each other. If we are divided, we will fight each other. What we need is not changing the borders, it's changing the mentality. Once people are educated, they can change the borders. The borders alone won't solve anything."

But most were simply looking for safety. As Waly, the Shabak mother in the Harsham camp put it, "We are ordinary people. Here it is safe, and we have rights and nobody is attacking us. The borders don't make any difference to us."

Neither Here nor There

Iraqi Kurdistan is a quantum country; like an object in physics that can exist as both a particle and a wave, it seems to shift and mutate depending on what angle or frame of reference you use to look at it.

It's a region of an internationally recognized nation-state called Iraq, though its relationship to that nation, and its physical shape within it, are contested. To a certain degree, it's also an independent country that passes all the common tests for statehood with flying colors: it's represented diplomatically in Washington and other foreign capitals on a higher and more comprehensive level than many UN members.

At the same time, it's also "southern Kurdistan," a part of a cultural nation—one of Benedict Anderson's "imagined communities" if ever there was one—called Greater Kurdistan, though cultural solidarity only goes so far. While Turkey's Kurds have been fighting a decades-long struggle—both armed and peaceful—for cultural and political rights, the Iraqi Kurdish Regional Government has emerged as a surprising ally of Ankara, reaching a controversial agreement to sell its oil via pipeline to Turkey without Baghdad's involvement. This got even more complicated with the emergence of the Syrian Kurdish PYD, which is ideologically aligned with Turkey's militant PKK, alarming the Turkish government. Relations between the PYD and the KRG have been tenuous at best, and occasionally outright violent. In March 2017, for instance, the Rojava Peshmerga, a Syria-based group affiliated with Barzani's Kurdish Democratic Party (KDP), fought with the Sinjar Resistance Units, a group affiliated with the PKK in Kurdish Iraq.[18]

On top of that, Iraqi Kurdistan is also internally divided into two political regions, each dominated by a political party associated with one of Kurdistan's political dynasties. The Kurdish Democratic Party dominates western Kurdistan, including the capital, Erbil. Until recently it was led by President Masoud Barzani. His sons Nechirvan and Masrour serve as prime minister and chair of the security council, respectively. Eastern Kurdistan, including the region's second-largest city and cultural capital, Sulaymaniyah, is dominated by the Patriotic Union of Kurdistan (PUK), formerly led by the late Iraqi president Jalal Talabani, whose own heir, Qubad, is now deputy prime minister. The PUK is much more closely aligned with the the PKK (pictures of imprisoned PKK founder Abdullah Öcalan were everywhere in Sulaymaniyah when I visited), which complicates things even more since it's the KDP's rather than the PUK's territory that borders the Kurdish region of Syria.

After looking into this even briefly, it becomes very frustrating to hear American politicians talk about "arming the Kurds" as if they are a monolithic group. (When running for president, Donald Trump called himself a "big fan of the Kurds," though he also at one point confused them with the Quds Force, the Iranian paramilitary group.)[19] Talking about "the Kurds" as a single political entity makes about as much sense as talking about "the Arabs": they are represented by an alphabet soup of sometimes overlapping, sometimes conflicting political parties, groupings, governments, and militias.

"It's still very evident. We have one government but going to Su-laymaniyah is almost like going to another country," Qubad Talabani, the deputy prime minister and son of the former Iraqi president, told me. "You're going to go through a KDP checkpoint and then a PUK checkpoint. That is a stark daily reminder that we still haven't unified certain institutions of the state. It's not a good way to start. We can't say, oh, we'll address these things after the fact."

Looking back on Kurdish history, Talabani suggested that "Kurds have only been united when we were unified toward a goal. We've never been united out of our own will. Whenever we've been fractured, there's been a great power and a greater cause to unify us. Left to our own devices, we're inclined to not unify. What the world hasn't done to us, we tend to do to ourselves."

The emergence of ISIS as a threat presented such a cause as well as a challenge to the region's century-old cartographical status quo. In June 2014, ISIS fighters released footage of themselves bulldozing the barriers separating Iraq and Syria in a video titled *The End of Sykes-Picot*. In the video, a fighter proclaims that they have destroyed the artificial boundary imposed by Western imperialists and that now "we are all one country." He describes ISIS leader Abu Bakr al-Baghdadi as "the breaker of barriers."[20]

The 1916 agreement signed between British diplomat Mark Sykes and his French counterpart François Georges-Picot, with the assent of Russia, to divide up the Ottoman Empire into British and French spheres of influence is frequently used as a shorthand way to describe the "artificial" boundaries of the Middle East. The "end of Sykes-Picot" seems to be declared every time there's a new territorial challenge in the Middle East, though there hasn't been a major territorial adjustment in the region for decades. Sykes-Picot's totemic status is a little strange given that the map the two diplomats drew up bears very little resemblance to the Middle East today.

The French "A" area, which includes much of modern-day Syria, also included Mosul, the city that ISIS conquered with great fanfare in the summer of 2014. The British "B" area included not only much of modern-day Iraq but what is now Kuwait and part of the Gulf Coast of Saudi Arabia. The border that was eventually drawn between Iraq and Syria, which ISIS so dramatically destroyed, was based not on Sykes-Picot but on earlier Ottoman administrative divisions. As UCLA professor Asli Bali wrote when the group was at its peak, "ISIS now seeks to control a swath of territory that actually corresponds more closely to the French sphere of influence designated by the Sykes-Picot map, joining central and eastern Syria with the Mosul province of Iraq. Rather than erasing the Sykes-Picot border, ISIS has unwittingly sought to resurrect it."[21]

But nomenclature aside, ISIS did create an unprecedented challenge to the existing geographical order of the Middle East. It was not the first jihadist group to control territory. In fact, most contemporary jihadist groups spend only part of their time on activities that are traditionally considered terrorism, focusing much of their efforts on controlling and governing territory according to their ideological priorities. Hamas and Hezbollah, both designated terrorist groups by the U.S. government, expend more energy governing territory than they do plotting attacks. Al-Shabaab controlled a significant portion of Somalia before it was pushed out of its last major urban stronghold in 2013. Boko Haram at one point controlled, to varying degrees, an area the size of Belgium in Nigeria. Al-Qaeda–linked jihadists controlled a significant portion of northern Mali—including, with disastrous consequences, the city of Timbuktu, from 2012 until 2013, when they were pushed back with the help of a French military intervention.

French (A) and British (B) areas of control and influence under the Sykes-Picot agreement (courtesy of the National Archives, United Kingdom)

Still, ISIS differed from its predecessors in its emphasis on the conquering and governing of territory. At its height, it was less a terrorist group than a genocidal proto-state, carrying out ethnic cleansing in the areas it controlled and challenging the cartographical status quo of the region in its effort to carve out a pure Sunni state between Iraq and Syria.

ISIS's worst atrocities were perpetrated against minority ethnic and religious groups, including the Kurds, Christians and Yazidis—a small minority group living predominantly in northern Iraq. ISIS's slaughter of thousands of Yazidis, and its detailed and codified system of sexual slavery, have been described as acts of genocide. It was ISIS's expansion into Kurdistan and the imminent slaughter of a large group of Yazidis that finally prompted the United States to begin air strikes against the group in Iraq in August 2014, the beginning of a military campaign involving U.S., Iraqi, Syrian Arab, and Kurdish forces that eventually retook most of ISIS's territory, including its de facto capital—Raqqa, Syria—in October 2017.

ISIS may have represented the greatest threat to Kurdish security since the overthrow of Saddam—at one point in 2014, ISIS advanced as far as Makhmour, just seventy-five miles from Erbil, before being pushed back by a Peshmerga counterattack—but it also represented something of an opportunity. Though the pro-Western, free-market democracy gradually taking root in Kurdish Iraq couldn't be more different from ISIS's atavistic, apocalyptic vision, the two do share a desire to upset the cartographical stasis that has held in the Middle East for decades.

The emergence of ISIS and the ease with which it rolled through Sunni areas of Iraq bolstered the argument that Iraqi Kurdish leaders have been making for decades: that a centrally governed multiethnic Iraq is no longer a workable political reality. Moreover, the collapse of the Iraqi military and the relative strength of the Peshmerga allowed Kurdistan to make sought-after territorial gains, particularly in the long-coveted city of Kirkuk.

"It's not so much the war against ISIS that has changed minds and put the independence back in the public. It's more how Baghdad has dealt with the Kurdistan region and how it does not really believe in delegating to the Kurdistan region," argued Karim, the Kirkuk governor. "Baghdad is dead set against any other region forming in Iraq. It's more of a reaction to Baghdad's treatment of KRG."

"The whole world is trying to help Iraq and keep Iraq united despite the best efforts of Iraq to fail and separate," added Talabani. "Eventually there will be international fatigue for this effort to maintain something that doesn't exist. Iraq is anything but unified right now."

Despite the overwhelming support for statehood, Kurdish authorities had been reluctant to formally declare independence from Baghdad. There were a number of reasons for the slow pace. For one thing, the country was somewhat distracted by the ongoing fighting and the streams of refugees pouring into the region from the rest of Iraq and Syria. For another, the KDP was at odds with the PUK— which didn't really see the point of the referendum—over when and how it would be conducted.

The Kurdish region also wasn't in quite as strong a position as it had been a few years earlier. For about a decade after the 2003 invasion, relative stability and oil profits drove an economic boom in Kurdistan. Even if social services didn't quite keep up—Kurdistan has been jokingly referred to as a country of "first-world restaurants and third-world hospitals"—the glittering new skyscrapers in Sulaymaniyah and generally improving standards of living indicated that there was a path forward.[22]

But since oil accounts for 85 percent of the government's revenues, the fall in global energy prices hit the region hard. The Kurdistan Regional Government is more than $17 billion in debt, poverty is at a record high, and unemployment has tripled from 4.8 percent in 2010 to 13.5 percent in 2016, though the real numbers may be much higher.[23] Add to that the costs of the war against ISIS, the economic stress of settling millions of refugees, and a dispute between Erbil and

Baghdad that has led to Kurdistan not receiving its 16 percent share of the Iraqi budget, and the region was mired in a full-blown economic crisis. It was not, to put it kindly, an auspicious moment to launch a new country, and current conditions have raised concerns internationally that an independent Kurdistan could repeat the not-so-inspiring examples of South Sudan, East Timor, and Kosovo as a newly independent economic and political basket case.

Many Kurds saw the future of a viable Kurdish state in Kirkuk, an oil-rich, culturally diverse northern Iraqi city just outside KRG territory. Starting in the 1970s, Saddam Hussein's regime began an Arabization campaign in the area around Kirkuk, evicting Kurdish, Yazidi, and Turkmen families and replacing them with Arab families from southern Iraq. Dozens of villages were bulldozed.

Kurds returned en masse to the city after the fall of Saddam and, according to article 140 of the 2004 constitution passed by the Iraqi government, a referendum was to be held by 2007 on whether Kirkuk should be joined with Iraqi Kurdistan or remain an Iraqi province. The referendum never happened, but in the meantime, Kirkuk's status changed anyway.

In the summer of 2014, Iraqi government forces in Kirkuk fled their posts as ISIS invaded the country and the Kurdish Peshmerga swept in to take over. When I visited in the summer of 2016, Peshmerga security forces were firmly in control of the city and Karim, a veteran of Kurdish politics dating back to the 1970s, was serving as its governor.

Behind several layers of blast walls and checkpoints, the Kirkuk governor's palace was one of the most heavily fortified facilities I've visited—the precautions seemed a little excessive at the time, but not in October when central Kirkuk came under attack by ISIS in the early days of the battle of Mosul. In his windowless, ground-level office, below a massive portrait of Masoud Barzani, Karim told me the reattachment of Kirkuk to Kurdistan was a necessary precondition of Kurdish independence. "If Kurdistan were to become independent, I think it has to have Kirkuk in it. Who's going to defend Kirkuk if there's Arabization? But if the Kurdistan region stays part of Iraq, we may want it to become a region for a couple of years," he said. He also worried about the increasing number of Arab refugees who had settled around Kirkuk, saying he sensed a new strategy of deliberate Arabization from Baghdad. "In six months, people who are in Fallujah will be able to become citizens of Kirkuk and Kurds will become a minority."

As I walked around Kirkuk's dusty bazaar following the interview, the fault lines dividing the city were clear. Nearly every Kurd I spoke with favored Kirkuk being part of an independent Kurdistan. Nearly every Arab argued that Iraq should stay undivided.

Redrawing the Lines

"Sometimes borders are treated as sacred. There's nothing sacred about them. As a Kurd, it's my job to remind people of that," Bayan Sami Abdul Rahman, the KRG's representative in the United States, told me in an interview in her office in Washington, DC, shortly before my departure for Kurdistan. I couldn't agree more: the lack of questioning of how borders are currently drawn on the earth today is exactly what motivated me to write this book. All borders should be questioned, and if they aren't serving the people who live within them, there's no reason to preserve them for their own sake.

But in the age of stasis there's another, equally troubling tendency: to assume that the redrawing of borders will be a solution to ethnic violence rather than the cause of more. The emergence of ISIS and the collapse of Libya, Yemen, Syria, and Iraq brought about a new wave of this thinking. Joe Biden's 2006 plan for the federal partition of Iraq was dusted off and given a more positive reappraisal than it had initially received.[24] American journalists, including Jeffrey Goldberg of the *Atlantic* and Robin Wright of the *New York Times,* discussed possible scenarios for carving the Middle East again.[25]

Wright's version imagined the Syrian and Iraqi Kurdistans combining into one independent state, a "Sunnistan" comprising much of current Iraq and Syria (corresponding roughly with the territory ISIS controlled at its peak), an Alawitistan in western Syria for Bashar al-Assad's sect, and a Shiastan in eastern Iraq. North Yemen and South Yemen would be split in two, as they were until 1990. Saudi Arabia, on Wright's map, is split into five countries corresponding with its pre-monarchy tribal divisions, which she concedes is a "fantastical idea," given that the country has comparatively little ethnic strife.

Goldberg made a case that most Kurds would wholeheartedly agree with: "I don't think it is worth American money, or certainly American lives, to keep Iraq a unitary state. . . . Westphalian obsessiveness—Iraq must stay together because it must stay together—just doesn't seem wise," he wrote.

Fair enough, even if there's some paternalism inherent in Americans making the case that the borders of the Middle East should be reshaped to correspond with more natural ethnic groups when they would never make the case that Americans shouldn't be expected to live with people of another ethnic group or be governed by them.

But still, we can acknowledge that at a certain point, the borders are no longer working. So why not just draw new ones? Unfortunately, there are a lot more bad partitions in history than good ones. Most infamously, there's the division of India and Pakistan, which resulted in months of slaughter that killed between two hundred thousand and 1 million people and uprooted 14 million, not to mention the nearly 3 million killed when Bangladesh later split from Pakistan.

Border changes are almost always invitations to more ethnic cleansing and violence. The problem is the same as it was in Wilson's time: people don't group themselves in cleanly divisible geographical units, and any attempt to divide them will leave certain people living on the wrong side of the line. Kurdistan is not immune from this problem.

The ISIS war made Kurdistan far more diverse, thanks to an influx of both Arabs and other minorities.

"Most of these people will not return back," said Khidr Domaly, a Yazidi journalist and minority rights activist. "Not to Mosul, not to Sinjar, not to Fallujah. The things they have found here, they will not find in that area, even ten years from now."

"ISIS didn't come from space, it came from those villages," said Johana Towaya, an advocate for Kurdistan's Christian community. "I'm calling on people to go back to their areas, but they need guarantees. They don't feel safe."

Talabani agrees. "These crimes were done by their neighbors. For them, the checklist for their level of comfort is very different. They're thinking, 'Do I want to go home and live next to that son of a bitch who raped my wife?' It's so difficult for governments and organizations to comprehend the psychological impact on these people."

Even in defeat, ISIS has permanently altered Iraq's ethnic balance, unsettled its already uneasy population, and perhaps permanently crippled it as a viable nation.

Though Kurdish authorities vociferously deny it, human rights groups have also documented cases of the destruction of property belonging to Arabs in areas liberated by the Peshmerga. According to a November 2016 Human Rights Watch report: "Based on witness accounts and satellite images, Human Rights Watch concluded that KRG forces, for the most part Peshmerga, demolished buildings in at least 21 villages and towns after recapturing them from ISIS, in apparent violation of the laws of war. The extent and timing of much of the destruction in the cases reviewed in this report suggest that it cannot be explained by ISIS-planted IEDs or damage from coalition air strikes, shelling or other actions during battle."[26] One European diplomat told Sara Elizabeth Williams of *Foreign Policy* magazine, "It's wholesale ethnic cleansing. . . . If you overlay this with the wider map of Kurdistan, you can predict which villages will fall next, where they will draw the buffer zone, and when it will stop."[27]

Kurdish officials denied there was a deliberate policy to remove Arabs from Kurdistan and insist that non-Kurdish minorities are welcome in their territory. (In fairness, the KRG has a far better record on this than other areas in the region and has been genuinely welcoming to non-Kurdish refugees.) They also insist that non-Kurdish minorities will be given a voice in an independent Kurdish state.

Karim, the then Kirkuk governor, conceded, "I think Arabs and Turkmens, probably, as of today, probably will not be for Kirkuk joining Kurdistan. The Kurdistan parliament should pass legislation to assure Arab and Turkmens that their rights will be protected. It should spell out how non-Kurds of Kirkuk will be represented in the Kurdistan parliament."

All the same, it's not hard to imagine large-scale population transfers should Kurdish independence ever become a reality.

Forty-six-year-old Shaha Ghazi from Mosul, who was living in the Dibaga IDP camp at the time I visited, said her husband, a former truck driver, was arrested when the family arrived in Erbil because some of his relatives had joined ISIS. "We don't have a problem with food or shelter here, but my children are crying for their father. My husband is innocent. With my husband in prison, I'm like a bird whose wings are broken."

Maryam Mahmoud, who arrived at Dibaga in 2015, recalls, "When we first came here, some children were shouting at us, 'You are Daesh.' But we said no, we were killed by Daesh. Not all of us are ISIS. My son was martyred fighting with you against Daesh."

And it's not just an issue for Sunni Muslim Arabs. Not everyone who lives within the KRG's territory identifies with the cause of Kurdish independence. Towaya, the advocate for Kurdistan's Christian community, told me, "The Christian community doesn't care about [independence]. They have their own connections with Baghdad and the central government and they have their own culture here. We have nothing to do with this matter at all."

He says there's been record emigration of Iraqi Christians from both Kurdistan and the rest of Iraq. "The Christian community doesn't trust the Kurds or the central government." He added that Christians often face political and economic discrimination in Kurdistan, despite the region's reputation for tolerance. "They're pretending to be good with the Christians to get support from Western countries," he said. "Christians are badly treated in many cases. The problem is historical. Kurds are taking our lands. The problem is not a new political one. It's long term."

Kurdistan isn't worse than other aspiring states on the question of how minorities will be absorbed into the new state. It's inarguably far better. But it's not a complete exception to the rule. Many people in Kurdistan were wary about what independence would mean for them.

Rojava

Iraqi Kurdistan may end up being beaten to the punch in its aspiration for political autonomy by its counterparts across the border in Syria. Like his Ba'ath Party counterpart in Iraq, Syria's Bashar al-Assad did his utmost to suppress Kurdish culture and national aspirations. Hundreds of thousands of Kurds were denied Syrian citizenship, land was redistributed in an attempt to Arabize Kurdish regions, and the Kurdish language was banned in Syrian schools. In 2004, the regime put down Kurdish nationalist demonstrations in the city of Qamishli, killing more than thirty people.

The collapse of the regime's political authority changed all that. The Democratic Union Party quickly established itself as the main political force in the Kurdish region, declaring an autonomous government in 2014. The People's Protection Units, or YPG, became the primary armed group in the region, seeing some of the heaviest fighting against ISIS, including at the brutal battle of Kobane in 2014.

Secular, feminist, and mostly democratic in its stated ideology, the Rojava government, led by a group called the Democratic Union Party, or PYD, gets extremely good press. It's a rare cause that's championed by neoconservative U.S. senators and anarchist academics alike, both of whom gloss over some of its darker aspects, including reports of the use of child soldiers, the torture of enemy prisoners, the marginalization of political opposition, and a tacit partnership with Bashar al-Assad's regime.

Its emergence has also alarmed Turkey, which views the YPG as the Syrian branch of the PKK. In a 2016 speech to the UN General Assembly, Turkish president Recep Tayyip Erdoğan included the YPG along with ISIS and al-Qaeda–linked Al-Nusra Front on a list of terrorist groups carrying out attacks in Syria. The YPG denies having any operational connection to the PKK, though it does revere the group's imprisoned founder Abdullah Öcalan: his photo was prominently displayed on the wall when I visited the group's mission in Iraq.

Also in 2016, Turkish ground forces launched an offensive into Syria with the dual aims of fighting ISIS and containing the YPG's advances. All this put the United States in an awkward spot. Washington has provided aid and coordinated with the YPG, its main partner in the fight against ISIS, but this has put it at odds with Turkey, a key NATO ally. In the fall of 2017, SDF forces, assisted by the U.S. military, captured ISIS's capital in Raqqa, Syria. At the time of this writing, Kurdish forces control a significant amount of territory in northeast Syria. Confrontation with Assad's regime, which they've so far mostly avoided, seems inevitable now that the ISIS threat has been neutralized.

Unlike their counterparts in northern Iraq, the Kurds of Syria want not full independence but a federal state within Syria. When Syria's Kurdish-controlled northern provinces voted to seek autonomy—not independence—in March 2016, State Department spokesperson John Kirby condemned the move, saying, "We don't support self-ruled, semi-autonomous zones inside Syria. We just don't."[28]

In an effort to boost its profile, the regional government has opened a number of offices in the Middle East and Europe to represent its interests, including one in Sulaymaniyah, the PUK-dominated second city of Iraqi Kurdistan. "It's not really a diplomatic mission because we're still in Kurdistan," Sherzad Yazidi, the Rojava representative in Iraqi Kurdistan, told me in his office.

"It will be a federal democratic system," he said of the postwar order he envisions for Syria. "The unique experience of Rojava will improve all ethnicities and religions. It's a third plan—far from the regime and the opposition. We are against the division of Syria. Just raising the idea will be a cause for more conflict or more fighting. If the other parts of Syria go on fighting, we don't want to be the reason for it."

Federalism is obviously not a new idea, in the Middle East or anywhere else. Yazidi points to America, Canada, Russia, and Germany. But Rojava has no intention of surrendering its armed forces. For all that federalism is contested in the United States, Alabama can't take up arms to defend itself from the writ of Washington bureaucrats. If we still accept that a monopoly on the legitimate use of force is a baseline criterion of statehood, it's not clear what kind of country Syria could be postwar. I tried to press Yazidi on this.

"We seek to be represented in Damascus in the central government. We want to be partners, not followers. We want to be a factor of democratization in Syria," he said. "Of course Damascus will have some power in sovereignty and foreign relations. In the region there should be regional security and military—all these issues will be in the region. [Damascus] will have no authority over regional issues."

The strain of the Kurdish nationalist movement that holds sway in Rojava aims not for the establishment of a Kurdish nation-state but for a subversion of the nation-state itself. In January 2017, the *Washington Post* reported that in addition to military training, Arab recruits to the Syrian Democratic Forces, a Kurdish-dominated, U.S.-backed rebel group fighting ISIS in Syria, were obligated to study the teachings of Öcalan and embrace his central doctrine, known as democratic confederalism.[29] It's one of the great ironies of our age that the United States, in its attempt to restore stability and the regional status quo to this region, has openly partnered with a group of literal anarchists. In an alternative universe in which the Syrian civil war took place in the 1980s, it's not that much of a stretch to imagine the United States backing the "freedom fighters" of ISIS against the radical socialist Kurds.

Öcalan, the founder of the PKK, which has been locked in armed struggle with the Turkish state since the 1970s, has been imprisoned on an island in the Sea of Marmara since 1999. Öcalan was an orthodox Marxist, but while in prison has altered his ideology to favor a new system, "democratic confederalism." He was influenced, surprisingly, by the American anarchist theorist Murray Bookchin, who in

his most famous work, *The Ecology of Freedom,* goes beyond traditional Marxist critiques of capitalism to suggest the elimination of all
hierarchical relationships, including the patriarchy, racial supremacy,
and economic domination. Bookchin also calls for the replacement of
the nation-state with a model he terms "libertarian municipalism."[30]

Taking a cue from Bookchin, Öcalan argues in his prison writings
that "the nation-state in its original form aims at the monopolization of
all social processes. Diversity and plurality need to be fought, an approach
that leads into assimilation and genocide." He feels that "fascism is the
purest form of the nation-state." In the Middle East in particular, he
writes, "The Palestine conflict makes it clear that the nation-state paradigm is not helpful for a solution." Rather than emulate the bloody independence struggles of the past, creating a Kurdish Israel or Kurdish South
Sudan, he argues instead for "federal structures in Iran, Turkey, Syria, and
Iraq that are open for all Kurds and at the same time form an umbrella
confederation for all four parts of Kurdistan." At a global level, he foresees
a "platform of national civil societies in terms of a confederate assembly to
oppose the United Nations as an association of nation-states under the
leadership of the superpowers."[31]

The PYD, the political party in power in the Kurdish region of Syria, and the YPG, its armed wing, deny an operational connection to
Öcalan's PKK, but take their ideological inspiration from him. His picture is everywhere in Rojava and in PUK-controlled Sulaymaniyah in
Iraqi Kurdistan. Given this, it's possible that Western powers haven't actually fully grappled with the radicalism of what's taking place in Kurdistan. In contrast to the statist approach favored by the KDP and the
Iraqi Kurds, Rojava represents a critique of the nation-state model itself.

This is sure to be controversial, and not only because the ideological figurehead of this viewpoint is an imprisoned terrorist whose
group, whatever the legitimacy of its dispute with the Turkish state,

has killed thousands of civilians over the course of three decades. Beyond that, it seems possible that Western nation-states don't even have a frame of reference for processing the demands of the Rojava Kurds.

"Libertarian municipalism" or "confederalism" is certainly not the stated goal of the government in Iraqi Kurdistan. "Independence is an aspiration in the heart of every Kurd," President Barzani has said. But there seems to be at least some contemplation of alternative future political arrangements among some of the Iraqi Kurdish officials I spoke with, including some on the opposite end of Kurdistan's political divide from the PYD. Rahman, the KRG's representative in Washington, described a possible future arrangement between Iraq and Kurdistan just short of statehood. "It would be pretty much sovereignty but keeping the borders intact. Let's say Iraq splits into three entities, these three entities would pretty much have sovereignty— control over our skies, control over our monetary and fiscal policy, the ability to buy weapons, these are the kinds of things that we would want sovereignty over. We could maintain, like the Emirates, the Iraqi border. There could be joint cabinet meetings. At the beginning maybe they could share a currency. It's almost outright sovereignty."

This could then impact relations between the various Kurdistans. "You could end up with four autonomous regions within four states, but these four regions could create a Kurdistan league, like the Arab League, as an umbrella organization," Rahman suggested. In other words, each of the four Kurdistans would be part of a larger nation-state—Iraq, Iran, Turkey, Syria—while also being part of a larger Kurdistan.

Najmiddin Karim was thinking along these lines too: "If there's sovereignty in Rojava and the Kurdistan region [in Iraq] holds a referendum and declares sovereignty rather than independence, two sovereign regions could confederate with each other. Then you could confederate with Iraq and Rojava could confederate with Syria. That may be something that will placate Turkey, Iraq, the United States, and Europe. They could say—okay, these countries are still the same."

Qubad Talabani suggested that Kurds in Iraq have "99 percent of independence already," and besides, "we're witnessing an era when borders are not as relevant as they were decades ago. The nation-state is no longer the preeminent identity. We're a test case in this. We're independent, but we're not."

I should stress again that this isn't the official position of the Kurdish government or any Kurdish party or political figure, including those I spoke with, who all share the dream of independence.

When I visited Kurdistan, I found it an optimistic place. Despite recent challenges and problems, the region and its people seemed closer than ever to achieving their long-held dream of independence. One year later, that dream turned into a nightmare.

On September 25 the Kurdish Regional Government finally held the long-awaited referendum on independence. The vote was conducted despite the opposition of the Iraqi central government, neighboring countries Turkey and Syria, and the United States, which urged Kurdish authorities to delay until the final defeat of ISIS. (The only country that supported the referendum was Israel, which didn't exactly help Kurdistan's credibility with its Arab neighbors.) Most controversially, the referendum was also held in Kirkuk and the other areas captured by the Peshmerga after 2014, a decision viewed by Baghdad as a de facto land grab.

While some commentators suspected Barzani was simply using the vote to gain leverage in talks for more autonomy from Baghdad, the referendum called for full independence. No intermediate options were included on the ballot.

Not surprisingly, in a 72 percent voter turnout, more than 92 percent of Kurds voted for an independent Kurdistan. Barzani's government did not immediately declare independence, instead calling for talks with Baghdad, but Iraqi authorities were in no mood to negotiate. Prime Minister Haider al-Abadi's government demanded the Kurds turn over control of their international airports and imposed a ban on international flights headed into the region. Turkey threatened to cut off the cross-border trade in food and oil—Kurdistan's crucial economic lifeline to the outside world—if the Kurds did not annul the referendum.

Then, in October, Iraqi government troops aided by Iranian-backed Shiite militias moved in to retake Kirkuk and the other newly occupied regions. There were some clashes between Iraqi and Kurdish forces, but for the most part the Peshmerga backed off.

The Iraqi offensive created yet another population of displaced people as tens of thousands of Kurds fled Kirkuk and the surrounding regions, headed for Erbil and Sulaymaniyah.

As of the time I'm writing this, Iraqi forces have not yet moved into areas controlled by the Kurds prior to 2014, though there have been calls in the Iraqi parliament for the government to put an end to Kurdish autonomy once and for all. What is clear is that the Kurdish government made a drastic miscalculation with the referendum, losing all of its post–2014 territorial gains—and the oil revenue that came with it—in the blink of an eye.

Kurdish authorities appealed to their coalition partners, particularly the United States, for help. But Washington stayed neutral. "We don't like the fact that they are clashing, but we're not taking sides," said President Trump at the White House. A statement from the U.S. embassy in Baghdad more or less endorsed the Iraqi government's moves: "We support the peaceful reassertion of federal authority, consistent with the Iraqi constitution, in all disputed areas."[32]

After his gambit had clearly backfired, Barzani resigned in November 2017. Despite the warnings he had received from Washington about holding the referendum, he publicly blamed the United States for allowing Iranian-backed Iraqi forces to attack the Kurds.[33] Self-serving or not, the accusation fit a long narrative of Kurdish disappointment in America.

At the moment, the future of Kurdistan is deeply uncertain. Once both sides cool off, tensions could abate and the situation could return to status quo. Or Iraq and its neighbors could continue to try to isolate the region, turning it into a sort of Middle Eastern Abkhazia. Or the conflict could erupt into full-scale civil war, a catastrophe that could threaten all the gains the region has made since the 1990s.

A year earlier, late at night in the Harsham camp on the outskirts of Erbil, I sat with Abu Saed, a sixty-year-old Kurdish man from Sinjar, Iraq, now selling vegetables in the camp. Like many Kurds of his generation, he has an Arabic name. He was something of an anomaly among the people I met in the camps, perfectly happy to identify as both Kurdish and Iraqi. He had also suffered as much as anyone from violence afflicting both his nations. Abu Saed had lost his leg fighting with Saddam's forces during the Iran-Iraq War. After ISIS took over Sinjar in 2014, he stayed for two days before fleeing with his family of twelve. "When they entered the city, they started killing people and kidnapping them and beheading them. So we were afraid and we fled," he said.

He said his family had "gotten used to the situation" in the camp, but still hoped to return home, as Sinjar had recently been recaptured by Kurdish forces. "Even if there are tents in Sinjar, we are ready to go back. A tent in Sinjar for us is better than a villa here." He pulled out his phone and showed me a shaky video, recorded by his neighbor, of his house back home, now destroyed.

Sinjar, in Nineveh province, was one of the towns taken over by the Peshmerga during the fighting against ISIS. It has since reverted to Baghdad's control. In 2016, Abu Saed told me that all things being equal, he would prefer to live in an area governed from Erbil, but he wasn't too hung up on the question. "I'm proud to be a Kurd, but I'm not racist. I don't have a problem with others. These problems are recent," he said. "I am Muslim and I still have Yazidi neighbors who I talk to on the phone. I'm optimistic that we can move back and live together. What we have together is stronger than what Daesh did to us."

When I asked Abu Saed if Kurds would be better off with an independent country of their own, he shrugged. "I am proud of the Kurdistan region but I think division will lead to more destruction," he said. "Governments come and go. What remains is the people."

Out of State

Mikhail Sebastian just wanted to go on vacation. The Californian barista didn't realize he was going to be stranded in American Samoa for over a year.

Travel is a little more complicated for Sebastian than it is for most of us. He's one of the more than 12 million stateless people living in the world today, meaning he's not a citizen of any country.[1] The last country Sebastian was a citizen of was the Soviet Union—he's an ethnic Armenian born in Azerbaijan. When ethnic conflict broke out in the late 1980s and his aunt was stoned to death, his family fled, ending up in Turkmenistan. This wasn't a good long-term option: Sebastian is gay and homosexuality is illegal in Turkmenistan, so in 1995 he came to the United States on a work visa, which he overstayed. He spent six months in jail in 2003 but was eventually released.

U.S. authorities might have preferred to deport him at this point, but with only a Soviet passport, he had nowhere to go. The United States is a signatory to the 1954 UN convention on statelessness, which prevents countries from expelling stateless people unless "on grounds of national security or public order."[2] So Sebastian was given a work permit.

"We all talk about illegal immigration, but people just ignore the issue of statelessness," Sebastian told me in a 2016 interview. More precisely, it irritates him when the U.S. government ignores its *own* stateless population. He recalls then secretary of state Hillary Clinton bringing up the issue of stateless refugees in a 2011 speech without any reference to the United States. It "really pissed me off. What authority do you have to tell Myanmar what to do when you can't help stateless people here in the United States?"

Though there are no solid numbers on America's stateless population, a UNHCR report stated that between 2005 and 2010, around 628 stateless people applied to the U.S. asylum court and around 1,087 presented themselves as stateless in immigration courts.[3] Stateless people in the United States are generally, like Sebastian, former Soviet citizens who never obtained citizenship in any of the new states, immigrants from the former Yugoslavia, Eritreans who came to the United States as Ethiopian citizens, or Palestinians born in other Middle Eastern countries.

Sebastian said most stateless people in America keep a low profile. "A lot of stateless people send me emails," he said. "A lot of them are scared to say anything. If you go to the immigration office and say, 'I am stateless,' the first thing they're going to do is put you in a detention center. You can sit there from six months up to a year, because there's no law protecting you. So they're just hiding."

Sebastian, though, loves to travel. This is a problem for stateless people, as the government considers it self-deportation if you leave the country, and will not let you back in. So for years he contented himself with traveling to U.S. overseas territories like Puerto Rico, Guam and, in 2012, American Samoa. What he didn't quite realize at the time, though, is that American Samoa is a bit different: unlike other U.S. possessions, it's not considered part of U.S. territory and its inhabitants are not automatically U.S. citizens. (Constitutionally, none of the residents of America's overseas possessions are entitled to birthright citizenship, a legacy of a series of blatantly racist court decisions of early twentieth-century cases that drew a distinction between North American territories destined for eventual statehood and the "unincorporated territories" like Puerto Rico and the Philippines recently acquired in the Spanish-American War. Birthright citizenship was eventually extended to the other territories via statute, with the exception of American Samoa. A 2015 appeals court decision upheld the constitutionality of this arrangement.)[4]

All this meant that when Sebastian tried to return, he was told by immigration authorities that he had self-deported. (It also didn't help his case that he had unwittingly spent a few hours in Western Samoa, not realizing until he got there that it was a separate, independent country.) He then spent over a year on the island, living with a local family on a $50-a-week stipend, spending most of his days at a McDonald's, the only place he could find Wi-Fi. Bizarrely, he wasn't even the only stateless person stranded in Samoa. He said he met an East German woman who had married, then divorced, a Samoan man, and then found herself unable to leave since the country on her passport no longer existed and she had missed the cutoff date to get a new Federal Republic of Germany passport.

Sebastian said that at one point, frustrated, he wanted to give up trying to return to the United States and asked the UN High Commission on Refugees to help him emigrate to Europe or New Zealand, but they thought he had a better case for going back to the United States, having already established himself there. Sebastian ended up being readmitted to the United States, but only after his story was featured on NPR and CNN. He was eventually granted asylum status and is currently awaiting legal residency.

Now in the coffee import business, Sebastian travels frequently for work and has visited Rwanda, Ethiopia, Cuba, Ecuador, Panama, Guatemala, and El Salvador. His travel stories are peppered with anecdotes of hour-long interrogations at airports and being pulled off buses at border checkpoints. "Every time I have to go through customs, I get detained," he said casually.

What I find remarkable about Sebastian is that in a situation in which most people would keep their head down rather than attract the attention of the authorities, he persists in asserting his right to travel freely, more than willing to expose himself to inconvenience and even risk to do so. He didn't view this as anything particularly unusual. After all, if the rest of us can travel for work and pleasure, why shouldn't he, just because he was born in a country that no longer exists?

In a speech defending Britain's exit from the European Union in October 2016, British prime minister Theresa May made the heavily criticized claim that "if you believe you are a citizen of the world, you are a citizen of nowhere."[5] Though meant to needle the jet-setting, neoliberal elites who were aghast at Brexit, the remark was seen as insulting to refugees, immigrants, and the ever-growing number of people in the world with more than one national identity. But it also reflects the unconscious biases of a world of countries in stasis: we assume today that every human being must be a citizen of somewhere.

The UN Declaration of Human Rights states, "Everyone has the right to a nationality," but a less benign way of putting it might be that in our current world system, everyone is *required* to have citizenship. People like Sebastian are an inconvenience and irritation to the nation-state system. As Ernest Gellner wrote, "A man must have a nationality as he must have a nose and two ears; a deficiency in any of these particulars is not inconceivable, and does from time to time occur, but only as a result of some disaster, and it is itself a disaster of a kind."[6]

Some countries have gone to bizarre lengths to deal with this "disaster." Kuwait, for instance, has a population of over one hundred thousand Bidun people, descended from nomadic Bedouin tribes, who were not granted citizenship when the country became independent in 1961. Though many have lived in the country their entire lives, they are considered illegal migrants by the Kuwaiti government and have been repeatedly rebuffed in their requests for citizenship. As noncitizens, they are barred from holding most jobs in Kuwait and are denied access to health care and education as well as many legal protections. In 2014, the Kuwaiti government announced that the Bidun would soon be eligible for citizenship—but not in Kuwait. Rather, the government plans to bulk-purchase "economic citizenship" for the Bidun from the East African island nation of Comoros, hundreds of miles away. Comoros, a member of the Arab League, has already provided passports to some stateless residents of the United Arab Emirates under a similar scheme.[7]

Comoros is one of a number of countries that sell passports for foreigners, many of them island countries like Malta, St. Kitts, Antigua, and Dominica. (The Maltese program, which sold citizenship for around $865,000, was slammed by EU officials who argued, "Citizenship is something that has to be earned, not simply handed out to people with deep pockets," and worried that the program might be used by Russian oligarchs and officials hoping to evade EU sanctions.)[8]

Another creative solution to the problem is the "world passport," issued by the Washington-based World Service Authority (WSA). Only about six countries formally recognize the passport although, according to the WSA, more than 180 countries, including South Africa, have accepted them on at least one occasion. The world passport was the creation of American-born former Broadway actor and world government advocate Garry Davis, who in 1948 renounced his U.S.

citizenship at the U.S. embassy in Paris and declared himself a global citizen. (Americans can renounce their citizenship only at embassies in foreign countries in order to avoid more stateless citizens within the country.) Davis managed to travel widely, though he was frequently arrested, and became a minor celebrity for stunts like stealing $47 worth of lingerie from a French department store in order to be arrested and avoid deportation. Davis eventually settled in Vermont, where he died in 2013.[9] In his later years, he had world passports sent to international fugitives Julian Assange and Edward Snowden. The passport made news in early 2016 when the rapper and actor Yasiin Bey, better known as Mos Def, attempted unsuccessfully to use one to travel from South Africa to the United States.[10] As Bey eventually did return to the United States to play some concerts, he evidently never gave up his American passport. Sebastian also has a world passport but said he rarely uses it as few countries will accept it.

As the journalist Atossa Araxia Abrahamian writes in her recent book on global citizenship, *The Cosmopolites,* "Increasingly ours is a world of stateless natives and citizen-strangers. . . . More than ever, people want or need to belong to, or be accepted in, places they were not assigned to by the accident of birth."[11]

This is becoming even more the case in the midst of an unprecedented global child refugee crisis. In 2014, the UNHCR reported that 75 percent of the Syrian refugees born in Lebanon since 2011 had not been properly registered, making them effectively stateless. The issue of people not properly recognized in the global country system is set to become a major crisis in years to come.[12]

As for Sebastian, he said life has improved immeasurably since his status was formalized. "I became more like a human," he said. "My human rights as described in [the UN Declaration of Human Rights] are restored because I have the freedom to move freely."

He said he still has difficulty explaining his predicament when questioned by officials, who simply can't conceive of someone not being a citizen of any country. He recalls asking one immigration officer to imagine what would happen if, like the Soviet Union, the United States one day broke up into fifty separate republics. "All of those republics are going to make their own immigration law. So a citizen of New Hampshire can't enter Connecticut without a visa. Say you're in California but you were born in Texas. California won't let you stay, but Texas won't give you citizenship because your papers say you were born in the United States. You would become stateless!"

What Sebastian was asking, essentially, was for an American to imagine herself subject to the vagaries and legal complications of a post-stasis world map.

Her answer? "Don't be a smart-ass."

5

The Country Vanishes

While I was visiting Kiribati, the local cell provider, ATH, was running an ad campaign with the tagline "The Future Is Here." I knew what the line, below a photo of a mother with a smiling baby, meant. Smartphones and tablets were finally becoming ubiquitous in this remote nation of 110,000 people living on thirty-three atolls in the central Pacific Ocean, which only recently got widespread Internet access. But given the challenges Kiribati faces, I couldn't help reading the slogan with a different emphasis: "The future is *here.*" As in "The future will be here." Or "In the future, there will be a here."

Kiribati isn't well known outside the Pacific. Known under British colonial rule as the Gilbert Islands (the name Kiribati, pronounced *Ki-ri-bahss,* is a local transliteration of "Gilberts"), it's located about fourteen hundred miles north of Fiji. The atoll of Tarawa, which I visited, was the site of one of the bloodiest naval battles of World War II. But if outsiders have any concept of Kiribati today, it's as a doomed country, first in line to be wiped out by the impacts of climate change.

As one of the smallest nations in the world, spread across formidable distances with few natural resources to rely on, the very existence of Kiribati seems unlikely. It's one of the newest countries in the world, having achieved independence from Britain only in 1979, at the tail end of the twentieth century's decolonization wave. But Kiribati could be at the forefront of the next major wave reshaping the map of the world, this one challenging physical as well as political boundaries and eliminating rather than birthing countries.

The reasons I traveled to Kiribati are different than what brought me to Abkhazia, Somaliland, and Kurdistan—countries fighting to be recognized as independent states. Its situation is a little closer to that of Akwesasne, a tiny outpost fighting for national survival. But Kiribati and small island states like it are facing a new problem. Countries can be conquered by other countries, though in the age of stasis, that isn't really tolerated. When Saddam Hussein's Iraq invaded Kuwait in 1990, for instance, the international community continued to recognize Kuwait as an independent country until Iraqi troops were forced out and the Gulf state's government was restored. Countries can also collapse into near anarchy: from 1991 until 2012 the Republic of Somalia effectively had no central government and still doesn't control much of its nominal territory, but it continued to be recognized as a state (at Somaliland's expense) by the international community. Countries can be split in two, as Czechoslovakia was in 1992, or joined together, like East and West Germany in 1990. Countries cannot be destroyed; they can only become other countries, the land they occupy now controlled by someone else. But what if there is no more land?

At a bare minimum, a country needs a government and a population to exist. But even more fundamentally, a country is a piece of real estate within a defined territory: the boot of Italy, the hanging diamond of India, the narrow strip of Chile. Generally the shape of a nation has long been defined by two kinds of lines: the borders that separate it from other countries and the coastlines that separate it from the sea. We may understand intuitively why political borders are subject to change—though as the other chapters in this book have demonstrated, this happens a lot less often than it used to—but in an era of rising seas and increasingly extreme weather and natural disasters, we now have to get used to the fact that coastal boundaries can't be taken for granted either. Indeed, our land-water borders are changing quickly and significantly, and in ways that will likely never be reversed.

According to the projections of the Intergovernmental Panel on Climate Change, even if the world were to meet the now seemingly hopelessly optimistic target of limiting global climate change to two degrees Celsius, global sea levels will rise between twenty-six and eighty-two centimeters by the end of this century.[1]

In the century to come, we're likely to see dramatic changes to the physical shape of the world as we know it, thanks to the impacts of climate change. But the immediate-term challenges faced by most countries pale in comparison to those of Kiribati, which has an average elevation of less than two meters.

According to the Kiribati government's own climate action plan submitted to the 2015 UN Climate Change Conference in Paris, Tarawa, where nearly half the country's population lives, could soon be substantially underwater. "By 2050, 18–80% of the land in Buariki, North Tarawa, and up to 50% of the land in Bikenibeu, South Tarawa could become inundated," it reads, referring to the two main islands making up the atoll of Tarawa. The smaller outlying islands of the country could be wiped out even sooner. The report continues: "The results of sea level rise and increasing storm surge threaten the very existence and livelihoods of large segments of the population, increase the incidences of water-borne and vector-borne diseases undermining water and food security and the livelihoods and basic needs of the population, while also causing incremental damage to buildings and infrastructure."[2]

Small island states like Kiribati have become global symbols of the potential impacts of global warming, and at the United Nations level have acquired a surprising amount of influence. At the 2016 Paris climate summit, it was the small island nations that pressured larger countries to accept the goal of limiting global warming to one and a half degrees Celsius rather than two degrees over preindustrial levels. (It's mostly a symbolic victory: barring unforeseen circumstances, both targets are likely to be exceeded.) They are also working to develop first-line defenses against the effects of sea-level rise, including planting mangroves to prevent coastal erosion and improving rainwater-collection systems to protect water quality.[3]

But if none of that works, they may have to consider more drastic options. In June 2014, Kiribati purchased 20 square kilometers (or about 7.7 square miles) on the Fijian island of Vanua Levu for a little less than $9 million. The country's president, Anote Tong, told the media that if worse came to worst, this would become the new home for the nation's inhabitants, known as the I-Kiribati. "We would hope not to put everyone on [this] one piece of land," Tong told the Associated Press, "but if it became absolutely necessary, yes, we could do it."[4] At the Paris climate summit, Tong thanked the government of Fiji, saying, "It's so heartening to hear that Fiji has undertaken to accommodate our people of Kiribati in the event that climate change renders our homes uninhabitable."[5]

The relocation of people due to climate change isn't entirely unprecedented. Papua New Guinea has already begun the relocation of the population of the Cartaret Islands, a group of low-lying atolls off the country's coast, to the mainland. But this would be the first time that an entire country has had to be relocated because the land on which it is built no longer exists. This raises a new and frightening question: if a country no longer exists in physical form, can it still exist as a political unit? Can a country just up and move?

I went to Kiribati to explore these questions, expecting to find a place sinking beneath the waves, with panicked inhabitants contemplating whether their country has a future. I wanted to see what a country in its death throes looked like. But that's not exactly what I found.

Trouble in Paradise

Viewed from the plane—biweekly flights from Fiji are the country's main connection to the outside world—the atolls of Kiribati are gorgeous. An atoll is a protruding ring of coral reef surrounding a lagoon. Arthur Grimble, the islands' British colonial administrator in the early twentieth century, poetically described one as "a ribbon of palm green . . . the regular golden circle of its beaches, closed save for one tidal passage, encompasses a lake forever exquisitely at rest."[6]

The land area of Kiribati's thirty-three atolls is about 300 square miles—about the same size as New York City—spread over a distance of 2,050 miles, roughly the distance from New York City to Los Angeles. Located where the equator meets the international dateline, Kiribati is the only country in the world with territory in all four hemispheres. More than half of the country's 110,000 people live in the southern part of Tarawa, an atoll consisting of a string of islands connected by causeways with an area of just 6 square miles.[7] It's cramped and getting more so as people relocate from the outer islands in search of economic opportunities in the relatively urbanized capital. A road, repaired with the help of Australian aid money a few years ago, connects the islands, which has been a major improvement for the inhabitants. Getting around is easy: just hop on one of the privately run buses that run up and down the sole road.

Most inhabitants of Tarawa live in slum conditions and sanitation is an issue. The azure-blue lagoon that looks so inviting is actually hazardously polluted with sewage. There's an active debate over whether much of the flooding that's been attributed to global warming is actually the

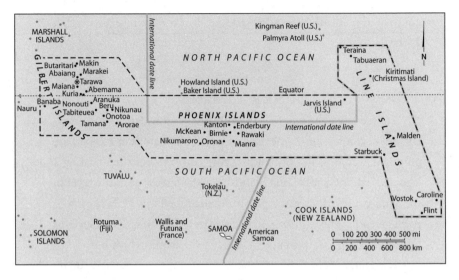

Kiribati

result of people building in flood-vulnerable areas because of over-crowding.

Most I-Kiribati are descended from Samoans who migrated to the islands between the eleventh and fourteenth centuries, but Micronesians lived there for hundreds of years before that. There was some interaction with Samoans, Tongans, and Fijians as well as evidence of some Chinese influence in the centuries following the Samoan migration. Europeans arrived in the eighteenth century.[8]

The territory was ruled as a British protectorate—the Gilbert and Ellice Islands—from 1892 to 1976. The Ellice Islands became the modern country of Tuvalu, while the Gilberts became Kiribati. Missionaries began arriving in the 1880s and the country is deeply religious today, though surprisingly diverse, with healthy representation of Protestants, Catholics, Seventh-Day Adventists, and Mormons.

(The fresh-faced young Mormon missionaries riding their bikes down Tarawa's main road were both the only people I saw wearing ties on the island and the only white people I encountered who could speak the I-Kiribati language.)

In colonial times, the main export of the island was phosphate, mined from the island of Banaba—a rarity among Kiribati islands in that it's not an atoll and has some elevation. The island was gradually hollowed out from the center and is now mostly abandoned, its inhabitants settled in Fiji in what may be a preview of what is to come for the rest of Kiribati.

Today, Kiribati's main resource is what's pulled out of its vast ocean territory. One local politician I spoke with said optimistically that the country has the potential to be the "Saudi Arabia of fish," and it does collect around $200 million per year from fishing licenses, though illegal fishing in Kiribati waters is also rampant and enforcement is lax: not only is there no coast guard or navy but—incredibly for a country consisting almost entirely of water—the government of Kiribati doesn't own a single boat.

Ordinary people, particularly on the outer islands, often make their living collecting copra, the dried meat of the coconut from which oil is extracted. In rural villages in North Tarawa, you can see the extracted coconut meat drying on racks outside many homes. In recent years, the government has increased the subsidy paid to villagers for copra to more than $1 over the world market price. This economically untenable scheme is seen by many as a way of convincing people who've moved to overcrowded Tarawa to go back to the outer islands where coconuts are plentiful and there's less competition. Many Kiribati men also spend much of the year working cargo ships—it's not unusual to meet people at bus stops in Tarawa with stories of misspent nights in Baltimore, Hamburg, or Shanghai.

From the right angle on the right day, despite its poverty, Tarawa is a heartbreakingly beautiful place, with palm trees swaying gently on the beaches, children playing joyfully in the surf. But reminders of its vulnerability, as well as the callous disregard with which the world treats small island countries, aren't hard to fined.

On my third day in Kiribati, I was invited by friends of my hosts to a party held by a local NGO for assisting people with disabilities. The party, like most formal functions in Kiribati, was held in a *manaeba,* a raised platform with a thatched roof and open walls that forms the center of traditional I-Kiribati social life. After a few rounds of beauty pageants and dance contests—under severe peer pressure I participated in the dance contest but, sadly, didn't win—it was time for the meal. At one point, an elderly man, walking with the assistance of a cane, came over to where I sat, stuffing my face with bread-fruit and fish, to show me the tattoo on his forehead: "USA" it read in faded letters between his eyebrows. Through an interpreter he explained that he remembered the arrival of U.S. troops following the recapture of Tarawa in the Second World War. "USA" had been stenciled on the emergency supplies airlifted in during the years after the battle—symbolizing relief and rare attention from the outside world.

On the island of Betio, the western tip of the Tarawa atoll, people live amid the scars of war. Japanese bunkers and pillboxes, overgrown with grass, sit surrounded by slums. On the beaches, artillery positions sit rusting, pointed out toward the horizon. At low tide, you can see the waterlogged hulks of the Amtrac amphibious assault vehicles that brought U.S. Marines ashore, still where they landed in November 1943. Tarawa was one of the most fortified Japanese positions captured by the United States during the Pacific campaign in World War II. Here for the first time during the war U.S. forces were fired upon during the initial invasion of an island. In addition to the heavy resistance, the landing party faced a shallower than normal tide, forcing them to abandon landing craft far out on the reef. More than a thousand U.S. troops were killed in what was one of the bloodiest days in the history of the Marine Corps.

The battle has been heavily documented, but few accounts describe in any detail how the residents of Tarawa were forced to flee during the clash between two superpowers that happened on their island. The island itself is treated as almost incidental in histories of the war, characteristic of the attitude the world tends to take toward small island states.

Those of us who live on the mainland attach a certain exotic romance to remote islands, celebrated in culture from the adventure stories of Robert Louis Stevenson, who himself stopped by the Gilberts in 1890, to the lush erotic scenes of Paul Gauguin's paintings. But such islands are also, shamefully, often treated as afterthoughts. Island countries—or "Small Island Developing States" in modern NGO parlance—are the places where the effluvium of global capitalism and militarism finally washes up. During the Cold War, it was on Pacific islands where the most powerful weapons ever devised were tested. The United States, famously, tested its bombs at Bikini Atoll in the Marshall Islands. France carried out nearly two hundred nuclear tests between 1960 and 1993 on the same islands in Polynesia that had inspired Gauguin. Britain carried out more than thirty nuclear tests between 1957 and 1962 on Kiribati's easternmost atoll, Christmas Island. Unlike in the other tests, Christmas Island wasn't evacuated during the trials—islanders were instructed merely to turn their backs to the blasts, not even to go indoors, likely exposing many to dangerous levels of radiation.[9]

Phosphate mining was equally devastating in the islands where it took place, notably Banaba in Kiribati and the independent nation of Nauru, three hundred miles to its west. Nauru, the smallest island country on the globe, had during the 1960s the second-highest GDP per capita in the world after Saudi Arabia, thanks to the phosphates mined from its center. But the island was stripped bare by mining, phosphate prices decreased, and the government made a series of ill-advised investments (including one in a West End musical that flopped), and the island was left with a devastated economy and a mostly uninhabitable homeland except for a narrow strip around the coastline. In the past decade, Nauru has made international headlines again as a dumping ground for refugees trying to reach Australia; they have been kept in dire conditions, suffering poor health and abused by guards.[10]

Western diets have also had a debilitating effect on island countries. The traditional diet in Kiribati is extremely limited but pretty healthy—breadfruit, coconut, and fish—but the islands are now awash in inexpensive flour and rice. The country's population is ranked the eighth most obese in the world. The top ten on this listing, with the exception of Kuwait, are all small islands—places where, due to centuries of relative isolation, people are physiologically unused to globalized, industrialized diets. Rates of diabetes are as high as 20 percent in the adult populations of Kiribati, Tuvalu, and Samoa.[11]

Island countries are often treated as a no-man's-land, far from the prying eyes of mainland media. This was true from the days of Devil's Island to the war on terrorism, when the CIA interrogated terrorist suspects in secret on Diego Garcia, an island in the British Indian Ocean Territory. (It was from here that the Chagos Islanders, one of the participants in the ConIFA World Cup, were displaced in the 1960s and 1970s.)

Today, the most glaring and obvious example of small islands suffering the consequences of the actions of larger countries is climate change. "Small Island Developing States," although they contribute only about .03 percent of global carbon emissions, find themselves on the front lines of a global catastrophe.[12] As former Kiribati president Teburoro Tito—a man whose complex environmental views I will get to shortly—memorably put it, "It's like the ants making a home on a leaf floating on a pond. And the elephants go to drink and roughhouse in the water. The problem isn't the ants' behavior. It's a problem of how to convince the elephants to be more gentle."[13]

Ants in the Pond

The world got a decidedly PG-rated preview of events to come in March 2010, when scientists announced that New Moore Island had ceased to exist. This wasn't an event of particular geological significance because the island, two miles long and one and a half miles wide, located just off the coast in the Bay of Bengal, had long been more of a sandbar. It had only come into existence in 1970, when the Bhola cyclone, a devastating storm that killed over five hundred thousand people, deposited sand into the bay. But the island took on political importance after 1971, when Bangladesh declared independence from Pakistan and began to recover from its long and bloody war. New Moore, or South Talpatti, as it's known in Bangladesh, sat about four kilometers south of the mouth of the Hariabhanga River, which serves as the border between Bangladesh and India. Bangladesh argued that the main flow of the river passed to the west of the island, which was a natural extension of its landmass. India claimed it flowed to the east of the island, which was after all closer to Indian territory.[14]

The island itself wasn't the real issue. Possession of the uninhabited patch would determine the maritime border between the two countries, a distinction that would have major economic ramifications if natural resources were ever discovered anywhere on or near it. The dispute became a media sensation in both countries, and in 1981 India even dispatched troops on a naval frigate to plant the country's flag on the narrow sand spit. Bangladesh responded with six naval ships of its own. Things later calmed down, but as recently as 2003, Bangladesh's parliament instructed the navy to ensure the country's sovereignty over the island. It took a far more dramatic intervention, from the sea itself, to finally end the dispute.[15]

Beginning around 2000, sea levels had been rising around New Moore by about five millimeters per year, so it was no surprise when the land finally became completely submerged only a decade into this century. As Suagata Hazra, an oceanographer at Jadavpur University in Kolkata, pointed out to the Associated Press, "What these two countries could not achieve from years of talking has been resolved by global warming."[16] Four years later, the waters around the former island were finally awarded to Bangladesh by a UN tribunal. The case of New Moore Island is thus an obscure and not particularly consequential territorial dispute that was resolved in an unusual way, but it's a reminder that the physical world map is becoming more fluid and dynamic, even as the political map stays frozen in an age of stasis. (The impact of global warming is not usually so benign: in 2017, the Venezuelan government blamed climate change for shifting the course of a river, resulting in some of its troops briefly invading Colombia.)[17]

On March 16, 2015, the Pacific Island nation of Vanuatu was nearly wiped off the map. When Tropical Cyclone Pam, a category 5 storm more powerful than any Atlantic hurricane ever recorded, blew through this tiny archipelago with a land area about the size of Connecticut, it was about as close to a knockout blow as a country can receive. Though only 17 people were killed, more than half of the country's buildings were badly damaged, affecting two-thirds of Vanuatu's 266,000 people. In the capital city, Port Vila, 90 percent of the buildings were destroyed. Forests were blown apart. Crops were uprooted. Water stocks were contaminated. "All the development that has taken place, all this development has been wiped out," said the country's president, Baldwin Lonsdale.[18]

Lonsdale, ironically, missed the storm because he was attending a disaster preparedness conference in Japan, where he was a bit belatedly informed that his capital, Port Vila, is the most natural disaster–prone city on the planet. Then, in a moment of foreboding clarity, Lonsdale suggested that perhaps the disaster wasn't so natural after all. "We see the level of sea rise. . . . The cyclone seasons, the warm, the rain, all this is affected," he told the BBC. "This year we have more than in any year. Yes, climate change is contributing to this."[19]

Vanuatu's fate prompted international affairs blogger Mark Leon Goldberg to suggest in the immediate aftermath that Vanuatu might be "the first country to vanish due to climate change."[20] He was being too pessimistic, but not by much. Vanuatu will continue to exist, though its economy, which is highly dependent on tourism, will take years to recover.

Tropical Cyclone Pam and the havoc it wreaked on Vanuatu is just the latest reminder of the dire predicament facing small island countries thanks to rising sea levels and increasingly unpredictable weather. According to the World Bank, two-thirds of the countries that suffer the worst yearly damages due to natural disasters are small island states. These countries lose between 1 and 9 percent of their GDP every year from disasters.[21] If conditions continue on their current path, Vanuatu's devastation won't be the last or the worst incident of its type. The devastation wrought by Hurricane Maria in Puerto Rico in 2017 has also accelerated the U.S. territory's already chronic outmigration.

Island states aren't the only countries facing existential threats. For instance, hovering over the ongoing territorial conflict between Ukraine and Russia is the inexorable trend that Ukraine's population is aging and shrinking at a remarkable clip. Like the populations of most former Soviet countries, Ukraine's has shrunk since the end of Communism, thanks to factors including high rates of alcoholism and smoking among working-age males, high rates of HIV, and low fertility. But Ukraine's decline has been the most dramatic. Its population is shrinking at the second-fastest rate in the world after Japan, which is on much surer economic footing. With Ukraine's death rate exceeding its birth rate, the country's total population is forecast to drop below 34 million in 2050, less than two thirds of what it was at independence—a demographic hollowing out that may ultimately prove a greater threat to its independence than Russian aggression.[22] (Russia faces similarly bleak demographics, though birth rates have picked up in recent years amid a government-led fertility campaign.)

Reflecting on Ukraine's demographic trends in 2013, the economist Edward Hugh wrote that he wondered "whether it is not possible that some countries will actually die, in the sense of becoming totally unsustainable, and whether or not the international community doesn't need to start thinking about a country resolution mechanism somewhat along the lines of the one which has been so recently debated in Europe for dealing with failed banks."[23] Of course, that was written before Russia's annexation of Crimea and the effective splitting-off of the country's eastern regions by Russian-backed armed separatists. Today, the answer of what will happen if the Ukrainian state is no longer demographically sustainable is more obvious: it will be absorbed in whole or in part into other countries.

Regions becoming depopulated is not unheard of in human history: several islands off the coasts of Scotland and Ireland, for instance, once had permanent populations but are now abandoned. But current population trends—declining fertility in nearly all of the developed world and rapidly declining populations in the former Communist countries and East Asia—are likely to pose a challenge to cartographical stasis by forcing some unsustainable countries to be absorbed into other ones. Some leaders are starting to come to terms with this once seemingly far-fetched reality. The president of Latvia, Andris Bērziņš, acknowledged in a 2013 speech that if the country's population continues to decline at current rates and its young people continue to emigrate, Latvia might not be viable as an independent state in ten years.[24]

Still, the land these countries occupy isn't going anywhere. The prospect of absorption into neighboring countries may be a grim one for independent states—particularly ones that gained their hard-won independence from Moscow only recently—but people will remain on the land under one government or another. The prospect of the land itself disappearing, of *no* state existing on a spot where once there was one, is a fate currently facing only the small island countries. And it's a fate that's fast approaching.

Leaving on a Jet Plane

"One of the most difficult things I've had to accept is planning for the demise of my country," Anote Tong told me.

I knew Tong by reputation from the impassioned speeches he became known for delivering at UN General Assemblies and climate change conferences during his time as president between 2003 and 2016. When I met with him one afternoon in Tarawa, he had just come in from fishing and was relaxing in shorts and sleeveless T-shirt in the manaeba outside his family's home in a crowded residential neighborhood. Signs of ostentatious wealth or status are conspicuously absent in Kiribati: the former president's residence doesn't look all that different from his neighbors'. With John Denver playing softly from a Bluetooth speaker, we spoke for some time about the apocalyptic fate awaiting his country.

"Whatever happens, we must do everything possible to try to stay. That's what I've been doing over the entirety of my term in office," he said, adding ruefully: "The science is pretty clear: zero emissions, we'll still go underwater. Unless some drastic work is undertaken, there will be no option [but relocation.]. That's the reality. It's not a hope. It's not a desire. It's the brutal reality."

Tong made international headlines in 2014 with the purchase of the fifty-five-hundred-acre plot of land on the Fijian island of Vanua Levu. Kiribati is frequently described as the only country to have purchased land abroad specifically for relocation due to climate change. It quickly became clear, however, that there was more to the story than what was typically reported. This was not exactly a "land without people for people without a land." For one thing, the land in question is already home to several hundred Solomon Islanders who were brought to Fiji in the nineteenth century to work as slaves on a nearby coconut plantation. For another thing, Kiribati, one of the poorest countries per capita in the world, may have paid as much as four times more per acre to the land's owner, the Church of England, than other buyers did for similar nearby properties. Moreover, most of the estate consists of steep hills and mangrove swamps, not particularly inviting for either habitation or agriculture.[25]

Tong's government changed its story several times throughout his presidency in characterizing what exactly the land was for. Sometimes for resettlement, sometimes for agriculture to provide food security to isolated Kiribati. When I asked Tong which it was, he told me, "It's all of those. It's a very large statement to the international community that our situation is serious. But apart from that, it's a damn good investment." When I said that most of the international community was under the impression that Kiribati's 110,000 people are planning to live on the plot one day, he responded, "The media makes their own interpretations and I allow them to do that."

I'll leave it to others to assess Tong's real estate savvy. In defense of the international media, Tong's speech to the United Nations certainly gave the impression that the land was meant for relocation. If nothing else, the purchase was effective as a kind of performance art, forcing the world to contemplate the prospect of an entire sovereign nation picking up and relocating. His administration also emphasized the concept of "migration with dignity," a process to provide citizens with skills so that they could work abroad on their own terms. "I don't like the term 'climate refugee,'" he said. "Refugees are regarded as second-class citizens, thought of as no longer belonging. I want people to be not only belonging but in control." Fiji Prime Minister Frank Bainimarama also said at a climate conference in 2017 that i-Kiribati would be welcome in his country and "will not be refugees" should they be forced to relocate.[26]

But could Kiribati continue to exist if its original landmass was no longer habitable? "You can have loss of state, the literature deals with that," he said, "but not this. I cannot really answer whether we will remain a sovereign state outside of here. There would be a lot of resistance to it."

One of the biggest questions is what would happen to Kiribati's "exclusive economic zone" (EEZ), the sea zone granted to countries around their territory by the Law of the Sea. Kiribati, as I mentioned earlier, despite its tiny land areas, is something of a sea superpower. Would the people of the country, wherever they ended up living, still get to take advantage of the riches drawn from their waters? "The world politics and world rules would have to change. At the moment I don't see that happening," Tong said. "What will happen to [our] EEZ? As far as we're concerned, it remains ours. We've just got to let it be known that in the absence of any letter or charter, we believe it's ours."

Tong isn't willing to give up on Kiribati quite yet, however, but his vision for his country's future entails nothing short of a full-scale physical transformation of the islands. In contrast to most Kiribati leaders, who want to preserve the settlements on the outer islands, he believes that the future for the Kiribati people is on Tarawa, and not only that, he's calling on the international community to physically reinforce the island to raise it further above sea level. He points to China's strategic island building in the South China Sea as evidence that this is possible. "It's very doable. China demonstrated that. Given the will, it's very doable. It's a question of applying the resources," he said.

Tong envisions an urbanized, densely populated, artificially reinforced Tarawa that sounds more like Dubai or Singapore than the laid-back underdeveloped island I was visiting. "The rural area that exists today will no longer be there," he said, conceding, "It's about building a new society. We have to learn to live in a different way."

Kiribati has had five presidents since independence and they don't seem to go away once they've finished their term. During my short visit to the country, I met three of the five. (The current president, Taneti Mamau, was unfortunately traveling on another island at the time.) Though the country doesn't exactly have fraught partisan politics—most politicians seem pretty amiable toward each other—it's fair to say that Teburoro Tito, president from 1994 to 2003 and now a senator, is on the opposite end of the country's political spectrum from Tong.

If the Fiji land purchase is Tong's claim to fame, the zigzag in the center of the international dateline is Tito's. The dateline that used to leave Kiribati's easternmost islands a day behind its western part was an economic nuisance, so in 1994, Tito simply announced that the dateline would run along the eastern boundary of the country.[27]

This might not seem like the sort of thing a country can decide on its own—and many authorities, including at the U.S. Naval Observatory, still don't technically recognize the adjustment—but most maps now show the dateline squiggling around the country. In 2000, Kiribati took advantage of the change, promoting Christmas Island as the first place to greet the new millennium.[28]

Not every president can successfully bend time to his will, and Tito brings up the change when, to his evident annoyance, I start asking him about climate change. "I wouldn't have done that if I had imagined that these islands are going to disappear," he tells me. "Our future is bright: we shouldn't be running away." He's dismissive about the international prestige his successor, Tong, got from talking about the islands' imminent disappearance. "He told the world that we're in trouble. He created a lot of panic." He dismisses Tong's notions of island building as "science fiction."

Tito may have made the famous remark about the ants and the elephants, but he often sounds more like an oil-company-backed American Republican denialist when he talks about climate change. "I don't believe that this nation will disappear from the map of the world," he said. "We're strong in our Christian faith. We think we will be here until the end of time. We won't be removed by, what, by the polar ice caps melting? I don't think the creator who put us here planned that."

As for the topic of this chapter, whether Kiribati could exist as a nation in another physical location, he's dismissive. "It's a good academic subject. Interesting to imagine. I wish you well with your book. The government doesn't have time to deal with this."

In my visit to Tarawa, I found that most Kiribati people were generally closer to Tito's view of things. It wasn't outright denial, just a kind of generalized indifference. For all that countries like Kiribati have provided effective advocacy on climate change at the global level and are often viewed as the canaries in the coal mine that will first show its effects, they don't evince any greater sense of urgency about the issue than people in the United States. People for the most part agreed that the climate is changing, pointing to shifting rainy seasons and irregular fishing patterns, but they usually didn't believe that the islands would come to an end.

I heard several odd pseudoscientific arguments from Kiribati people during my time there, including that hotter weather would just evaporate all the water caused by the melting ice caps, and that the coral in the Kiribati atolls would help the islands simply float as the water rose. But these theories aside, it *is* true, as many people pointed out, that the shape of the islands regularly shifted and altered before sea-level rise and that so far the impacts of climate change had been difficult to disentangle from other factors.

But usually what I heard was frustration that the rest of the world seems to take notice of them only to tell them they're doomed. On several occasions, people I spoke with had already given several interviews about the topic of climate change to foreign reporters. "In my case, you are the fifth person," remarked Teewata Aromata, the director of Te Toa Matoa, the NGO for people with disabilities whose party I attended.

"People come and ask us the same questions. They see pictures of us and think we are drowning in the ocean. Kiribati isn't sinking. Climate change is happening. We experience this, the saltier seawater, and the land is changing as well. But it is not sinking." Like many, she attributed much of the erosion of land and flooding on Tarawa to the overcrowding of new arrivals from the other islands, saying the problem would go away if people went back to where they came from.

Sentiments like these made me feel a bit guilty for my project. How typical of the mainland's general ambivalence to island countries to take note of them only as symbols of a larger global problem, as martyrs to a cause. Even the often used phrase "canaries in the coal mine" implies that the death of nations is nothing more than early warning signs for the fates awaiting larger, more important countries. This kind of reduction to symbolism seems only marginally better than the utter indifference of others. (When Rupert Murdoch was asked about the effects of climate change during a Sky News interview, he dismissively answered, "The Maldives might disappear, but we shouldn't be building windmills and all that rubbish.")[29]

But the stubborn fact remains that as much as we would prefer not to think about it, countries like the Maldives and Kiribati likely *are* disappearing and not that long from now. I came to Kiribati expecting to find a place planning for its own destruction, but instead I found something more dispiriting: a place that (understandably) *isn't* even contemplating that destruction. With a few exceptions, of course. "Who wants to believe that their home won't be here? People here don't even like to plan for next week. But we've got to be hardheaded about it," said Tong.

The mental block that prohibits thinking about what will happen when the island is no longer inhabitable seems to be a major impediment to planning for that eventuality—in this regard, too, Kiribati is a microcosm of the world's unwillingness to face the reality of the future. A nation disappearing off the map is something that's never happened before and, so far, is something people seem unable to imagine.

Land without a Land

Early in our conversation, Secretary of Foreign Affairs Akka Rimon made the joke I had been afraid to: "Climate change really put us back on the world map. The irony is that we're being erased from the world map." Just a week before my visit to the country, Kiribati weightlifter David Katoatau got international attention at the Olympic Games in Rio de Janeiro with his exuberant dancing at the opening ceremony. He told Reuters, "Most people don't know where Kiribati is. I want people to know more about us so I use weightlifting, and my dancing, to show the world. I wrote an open letter to the world last year to tell people about all the homes lost to rising sea levels. I don't know how many years it will be before it sinks."[30]

In contrast to some of her counterparts, Rimon was willing to think through the possibilities of what relocation could entail, though she didn't really have answers for how Kiribati's nationhood could be preserved. She was somewhat optimistic that the issue was starting to come to the fore, saying, "Now I see the switch to people talking about EEZs and sovereignty rights." One possibility she suggested was building artificial structures, or even building up several islands themselves, to preserve the nation's borders if it began to lose land territory. "We don't have the answer. There doesn't seem to be any entity that looks after that. Sovereignty exists within the borders of your nation, but what happens when that changes? Nobody has the answer to that," she said.

A fictional version of such a scenario is imagined in a 2017 short story by Kanishk Tharoor, "A United Nations in Space." The story imagines the world in the final throes of a climate change apocalypse, in which the United Nations has been relocated from flooded Manhattan to the MaidenX, a luxury hotel orbiting the earth. As one by one, the delegates look out the window to see their nations succumbing to war or natural disaster, the delegate from Kiribati takes on a kind of elder statesman role as a representative of one of the first countries to disappear completely, a diplomat for a place that no longer exists:

> We knew for many years that our islands were doomed, that the ocean would take them . . . but we thought it would happen gradually: an atoll here and there, a beach eaten away, until the sea seeped into our groundwater and made life impossible. Then the day came. . . . I was already up in the MaidenX so I've only heard the stories and seen some of the videos. . . . They say it was difficult to know what was what, to tell the tsunami from the storm, that it seemed like an unbroken mass of water and wind rising to the roof of the sky. Dreadful, Kenya shakes his head. Jordan says something grave, one assumes along the same lines. Only with satellite images, Kiribati says, can you see the outlines of my underwater islands, faint like a footprint, the suggestion of a country no longer there.[31]

The topic is starting to receive some academic interest as well. Environmental law scholar Maxine Burkett of the University of Hawaii has taken up the question of what the international political order will look like when nations begin to disappear. She has proposed a model of "ex-situ nationhood" under which governments, with some financial support from the international community, would continue to represent their populations on an international level at bodies like the United Nations, although without any connection to a physical territory.[32] The government of the ex-situ Kiribati could ensure that the concerns of I-Kiribati are still heard at a global level as the international community works to address the catastrophic effects of climate change. I-Kiribati would retain some rights as citizens, even as they likely disperse around the globe. "A number of us understand the modern notion of citizenship, where people have ties to more than one country," Burkett told me in a 2014 interview. "But the notion of that happening without a physical territory is quite novel."

In a 2013 essay, University of Colorado law professor Jenny Grote Stoutenburg recommended that, in order to maintain international recognition, island states facing destruction reinforce their territory to maintain at least some physical structure above water and keep a small group of inhabitants behind, even if the bulk of the population has relocated.[33] The Kiribati of the future, in other words, may be little more than a skeleton crew, a reinforced platform with a flag perched in the open ocean after the rest of the country's population has moved to another piece of land or dispersed to several of them. This is a very different notion of national sovereignty than anything the world has seen before.

There are understandable motivations behind plans like these: the people of small island states want to continue to have political representation in the international community, and they have economic interests to protect—rights to fisheries and natural resources in their former territory, for instance. But these plans also offer a version of cartographical stasis taken to the extreme, or even to the point of parody: the erection of a fig leaf physical presence in the middle of the ocean just so that maps showing a country in a particular place will be technically correct.

Given that the die is likely cast, and it's probably too late to counter the reality of sea-level rise, it's time to start thinking more creatively about what defines a country. When the era of stasis is confronted by the era of climate change, we'll have to revisit the question of whether a country needs a physical territory to be a country. In imagining what an "ex-situ nation" might look like, some international law scholars have dusted off an unlikely precedent: the Knights of Malta. Burkett's writing specifically cites the order as a rare example of nonterritorial nationhood. If the vanishing countries of the future are to survive in any form, it's likely to be something that looks less like a contemporary nation-state than something like the Order of Malta, a political creation set up to represent a group of people and their political interests who will be increasingly dispersed both geographically and culturally. A nation ending entirely, with no successor, might be a wholly new event in human history, but to react to it, it may be worth dusting off some concepts that predate the age of stasis.

The concept of "climate refugees" is starting to receive a lot more attention, and may be applicable to places much larger than Kiribati. The year 2016 was the deadliest yet for migrants crossing the Mediterranean, with more than five thousand deaths.[34] This particular exodus isn't usually associated with climate change, but climate scientists argue that droughts played a role in sparking and worsening the conflict in Syria—one of the main countries of origin of the migrants attempting to reach Europe—and poor weather certainly contributed to economic distress in Somalia (including Somaliland), another major country of origin.

In the summer of 2014, the U.S. media suddenly woke up to the crisis of hundreds of unaccompanied children from Central America massing on the southern U.S. border. The main reason for the increased flow of migrants is the high murder rate in Central America, but the International Red Cross also warned in 2014 that drought in Honduras, the country where the largest number of the migrants came from, was putting around 3 million people at risk of malnutrition and was likely to increase the number of those looking to migrate.[35] Honduras sent around half a million migrants to the United States. The drought came after a period of *too much* rain that contributed to an outbreak of fungus that devastated the region's coffee crop. This, too, is rarely discussed as a climate issue, and there are undoubtedly other factors involved, but changing weather patterns are playing a role in driving mass migrations of people from poor countries to wealthy ones—which are struggling to absorb them.

This is where the plight of the island states becomes so critical as a warning. Unlike other countries, where the connection between climate and larger economic and social conditions is harder to demonstrate, a country that is literally sinking makes the situation rather obvious.

In the near term, countries like Bangladesh, Indonesia, and Mexico will still exist, unlike their small island counterparts, in their current political form. But over time, climate change will transform them physically by eroding coastlines, economically through impacts on agricultural production, and socially through increased migration. The nature and severity of these effects are difficult to predict, but it's certainly true that most governments haven't done nearly enough to plan for them.

"These countries may still have a placard at the General Assembly," said the University of Hawaii's Burkett, "so it's different in nature to the challenge facing countries like Kiribati and the Marshall Islands, but there are a number of ways in which even long-standing nation-states are seeing a juggling of their population with implications for the culture, implications for the economy, and also interesting implications of migration as an international challenge."

Thankfully, this is still a speculative scenario, but international law is also starting to come to grips with the population disruptions that changing environmental conditions will soon cause. A recent case in New Zealand serves as an indicator of the challenges climate refugees may soon pose. Ioane Teitiota, a farm laborer from Kiribati, immigrated to New Zealand in 2007 in search of work and because the island was becoming too difficult to live on due to rising sea levels, declining fish populations, and polluted groundwater. In 2011, he accidentally overstayed his visa and was in danger of deportation back to his sinking homeland. His lawyer, sensing an opportunity to affect international law, called for Teitiota to be granted protection under the 1951 UN convention on refugees, which confers refugee status on anyone with a reasonable fear of persecution for "reasons of race, religion, nationality, membership of a particular social group or political opinion." The argument was that climate change, caused primarily by wealthy nations and experienced so far primarily by poor ones, is a form of persecution. Teitiota became the first person to claim refugee status based on climate change.[36]

The case received international media attention and made an unassuming man the face of a looming global catastrophe. Ultimately, the argument was dismissed. In May 2014, a New Zealand appeals court rejected Teitiota's case, ordering that he and his family be deported. The court ruled that the international community itself cannot be a "persecutor" under the terms of the convention. In 2017,

New Zealand's new Labour Party–led government did propose creating a new category of visa for climate refugees, but the idea is still controversial.[37] But Teitiota's case will almost certainly not be the last of its kind. International efforts to address climate change will also involve some measure of wealthy countries acknowledging responsibility for causing it, and people forced to uproot their lives as a result of it, or entire nations that cease to function as a result, could look for compensation through international humanitarian law.

Estimates about "climate refugees" have been contentious, and those advocating more concerted action on climate change have at times been guilty of overhyping the data. The 2005 Intergovernmental Panel on Climate Change report estimated that the world would have to cope with 50 million refugees by 2010, a claim that was obviously premature and was dropped from subsequent drafts.

The term *climate migration* refers not to a single event forcing the movement of people but a long-term trend that's reshaping the world's population, and the development won't always be immediately obvious while it's happening. As former secretary of state John Kerry recently put it, "You think migration is a challenge to Europe today because of extremism. Wait until you see what happens when there's an absence of water, an absence of food, or one tribe fighting against another for mere survival."[38] That picture of a future world is distressing enough, but the more alarming question raised by the uncertainty over the current refugee crisis is whether we'll even know when we've entered that world—or if we're already in it.

As the extent to which sea-level rise will redraw the international map becomes more evident, some U.S. states are starting to think outside the box. In October 2014, officials in the city of South Miami passed a resolution in favor of splitting the state of Florida in half, in part because of frustration that the state government in Tallahassee isn't taking the threat posed by climate change seriously enough. South Florida is already facing more frequent floods, damaging roads and infrastructure and threatening water supplies. In another century, much of Miami could very well be underwater—one of the world's first major cities lost to climate change.

When the resolution passed, South Miami mayor Philip Stoddard told the *Orlando Sentinel*, "It's very apparent that the attitude of the northern part of the state is that they would just love to saw the state in half and just let us float off into the Caribbean. . . . They've made that abundantly clear [at] every possible opportunity and I would love to give them the opportunity to do that."[39] The proposal is mostly a symbolic gesture for now—there's little chance in the near future of Florida being cut in half—but the protest vote in South Miami may be a preview of more serious debates to come.

For all the talk of globalization and the blurring of borders, people of the modern era have a much less fluid concept of nationalities than their forebears. A country is still, first and foremost, a piece of land. But we have to adopt some flexibility in this notion in a world where the land is literally washing away from beneath our feet. Not all nations will survive the end of the age of stasis in physical form, and it's time to begin planning for what they will become.

Before I went to Kiribati I had naïvely hoped to visit several of the country's thirty-three atolls, but I quickly realized that the distances and travel hassles involved were prohibitive. But on my last day, most of my interviews already completed, I spent the day walking from South Tarawa to the less populated and developed north, separated from the south by a channel that changes in size and depth depending on the tides. I hitched a ride on a truck heading up the road from the guesthouse where I was staying, walked along a dirt road past a Taiwanese agricultural development (Kiribati is one of the few countries in the world that recognize Taiwan's sovereignty and has been rewarded with some conspicuous development projects), and arrived at a shallow channel where canoes were waiting to take travelers across to North Tarawa.

The other side of the channel was a dramatic transformation. There were no paved roads or vehicles, no billboards, no restaurants or hotels, just a narrow path winding through villages of manaebas and thatched-roof huts, copra drying in the blazing sun outside. You could have been in a past century, if not for the solar panels affixed to the thatched roofs and the ubiquitous smartphones. Walking further through salty marshes across an aptly named Broken Bridge, I saw ahead the town of Tabiteuea, perched on stilts over a channel between the islands. Being far from the sewage and pollution of South Tarawa, I slipped into the channel to swim across to the town, which was mostly empty as the locals had either headed south to shop or were out fishing. Aside from a few boys playing on the shore, there was little human activity to be seen, but movement was everywhere, the tide pushing the water up to the edge of the town, the waves lapping at the shore, the wind blowing sand across the sizzling hot beach.

I spend most of my time writing about structure—physical, political, and ideological—created by people on the landmass where we live amid a sea of blue. Dog-paddling in the channel at Tabiteuea as the tide rolled in, thinking only hazily in the back of my mind about how I was going to make it back to my guesthouse before the passage became impassable (I made it), it was more apparent than usual how fragile the physical space we live in can be, and how subject to rapid change.

The New Map

It wasn't clear at the outset if anyone in Abkhazia would actually care about the World Football Cup, but public excitement in Sukhumi grew as the tournament progressed, particularly as the home team continued to advance through the rounds. In the group stage, they narrowly beat Western Armenia and demolished the Chagos Islands. Then in the knockout stages, they took down Sápmi, followed by Northern Cyprus. The games attracted standing-room-only crowds and gawkers who stood on the ramparts outside the stadium.

In the finals, the Abkhazians were to meet Punjab, the UK-based team inspired by a Sikh emperor who ruled an independent empire from 1799 to 1839. In the surprise of the tournament, the Punjabis had seen off Somaliland and Sápmi in the group stage. They beat Western Armenia in a chippy quarterfinal game that ended in a three-way on-field brawl between the two teams and the police. They also managed to beat Padania, an early favorite that had won ConIFA's European championships in 2015. When I asked the team's manager, Harpreet Singh, the one who had asked me to imagine the death of my own family, how his players were handling the pressure, he responded cryptically, "This is all an illusion."

I had spent most of my time with members of the Somaliland team, who had been quickly eliminated from contention after losses to Sápmi and Punjab. They regained a bit of pride after beating Chagos in a makeup game to determine ConIFA's international rankings. (The woeful Chagossians, there mostly to make a political point about their displacement, were consistently irritated to find that rather than their own flag, the colonial flag of the British Indian Ocean Territory was flying above the field before their games. At one game I attended, the field staff didn't quite understand the problem until I explained to them that it was the equivalent of a Georgian flag being flown in Abkhazia.) Somaliland then lost a final game to Székely Land, a team representing the Hungarian minority in Romania.

It wasn't quite the result the team was hoping for, particularly as the organizers were hoping not only to raise Somaliland's profile on the international stage but also to get the Somaliland government itself to recognize them as a national team. The government was reluctant to participate in a tournament meant for not-quite countries, feeling it was a kind of forfeiture of its claim to full independence.

But the result was satisfying to Hassan Abdala, the senior member of the team's staff, particularly the fact that the country's flag had been raised on foreign soil, a rare feat for Somaliland. The video of the flag raising was viewed over twenty thousand times on YouTube during the tournament. Clearly, there was some notice being taken of the country.

I sat speaking with Abdala by the side of Lake Ritsa, Abkhazia's main tourist attraction. While the rest of the Somalilanders took out paddleboats on the gorgeous alpine lake where Joseph Stalin's personal yacht once sailed, I spoke with Abdala about sports and nationhood. Abdala had played for the Somalia national football team from 1977 to 1983. At a competition in Iraq, he left the team and traveled to Saudi Arabia. He moved to Norway in 1987 before coming to Britain, where he worked with young Somali players. He traveled between the UK and Somaliland from 1992 until he moved back to Somaliland a year before the tournament to run a football academy. He boasts of building Hargeisa's first artificial turf field.

Until 2016, Abdala was a member of Somaliland's Olympic Committee, a frustrating experience involving continual rejection from the IOC. "When we send applications they reject us, they say we are part of Somalia," he said. "All my country is talking about the flag coming here. The president will be very happy. One hundred percent everything will change."

For residents of places like Somaliland, Abkhazia, and Kurdistan, not to mention Palestinians, Northern Cypriots, and many Taiwanese, the idea of changing borders and allowing new countries into the exclusive club of recognized states is a hopeful one, the rightful acknowledgment that these places have earned the status of country. But for many others, tempered by a nightmarish history of wars over territory, the idea is a frightening one.

If you asked my grandfather Joe where he was from, he'd tell you, "the Bronx," a technically accurate answer that didn't quite explain the thick accent that people were actually asking about. Pressed a little more, he would probably say, "Poland," which was partly true.

He was born in 1908 in the town of Peremyshliany, or Premishlan in Yiddish, in the historical region of Bessarabia, at a time when it was part of the Austro-Hungarian Empire. But in 1918, when he was ten, it became part of Poland in the great postwar adjustment of borders, when Woodrow Wilson and others thought that redrawing national boundaries to correspond naturally with nations and peoples on the ground would prevent war. Unfortunately, Jews like my grandfather were a minority, no matter where the lines were drawn, and he immigrated to the United States from Poland in 1936. "Hebrew" is the race listed on his immigration papers and "Poland" the country of origin. Only Peremyshliany didn't stay in Poland for much longer. It was annexed by the Soviet Union after the invasion of Poland in 1939, then occupied by Nazi Germany from 1941 to 1944—during which time nearly all the remaining Jews in the area were killed. After the war, it was part of the Soviet Union once again until 1991, when it became part of the independent nation of Ukraine, which it remains today. In the twentieth century alone, Peremyshliany was part of five different countries.

During most of my grandfather's lifetime, and for hundreds of years before he was born, the fate of towns like Peremyshliany wasn't particularly unusual—they found themselves on one side of a border or another, part of one country or another, depending on the expansion and contraction of empires, the redrawing of boundaries in conference rooms hundreds of miles away.

But for the last quarter century or so, things have been different. We often think of this as an era of globalization, in which people and capital move around the world with a speed and freedom never before seen, when boundaries between nations and cultures have become more porous and our society more global. But at the same time, the actual lines on the map, the arrangement of countries that we live in, has been for the most part fixed and unchanging. A town in Poland can reasonably expect to remain part of Poland for the foreseeable future.

This has been an unusual time in human history, and also a relatively good one, corresponding with fewer interstate wars, fewer casualties from violence in general, and all the positive outcomes in health and human development that result from those conditions. As the 2013 Human Security Report, a widely cited annual analysis by the Peace and Conflict Studies research group and Simon Fraser University, put it, "High-intensity conflicts have declined by more than half since the end of the Cold War, while terrorism, genocide and homicide numbers are also down. . . . In the past 10 years, most of the few interstate conflicts we have seen—including one in 2011 between Cambodia and Thailand—have been very small compared to those taking place in the 1990s and at the turn of the century."[1] Most of the conflicts that do happen today are *intra*state, between governments and nonstate armed actors, rather than between two countries. Most of these are "low intensity," meaning fewer than a thousand battle deaths per year.

There are a lot of reasons for the so-called long peace, and whether it even exists is a topic of ongoing debate, but it's also probably not a coincidence that it corresponds with the age of cartographical stasis. Governments are understandably leery of letting the genie of territorial conflict out of the bottle again. When the United States is wary of supporting the breakup of Iraq, when the African Union looks skeptically at Somaliland, or even when the EU looks askance at Scottish or Catalan independence, it appears massively unjust to the people who live in those places, but it's hard to fault those who want to retain the status quo given how many towns like Peremyshliany were pulverized in wars over scraps of land during the last century.

But we also shouldn't necessarily assume that stasis is permanent. Often, what appears to be an endpoint of historical development is just a lull. Leo Tolstoy described another such lull, the period of relative stability following the Napoleonic wars, in the concluding chapter of *War and Peace:* "Though the surface of the historical sea seemed immobile, mankind moved as ceaselessly as the movement of time. Various groups of human connections were made and unmade; causes were prepared for the formation and decomposition of states, for the displacements of peoples."[2] We may very well just be living in another period where the surface—seen by us as the lines drawn on our maps of the earth's landmass—appears immobile, even as deeper movements are brewing underneath. After all, the displacement of people, the making and unmaking of social groups, and competition over territory have been constants in human history a lot longer than the notion of countries has existed.

Oxford political scientists Monica Duffy-Toft and Dominic Johnson go so far as to argue that competition over territory is an impulse that evolution has hardwired into animals, including humans, "a proxy through which organisms secure access to key resources and protect them from competitors."[3] As Duffy-Toft told me in an interview, "It comes back to survival and reproduction. There's an instinct that we need land in order to exist. We need to have the capacity to get resources to live our lives. . . . It's to our advantage to have borders, to delineate them and understand the basis of who lives where. [The model] may explain why it is that states go after territories that have no material basis, or that the costs are higher than what they will get out of them."[4] When those borders come into question, violence can be expected.

Competition for territory may be as old as human society, but we've made some modifications to the concept. One is the notion of state sovereignty, that the political task of the state is exclusive control of a fixed piece of territory and that every piece of territory on the earth's landmass should be controlled by a state. Another is nationalism, the idea that political and cultural units should be congruent. It is also now taken for granted, in theory anyway, that the legitimacy of a country is rooted in the consent of the people who live within its borders, not just the power of its rulers. This has raised the price of conquest and exchange of territory: people have a stake in the countries they live in and won't consent to those countries being traded away or reshaped as part of grand bargains between empires or local barons. After World War I, Wilsonian rhetoric raised nationalism to the level of grand strategy, putting forward the idea that global peace and stability depended on each ethnic group having a country of its own. This was followed by the great geographical trend of the twentieth century, the collapse of Europe's territorial empires.

Wilson's idea may have failed to create a lasting peace in his time, but in a way he wasn't wrong. There is even some empirical evidence to support the idea that groups are better off having their own state rather than sharing. A 2006 paper by economists Alberto Alesina of Harvard, William Easterly of New York University, and Janina Matuszeski of Oxfam America invented a measure of the "artificiality" of states, meaning the degree to which their political borders do not coincide with the "nationalities desired by the people on the ground." Simply put, they measured how "straight" or "squiggly" a country's borders are, the idea being that "squiggly" borders probably correspond to either geographical features or the desires of people who live there—think of Germany's borders, for instance—as opposed to straight borders, which were more likely drawn by outside powers without regard to realities on the ground. (Think of "Winston's Hiccup"—the squarish chunk cut out of the eastern border of Jordan by Winston Churchill "with the stroke of a pen, one Sunday afternoon in Cairo" after, as the legend goes, a "particularly liquid lunch.")[5] The countries with the squarest borders—Chad, Ecuador, Equatorial Guinea, Eritrea, Guatemala, Jordan, Mali, Morocco, Namibia, Niger, Pakistan, Sudan, and Zimbabwe—correspond pretty neatly with what you'd think of as "artificial" states, and these tend to have lower GDPs and more political instability than their squigglier counterparts. (The very straight border between the United States and Canada is a notable exception.)[6]

But the idea of "natural" borders is itself dangerous and deceptive. For one thing, ethnic groups are fluid categories. The fact that the eastern countries of the EU—Hungary, Poland, Slovakia, and the Czech Republic—are more hostile to large-scale immigration or accepting refugees than their counterparts to the west is often attributed to the fact that they're more ethnically homogenous. But they only got that way through a century of war, genocide, and mass displacement. Contemporary Europe in some ways vindicates Wilson's notion that having country borders divide national groups from each other will lead to peace. But at the same time the process by which it arrived at those borders also shows why his idea is so dangerous.

In light of all this, it's not surprising that the world's status quo powers feel the map should be kept the way it is. But it's becoming increasingly unclear whether this status quo can be preserved.

On February 22, 2014, Ukraine's Russian-backed president Viktor Yanukovych fled Kiev following months of protests of his decision to scrap an agreement with the European Union in favor of closer ties with Russia. A week later, unidentified gunmen in what appeared to be Russian combat uniforms seized key buildings in Simferopol, the administrative capital of Crimea. On March 16, Crimeans had gone to the polls in a hastily organized referendum and voted to join the Russian Federation rather than become independent. Remaining a part of Ukraine, as Crimea had been for twenty-three years, was not an option on the ballot. Two days later, President Vladimir Putin signed a bill absorbing Crimea into Russia. The entire operation was a textbook example of the Kremlin's hybrid war tactics, carried out by "volunteers" whose activities on behalf of Russian interests aren't formally acknowledged as they are taking place. Putin didn't admit until a year later that the annexation had been planned from Moscow and was not simply a spontaneous expression of the will of the Crimean people.[7]

The Crimea annexation was followed by a bloody months-long conflict in the heavily Russian-speaking regions of eastern Ukraine, again involving unacknowledged participation by Russian "volunteers" and the emergence of the self-declared independent republics of Donetsk and Luhansk. Although fighting between the Ukrainian government and the Russian-backed separatists has diminished since a ceasefire signed in early 2015, the status of the breakaway regions remains unresolved at the time of writing.

The annexation of Crimea was recognized by only a small handful of the usual suspects, including Cuba, Venezuela, Syria, and North Korea. No one (not even Russia, technically) recognizes Luhansk and Donetsk. In July 2017, separatist leaders announced the creation of a new state called Malorossiya (Little Russia) that would take the place of Ukraine and have its capital in Donetsk.[8] The international community hasn't exactly rushed to recognize the move, but it did indicate that Ukraine's territorial conflict is a long way from resolution.

While the international community has widely condemned Russia's actions, it hasn't been able to do much about them. The United States and Europe placed strict sanctions on Russian officials and businesses which, in conjunction with the falling price of oil, have had a severe impact on the Russian economy, but the Russian public has still largely supported Putin's actions. Unlike when Iraq invaded Kuwait in 1990, this time the United States and its allies weren't willing to start a shooting war with a nuclear power to protect Ukraine's territorial integrity. The harsh reality that few Western policy makers will openly admit is that the peninsula is today de facto part of Russia and is extremely unlikely ever to be returned to Ukrainian control.

It's possible that Crimea is simply a one-off situation, made possible by unique historical circumstances. It was, after all, a historically Russian area that had been joined to what was then the Ukrainian

Soviet Socialist Republic only in 1954 by Nikita Khrushchev. Putin, from the Russian point of view, was merely correcting one of the anomalies of the breakup of the Soviet Union. He got away with annexing Crimea in large part because Ukraine—in the midst of overthrowing its government—wasn't in any position to stop him and because no outside powers care about the place nearly as much as Russians do.

On the other hand, Putin effectively found a loophole in cartographical stasis, a way to take advantage of a chaotic situation to redraw the map. While the referendum in Crimea may have been rigged and bogus, the rhetoric that Russia has used to justify the annexation as well as to support the separatists in eastern Ukraine is straight out of the Wilsonian playbook. There's a direct line from the American president's argument for a readjustment of borders along "clearly recognizable lines of nationality" to the Russian president's argument nearly a century later that "in people's hearts and minds, Crimea has always been an inseparable part of Russia."[9]

Other powers with long-standing claims on neighboring territory are likely to take note. Russia's successful annexation of Crimea may mark a turning point: a major power, in spite of the legal, political, and military norms preventing the unilateral redrawing of the world map, managed to do so and get away with it.

In March 27, 2014, the United Nations voted on a resolution condemning the Russian annexation of Ukraine. Only eleven countries voted *against* the resolution—mostly reflexively anti-American governments like Syria, Cuba, North Korea, and Venezuela—and one hundred voted for it, but most notable may have been the fifty-eight abstentions.[10] This relative ambivalence was a noteworthy departure from the norm in the age of stasis, when the UN has tended to firmly come out against secessionism or unilateral border adjustments. The legal scholar Yuval Shany writes, "The less-than-universal opposition to the Crimean act of secession may represent a change of the international legal and political paradigm. It is a change that would allow self-determination to be invoked as a remedy to comparatively minor political grievances, to reverse historical dispositions of sovereign title over territory . . . or to simply advance the strategic interests of major states who are ready to flex their political and military muscles."[11]

The contradictions of the age of stasis are ripe for exploitation by a leader as canny as Putin.

Ukraine certainly isn't the only place where powerful actors are threatening to redraw the world map, or even where Russia is. In 2007, a Russian submarine placed a flag on the seabed underneath the North Pole, staking a claim to a seabed that could contain billions of dollars' worth of oil and minerals. The move, a conscious echo of the age of exploration, caused Canada's foreign minister to sniff dismissively, "This isn't the 15th century. You can't go around the world and just plant flags and say: 'We're claiming this territory.' "[12] But nonetheless, Canada, the United States, Denmark, and other Arctic powers are staking territorial claims of their own in an ongoing rush for securing energy resources that, in a perverse twist, have become more accessible because of the melting of Arctic ice caused by the burning of those very fossil fuels sought.

In the South China Sea, China has constructed more than two thousand acres of new land in the form of small artificial islands meant to bolster its claims over the area, contradicting competing claims by countries including Brunei, Malaysia, the Philippines, and Vietnam as well as the staunch objections of the United States. Outright war over the islands is unlikely, but the increasing militarization of the area has certainly raised the risk of a catastrophic military confrontation. China is involved in separate disputes with Japan over islands in the East China Sea, and Japan has recently begun fortifying its own tiny reefs to bolster its claims.

Despite Israeli and U.S. objections, more than 130 UN member states (more than 70 percent) now recognize Palestine as an independent state. Most countries in Europe and North America are still holdouts, but the parliaments of Spain, Ireland, Britain, and Sweden have all passed resolutions urging their governments to recognize Palestine. The U.S. veto on the Security Council prevents Palestine from gaining full membership to the United Nations, but it enjoys observer status and in September 2015, the Palestinian flag was raised outside the UN headquarters in New York. Citing a lack of progress in negotiations with Israel, Palestinian president Mahmoud Abbas has threatened to dissolve the Palestinian Authority, which has practiced limited self-rule over the West Bank in uneasy cooperation with Israel since 1994. Meanwhile, as outside powers increasingly recognize Palestinian independence, the Israeli government has become increasingly opposed to the idea of an independent Palestinian state, and voices in Israeli politics calling for maintaining full control of the West Bank have become more prominent. One way or another, the uneasy status quo in the world's most controversial land dispute is probably unsustainable in the long run.

Then there are the potential territorial disruptions brought on by the aftermath of the political upheaval that swept through the Arab world in 2011, which became known as the Arab Spring. At the time of this writing, Libya has two rival governments, each backed by a number of semi-autonomous militias, battling for control of a country that's been plunged into instability since the internationally backed overthrow of Muammar al-Qaddafi in 2011. Yemen, which has existed in its current form only since 1990, when North and South Yemen were joined, has been torn asunder again as Iranian-supported Shiite Houthi militias and a Saudi-backed government in the country's south fight for control. Calls for the country to be partitioned yet again have become more prominent.

And, of course, there are Iraq and Syria, where civil wars that have raged since 2011 and the resulting rise of the Islamic State have once again placed stress on national borders set up in the wake of World War II.

At the same time that borders have been under more stress than ever before, a wave of political leaders in the West has come to power promising to strengthen them. On June 23, 2016, the British voted to withdraw their country from the European Union after a campaign by nationalist politicians promising greater sovereignty and control over immigration and the country's economy. Four months later, American voters elected Donald Trump, whose signature promise was to build a wall on the U.S.-Mexican border. A new wave of far-right ultra-nationalist politicians throughout Europe is ascendant, sharing an opposition to immigration and a hostility to globalization. As French National Front leader Marine Le Pen put it after the Brexit vote, "This is the beginning of the end of the European Union. And I hope the birth of the Europe of nations."[13]

It shouldn't be surprising that this wave of nationalism is also more open to questioning the world map as we find it during the age of stasis. If this age was defined by a worldview holding that international borders should remain what they are, even as they become gradually less meaningful in our everyday lives, these leaders promise the opposite: a world in which borders are zealously guarded but also subject to change, either by agreement or by force.

The political map we all live within today is the product of path dependence, the result of thousands of small decisions over time creating institutions that it's very hard to unmake without massive disruption. It persists, and the world's institutions and superpowers exert enormous effort to preserve it, not because it is necessarily better than potential alternatives but because centuries of experience have taught us that redrawing boundaries is a bloody and dangerous process.

That being said, the current status quo leaves a lot to be desired. It locks in the decisions made by colonists in the nineteenth century in both Africa and the Middle East, and it contains ambiguities and prolonged stresses that can be exploited by both nonstate actors like ISIS and revisionist powers like Vladimir Putin's Russia.

The age of stasis was in part the result of an era of unquestioned American hegemony following the end of the Cold War. Russia's expansionism and China's island-building spree in the South China Sea suggest that emerging rivals for global power may not have the same interest in preserving the status quo.

It's hard to make the argument for a more flexible approach to world borders simply because it's so hard to imagine alternatives, not just to the nation-state system but also to the current arrangement of countries. The few historical examples of borders redrawn peacefully are far outnumbered by civil wars and wars of conquest. Attempts to diplomatically redraw political boundaries in a more rational way, such as the 1919 Paris Peace Conference, have usually proven unsuccessful. Even when intentions were good, they were undone by power politics, ethnic rivalry, and basic human nature. The idea of holding a grand congress today to redraw the boundaries of, say, the Middle East is unimaginable. So we continue operating with the map we've got.

I don't believe we can, or should, simply throw out the existing world map, but I do believe our priorities, as a country and as a global community, should be reordered. In 1992, the Carnegie Endowment concluded that "the United States and the world community continue to be shackled by the instinct that existing states and governments should be supported at almost any cost in their efforts to preserve the status quo."[14] That's still essentially the case today.

Even if the reasons for preserving this status quo are entirely understandable, it's still worth asking whether it's a state of affairs we *should* uphold. The existing countries in the world aren't good in and of themselves; they are useful to the extent that they help provide security and general welfare for the people who live within them as well as for the world as a whole. When they fail to do so, our first impulse should be to ask how they can be improved, not simply to state that they must be preserved.

It's not exactly clear *how* they can be improved given the current prevailing political norms, but some opportunities for creative thinking may soon present themselves. In the wake of Brexit, Scottish political leaders are calling for a new referendum on independence. The last such referendum, in 2014, failed, but Scots are overwhelmingly opposed to pulling out of the European Union. Northern Irish leaders are also reopening the question of whether the territory should be united with the Republic of Ireland rather than being pulled out of the EU along with the rest of the UK.

It's certainly not my place to judge the wisdom of any of these ideas. That's for the people who live there to decide. But I do think that international observers should reconsider their reflexive objections to this kind of territorial adjustment, what Jeffrey Goldberg has called "Westphalian obsessiveness." During the last Scottish referendum, the defenders of cartographical stasis made their presence felt. President Barack Obama called on Scottish voters to maintain a "strong, robust, and united" Britain.[15] European Commission president José Manuel

Barroso has said it would be "extremely difficult, if not impossible" for an independent Scotland to join the EU.[16]

On October 1, 2017, one week after Kurdistan held its independence referendum, Catalonia held a vote on whether to secede from Spain. Unlike in the Scottish case, the Spanish government refused to recognize the referendum, calling it unconstitutional. On the day of the vote, riot police attempted to stop balloting with truncheons and rubber bullets. The scenes of unrest broadcast around the world seemed like artifacts of an earlier, darker European age.

More than 90 percent of those who took part in the referendum voted for independence, but turnout was only 42 percent. Catalan leader Carles Puigdemont delayed an official declaration of independence, hoping for negotiations, but got nowhere with Madrid. On October 27, Catalonia officially declared independence. The Spanish government then invoked a never-before-used clause in the Spanish constitution to reestablish direct rule over Catalonia, dissolving its parliament and holding new elections. Madrid's gamble backfired: separatist parties won the new elections, even with many of their leaders in jail or in exile. Puidgemont was once again named leader of the region, despite being unable to set foot on Spanish territory for fear of arrest. As of this writing, the political crisis remains unresolved.

The assumption has been that if secession movements were allowed to succeed, it would open a Pandora's box of dangerous separatism. But it also would not be the worst thing to have at least one example of a peaceful, democratic adjustment of country borders in the modern era. (Czechoslovakia's 1993 "Velvet Divorce" is often cited as an example of this, but although the event was peaceful, it was not exactly democratic. It was the result of a backroom deal between nationalist politicians struck against the will of the majority of the population.)[17] The Scottish or Catalonian cases could be precedents for a new kind of democratic separatism—one involving peaceful, prosperous countries in which there is little risk of civil war or ethnic cleansing.

Another intriguing challenge to cartographical stasis is presented by the Rojava Kurds of Syria, America's main Syrian allies in the fight against ISIS, who claim to be seeking not a fully independent country but maximum political autonomy within a federalized Syria. Federalism is nothing new, of course, but Rojava seems to have something more radical in mind, a challenge to the notion that a nation can find its full political expression only through full political independence. Their answer to the question of whether to be part of Syria or an independent Kurdistan appears to leave the door open for other Kurdish regions to build political links with each other while still remaining nominally part of other countries. However, the fact that the Rojava idea of "democratic confederalism" is based on the writings of an imprisoned terrorist inspired by an American anarchist philosopher is not going to do much for its credibility. And there's reason to be skeptical about whether Rojava is quite as democratic and pluralistic as its rhetoric would suggest. But among some of the Iraqi Kurdish politicians I spoke to, I also detected a willingness to entertain alternative ideas of what Kurdish independence could look like.

Models of overlapping sovereignties already exist to some extent, as shown by the recent experience of American Indian nations. Given the tragic history that led to the current reservation system and the economic and social problems afflicting many of these communities, it's problematic to suggest them as a model, but it's also undeniable that many Indian nations have been remarkably successful in recent years at building sovereign political institutions outside of the global nation-state system. The works of Mohawk scholars like Audra Simpson and Taiaiake Alfred suggest that the transborder existence of their nation poses a threat to the international nation-state classification. But if nation-states took a less rigid view of sovereignty, they could also make that system more flexible and inclusive to political units that don't fit the standard definition of a country.

It might be best if a placard at the United Nations were not the be-all and end-all of country building, and if multilateral organizations like the UN could think more creatively about what a country looks like. While it's not on the international agenda to the same degree as the future of the nations mentioned above, the predicament of threatened small island states could very well force this kind of creative thinking. As climate change alters the physical boundaries of the earth's landmass and certain current countries become unsustainable in their current form, sovereign political entities that aren't based on physical territory might become more common and accepted— whether their status is premised on old ideas like the Knights of Malta or newfangled ones like Liberland or e-residency. Perhaps the countries of the future may not be pieces of land at all.

This raises the question of how such not-quite-country entities would be treated at an international level. Our global institutions are designed by countries that for the most part like to recognize and interact only with other entities that look like countries. In the early 1990s, when the breakup of the Soviet Union and Yugoslavia led many to believe, reasonably, that the divisions would continue indefinitely, Gidon Gottlieb of the University of Chicago, concerned by the global instability that the proliferation of new nations might cause, described a "futuristic scenario" in which the "[UN] General Assembly could establish a new status of 'Associated People of the United Nations' for nations that have no state of their own and that are politically organized in a democratic fashion. The members would negotiate the attributes of such status, which may include the right to address selected

UN organs (without a vote) and to display flags and other symbols of nationality."[18] Gottlieb turned out to be incorrect that the creation of ever more new countries would pose a serious problem, but the argument that global institutions need to accommodate more than a one-size-fits-all definition of countryhood is just as valid under the scenario that did come to pass: one in which the current number and arrangement of countries is largely frozen in place.

The people of the world's countries—almost all of us, in other words—have been given some contradictory messages. The ideology of nationalism has taught us that "peoples," however they self-define, ought to strive to have their own state. Liberal democracy has taught them they have the right to demand it. But the political order that has developed since the end of World War II enforced the norm that secession or adjustment of existing borders is a dangerous threat to stability that must be prevented. The contradiction can't last indefinitely.

Whatever form the future map of the world takes, for believers in multiculturalism, democracy, pluralism, the freedom of movement, and the free exchange of ideas, creative thinking is critical. If we can't find ways to make the world map work for the people who live on the planet, actors with more malevolent motives will change it in ways we can't predict or control.

As the clock ticked down, things weren't looking good for the home team. Abkhazia had breezed through the early rounds of the 2016 ConIFA World Cup to make it to the finals, but the players were trailing the Punjabis by one goal. It wasn't until the eighty-sixth minute that they managed to equalize, sending the overflowing crowd packed into every seat, stair, and square inch of Sukhumi's brand-new stadium (in defiance of any semblance of safety regulations) into a frenzy.

ConIFA rules eschew the normal overtime period of international football, so the game went straight to penalties; Abkhazia found itself down three goals to one in the best of five shootout. Then, in one of those stunning sequences of events that make the normal tedium and frustration of sports all worth it, Abkhazia's keeper came up with two clutch saves and his teammates two clutch goals to send the match to sudden-death penalties.

The electric stadium lights on that humid night heightened the green of the AstroTurf and the Abkhaz players' uniforms. The crowd's expectant agony was palpable. An entire country—let's not quibble with definitions for just this moment—sat on the edge of its seat. Earlier in the day, this event had felt very much like an oddball stunt featuring not-quite-professional football teams playing in an artificially propped-up rebel region. But now, somehow, it felt more like a proper athletic contest between nations, with all the stakes for national pride and glory that entails.

So it almost seems it was preordained that Abkhazia's goalkeeper would come up with one more save, and that Abkhazia's Vladimir Argun would catch the Punjabi goalkeeper off balance to score the winning goal.

As the crowd (and more than a few assembled international reporters) rushed onto the field, mobbing the players; as fans danced and waved the national flag; as Sukhumi's party continued long into the night—whatever your views of Georgia's history, of Vladimir Putin's territorial ambitions, of the global world order, of our very uncertain and scary future, at that moment, it was hard to deny that you were in a country.

Notes

Introduction

1. Shaun Walker, "World Cup for Unrecognised States Kicks Off in Abkhazia," *Guardian,* May 27, 2016.

2. "Kosovo and Gibraltar Join FIFA Ahead of 2018 World Cup Qualifying," *ESPNFC,* May 13, 2016.

3. Gidon Gottlieb, *Nation against State: A New Approach to Ethnic Conflicts and the Decline of Sovereignty* (New York: Council on Foreign Relations, 1993), 19, 2.

4. Neal Stephenson, *Snow Crash* (New York: Bantam Books, 1992).

5. Max Weber, "Politics as a Vocation," in *From Max Weber: Essays in Sociology* (Oxford: Oxford University Press, 1958), 78.

6. "Quotations from Mao Tse Tung: 5. War and Peace," Mao Tse Tung Internet Archive, 2000, marxists.org, https://www.marxists.org/reference/archive/mao/works/red-book/ch05.htm.

7. "Montevideo Convention on the Rights and Duties of States," The Avalon Project, Yale Law School, http://avalon.law.yale.edu/20th_century/intam03.asp.

8. Quoted in in Nicholas Stargardt, "Beyond the Liberal Idea of the Nation," in *Imagining Nations,* ed. Geoffrey Cubbit (Manchester: Manchester University Press, 1998), 22.

9. Benedict Anderson, *Imagined Communities* (London: Verso 1983).

10. Ernest Gellner, *Nations and Nationalism* (Malden, MA: Blackwell, 1983), 1.

11. Anthony D. Smith, *Nations and Nationalism in a Global Era* (Cambridge: Polity, 1995), 86.

12. Smith, *Nations and Nationalism.*

13. James Hardy and Sean O'Connor, "China's First Runway in Spratlys under Construction," *IHS Jane's Defense Weekly,* April 17, 2015.

14. "Transcript: Read the Full Text of the Fourth Republican Debate in Milwaukee," *Time,* November 11, 2015.

15. Julie Hirschfeld Davis, "Trump Seems to Side with Russia in Comments on Ukraine," *New York Times,* February 6, 2017; Josh Rogin, "Trump Campaign Guts GOP's Anti-Russia Stance on Ukraine," *Washington Post,* July 18, 2016.

16. Reena Flores, "Newt Gingrich: NATO Countries 'Ought to Worry' about U.S. Commitment," *CBS News,* July 21, 2016.

17. Caren Bohan and David Brunnstrom, "Trump Says U.S. Not Necessarily Bound by 'One China' Policy," *Reuters,* December 12, 2016.

18. Christopher Woolf, "Trump Outraged South Koreans by Saying Korea Used to Be Part of China. Is He Right?" Public Radio International, April 20, 2017.

19. Stephanie Kirchgaessner and Julian Borger, "Trump Aide Drew Plan on Napkin to Partition Libya into Three," *Guardian,* April 10, 2017.

Chapter 1. How Countries Conquered the World

1. Tony Azios, "Korean Demilitarized Zone Now a Wildlife Haven," *Christian Science Monitor,* November 21, 2008.

2. "Fatal Shooting at Abkhaz Administrative Border," *Civil Georgia,* May 20, 2016.

3. Charles King, *The Ghost of Freedom: A History of the Caucasus* (Oxford: Oxford University Press, 2008).

4. Clifford J. Levy, "Russia Backs Independence of Georgian Enclaves," *New York Times,* August 26, 2008.

5. Gerard Toal and John O'Loughlin, "How People in South Ossetia, Abkhazia and Transnistria Feel about Annexation by Russia," *Washington Post,* March 20, 2014.

6. www.kosovothanksyou.com.

7. "Transcript: Clinton Addresses Nation on Yugoslavia Strike," *CNN,* March 24, 1999.

8. Robert Lansing, "A Unique International Problem," *American Journal of International Law,* October 1917.

9. Rudmose Brown, "Spitsbergen, Terra Nullius," *Geographical Review,* May 1919.

10. "Norway in Arctic Dispute with Russia over Rogozin Visit," *BBC,* April 20, 2015.

11. Joseph Conrad, *Heart of Darkness* (New York: Everyman's Library, 1993), 9.

12. Azar Gat and Alexander Yakobson, *Nations: The Long History and Deep Roots of Political Ethnicity and Nationalism* (Cambridge: Cambridge University Press, 2013).

13. Mary Beard, *SPQR: A History of Ancient Rome* (New York: Norton, 2016).

14. Gat and Yakobson, *Nations.*

15. Tom Mashberg and Graham Bowley, "Islamic State Destruction Renews Debate over Repatriation of Antiquities," *New York Times,* March 30, 2015.

16. James R. Crawford, *The Creation of States in International Law* (Oxford: Oxford University Press, 2007), appendix 1.

17. Gat and Yakobson, *Nations,* 106–7.

18. Crawford, *The Creation of States.*

19. Derek Croxton, *Westphalia: The Last Christian Peace* (London: Palgrave Macmillan, 2013), 3, 4.

20. Robert Jackson, *Sovereignty: The Evolution of an Idea* (Cambridge: Polity, 2007).

21. Croxton, *Westphalia,* 13–14.

22. C. V. Wedgwood, *The Thirty Years War* (New York: New York Review of Books, 2005), 15.

23. Croxton, *Westphalia,* 358.

24. Martin Van Creveld, *The Rise and Decline of the State* (Cambridge: Cambridge University Press, 1999).

25. Jackson, *Sovereignty.*

26. Rory Carroll and Andres Schipani, "Bolivia's Landlocked Sailors Pine for the High Seas," *Guardian,* August 27, 2008.

27. Carlos Salazar, "Bolivian Navy Can Finally Sail out to Sea, Says Peru," *Independent,* October 20, 2010.

28. Anderson, *Imagined Communities.*

29. Crawford, *The Creation of States.*

30. Anderson, *Imagined Communities.*

31. Gellner, *Nations and Nationalism,* 1.

32. Hannah Arendt, *The Origins of Totalitarianism* (New York: Schocken Books, 2004), 230.

33. Quoted in James Mayall, *Nationalism and International Society* (Cambridge: Cambridge University Press, 1990), 27.

34. William Dalrymple, "The East India Company: The Original Corporate Raiders," *Guardian,* March 4, 2015.

35. Chris Baker and Pasuk Phongpaichit, *A History of Thailand* (Cambridge: Cambridge University Press, 2014).

36. Thomas Pakenham, *The Scramble for Africa: White Man's Conquest of the Dark Continent from 1876 to 1912* (New York: Harper Collins, 1991).

37. *City of Sherrill v. Oneida Indian Nation of N.Y.* (03–855) 544 U.S. 197 (2005).

38. Crawford, *The Creation of States.*

39. President Wilson's Fourteen Points, in *The World War I Document Archive,* ed. Richard Hacken, Brigham Young University Library, February 28, 2008, https://wwi. lib.byu.edu/index.php/President_Wilson's_Fourteen_Points.

40. Quoted in David Milne, *Worldmaking: The Art and Science of American Diplomacy* (New York: Farrar, Straus and Giroux, 2015), 111.

41. Erez Manela, *The Wilsonian Moment: Self-Determination and the International Origins of Anticolonial Nationalism* (Oxford: Oxford University Press, 2007), 22.

42. Manela, *The Wilsonian Moment,* 19, 288.

43. Merrit Kennedy, "Princeton Will Keep Woodrow Wilson's Name on School Buildings," *NPR,* April 4, 2016.

44. Manela, *The Wilsonian Moment,* 51.

45. Manela, *The Wilsonian Moment.*

46. Margaret MacMillan, *Paris, 1919: Six Months That Changed the World* (New York: Random House, 2003), 11.

47. MacMillan, *Paris, 1919.*

48. Timothy Snyder, *Black Earth: The Holocaust as History and Warning* (New York: Tim Duggan Books, 2016), 144–45.

49. Crawford, *The Creation of States.*

50. United Nations, *Charter of the United Nations,* October 24, 1945, http://www. un.org/en/charter-united-nations/.

51. Crawford, *The Creation of States.*

52. Elizabeth Pisani, *Indonesia, Etc.: Exploring the Improbable Nation* (New York: Norton, 2015).

53. Van Creveld *The Rise and Decline of the State.*

54. Crawford, *The Creation of States.*

55. "Address by President of the Russian Federation," Kremlin.ru, March 18, 2014.

56. King, *The Ghost of Freedom,* 220, 188–89.

57. King, *The Ghost of Freedom.*

58. Human Rights Watch, *Georgia/Abkhazia: Violations of the Laws of War and Russia's Role in the Conflict,* March 1995, https://www.hrw.org/report/1995/03/01/georgia/abkhazia-violations-laws-war-and-russias-role-conflict.

59. ICRC, Customary IHL Database, https://ihl-databases.icrc.org/customary-ihl/eng/docs/v2_rul_rule129_sectionc.

60. Joshua Keating, "Did the Age of Genocide Begin in Sochi?" *Slate,* February 5, 2014.

61. Benjamin Lieberman, *Terrible Fate: Ethnic Cleansing in the Making of Modern Europe* (Lanham, MD: Rowman and Littlefield, 2013).

62. See maps created by Michael Izady for the Gulf/2000 project: Columbia University School of International and Public Affairs, 2013, http://gulf2000.columbia.edu/maps.shtml.

Outlier: Knights of the East Side

1. https://www.orderofmalta.int/history/.

2. Miles Davis with Quincy Troupe, *Miles: The Autobiography* (New York: Touchstone, 1989), 388.

3. Martin A. Lee, "Their Will Be Done," *Mother Jones,* July–August, 1983.

4. Blake Hounshell, "Seymour Hersh Unleashed," *Foreign Policy,* January 28, 2011.

5. Norman Davies, *Vanished Kingdoms: The Rise and Fall of States and Nations* (New York: Penguin Books, 2012), 127.

6. Stephen J. Kobrin, "Back to the Future: Neomedievalism and the Postmodern Digital World Economy," *Journal of International Affairs,* Spring 1998.

7. Nicole Winfield, "Knights of Malta Insist on Sovereignty amid Papal Takeover," *Associated Press,* January 27, 2017.

8. Damian Thompson, "Pope Seizes Power from the Knights of Malta, Brutally Ending 900 Years of Their Sovereignty," *Spectator,* January 25, 2017.

Chapter 2. A Nation between Countries

1. Kathryn Blaze Baum, "Federal Government Urged to Rethink Cornwall Border Crossing's Relocation," *Globe and Mail,* May 3, 2013.

2. *You Are on Indian Land,* dir. Michael Kanentakeron Mitchell (National Film Board of Canada, 1969).

3. Shannon Burns, "Re-introducing Grand Chief Michael Kanentakeron Mitchell," *Indian Time,* February 11, 2010, http://www.indiantime.net/.

4. Bob Joseph, "21 Things You May Not Know about the Indian Act," *CBC,* April 13, 2016.

5. David. E. Wilkins, *American Indian Politics and the American Political System* (Lanham, MD: Rowman and Littlefield, 2010).

6. Quoted in Wilkins, *American Indian Politics,* 54.

7. Quoted in Wilkins, *American Indian Politics,* 48.

8. Charles F. Wilkinson, *Blood Struggle: The Rise of Modern Indian Nations* (New York: Norton, 2006), xiii.

9. Kate Wheeling. "A Closer Look at Poverty across the United States," *Pacific Standard,* December 10, 2015.

10. Wilkinson, *Blood Struggle,* xiv.

11. Wilkins, *American Indian Politics.*

12. Bill Harlan, "Lakota Group Secedes from U.S," *Rapid City Journal,* December 19, 2007.

13. Dean Snow, *The Iroquois* (Hoboken: Wiley-Blackwell, 1996).

14. Snow, *The Iroquois.*

15. Snow, *The Iroquois.*

16. Snow, *The Iroquois.*

17. Collected in Edmund Wilson, *Apologies to the Iroquois* (New York: Random House, 1959), 3.

18. Akwesasne Notes, ed., *Basic Call to Consciousness* (Summertown, TN: Native Voices, 2005).

19. Laurence M. Hauptman, *The Iroquois Struggle for Survival: World War II to Red Power* (Syracuse: Syracuse University Press, 2015), 5.

20. Snow, *The Iroquois.*

21. Published in Thomas King, *One Good Story, That One* (Toronto: Harper Perennial Canada, 1993), 137–38.

22. Thomas Kaplan, "Iroquois Defeated by Passport Dispute," *New York Times,* July 16, 2010.

23. Kathryn Blaze Carlson, "Ottawa in 'Explosive' Situation over Rejected Iroquois Passport," *National Post,* July 11, 2011.

24. Snow, *The Iroquois,* 201.

25. Moises Naim, *Illicit: How Smugglers, Traffickers, and Copycats Are Hijacking the Global Economy* (New York: Anchor, 2005), 261.

26. Tom Blackwell, "Contraband Capital: The Akwesasne Mohawk Reserve Is a Smuggling Conduit, Police Say," *National Post,* September 22, 2010.

27. Tim Johnson, "Indian Reservations on Both U.S. Borders Become Drug Pipelines," *McClatchy,* June 16, 2010.

28. Samantha Schmidt, "A 75-Mile-Wide Gap in Trump's Wall? A Tribe Says It Won't Let It Divide Its Land," *Washington Post,* November 15, 2016.

29. Dana Liebelson, "Canada Responds to Scott Walker: 9/11 Terrorists Had U.S. Visas," *Huffington Post,* August 31, 2015.

30. "St. Lawrence River Smuggling in Spotlight After Drownings," *CBC News,* September 5, 2015.

31. Giuseppe Valiante, "Akwesasne Creates First Court in Canada for and by Indigenous People," *CBC News*, October 2, 2016.

32. Giuseppe Valiante and Peter Rakobowchuk, "Oka Crisis, 25 Years Ago, Inspired Native Movements around the World," *Huffington Post*, July 7, 2015.

33. Adrian Morrow, "Military to Apologize for Listing Radical First-Nation Groups among Terrorists," *Globe and Mail*, December 22, 2010.

34. James Scott, *Seeing like a State: How Certain Schemes to Improve the Human Condition Have Failed* (New Haven: Yale University Press, 1999).

35. Audra Simpson, *Mohawk Interruptus: Political Life across the Borders of Settler States* (Durham, NC: Duke University Press, 2014), 11.

36. Taiaiake Alfred, *Wasase: Indigenous Pathways of Action and Freedom* (Toronto: University of Toronto Press, 2005), 158. Onkwehonwe is his preferred term.

37. German Lopez, "The Big, Nearly 200-Year-Old Legal Issue at the Heart of the Dakota Access Pipeline Fight," *Vox*, March 13, 2017.

38. "Pawnee Nation Sues Oklahoma Oil Companies in Tribal Court over Earthquake Damage," *Associated Press*, March 4, 2017.

Outlier: Virtual Countries, Real Borders

1. Lily Hay Newman, "Soon You'll Be Able to Apply for Estonian E-Residency, Whatever That Is," *Slate*, October 8, 2014.

2. Uri Friedman, "The World Now Has Its First E-Resident," *Atlantic*, December 1, 2014.

3. Charles Brett, "My Life under Estonia's Digital Government," *Register*, June 2, 2015.

4. John Perry Barlow, "A Declaration of the Independence of Cyberspace," Electronic Frontier Foundation, February 8, 1996.

5. "China's Internet: A Giant Cage," *Economist*, April 6, 2013.

6. Julian Assange, "State and Terrorist Conspiracies," iq.org, November 10, 2006, https://cryptome.org/0002/ja-conspiracies.pdf.

7. Jonathan Stempel, "Microsoft Victory in Overseas Email Seizure Case Is Upheld," *Reuters*, January 24, 2017.

8. Lily Hay Newman, "Quick Review for Donald Trump: The Internet Isn't 'Ours,'" *Slate*, December 15, 2015.

9. Ewan MacAskill, "Putin Calls Internet a 'CIA Project,' Renewing Fears of Web Breakup," *Guardian*, April 24, 2014.

10. "Iran Rolls out Domestic Internet," *BBC*, August 29, 2016.

11. Anthony Boadle, "Brazil to Drop Local Data Storage Rule in Internet Bill," *Reuters,* March 18, 2014.

12. Isabel Coles, "Iraq's Kurds Declare Independence in Cyberspace with .krd Domain Name," *Reuters,* April 14, 2016.

13. Adam Taylor, "Russia Accuses Google Maps of 'Topographical Cretinism,'" *Washington Post,* July 29, 2016.

Chapter 3. The Invisible Country

1. Graeme Wood, "Limbo World," *Foreign Policy,* December 18, 2009.

2. American-Israeli Cooperative Enterprise, "Israel International Relations: International Recognition of Israel," *Jewish Virtual Library,* http://www.jewishvirtuallibrary.org/international-recognition-of-israel.

3. Annalisa Merelli, "The Vatican Has Officially Recognized the State of Palestine," *Quartz,* May 13, 2015.

4. Courtney Brooks, "To Recognize or Not to Recognize Abkhazia? That Is Vanuatu's Question," *Radio Free Europe/Radio Liberty,* August 26, 2012.

5. Joshua Keating, "How Does the U.S. Decide Which Governments to Recognize?" *Foreign Policy,* April 13, 2010.

6. L. Thomas. Galloway, *Recognizing Foreign Governments: The Practice of the United States* (Washington, DC: American Enterprise Institute, 1978).

7. Joshua Keating, "Does the U.S. Recognize Assad as Legitimate Now? Did It Ever Not?" *Slate,* September 13, 2013.

8. Joshua Keating, "How to Start Your Own Country in Four Easy Steps," *Foreign Policy,* February 26, 2008.

9. U.S. Department of State, "Somalia Travel Warning," January 11, 2017, https://travel.state.gov/content/passports/en/alertswarnings/somalia-travel-warning.html.

10. "Somaliland Condemns Two to Death for Slain Aid Workers," *Reuters,* April 19, 2007.

11. "Deadly Car Bombings Hit Somaliland," *BBC,* October 29, 2008.

12. Mark Tran, "Inside Somaliland's Pirate Prison, the Jail That No Country Wants," *Guardian,* August 23, 2012.

13. David D. Laitin and Said S. Samatar, *Somalia: Nation in Search of a State* (Boulder: Westview, 1987).

14. Ioan M. Lewis, *A Modern History of the Somali: Nation and State in the Horn of Africa* (Oxford: James Currey, 2002), 163.

15. Lewis, *A Modern History of the Somali.*

16. Joshua Keating, "The Post-colonial Hangover," *Foreign Policy,* January 3, 2012.

17. Ioan M. Lewis, *Understanding Somalia and Somaliland* (New York: Columbia University Press, 2008).

18. Lewis, *Understanding Somalia and Somaliland.*

19. Lewis, *Understanding Somalia and Somaliland.*

20. Nicholas D. Kristof and Sheryl WuDunn, *Half the Sky: Turning Oppression into Opportunity for Women Worldwide* (New York: Vintage Books, 2010).

21. Kate Grant, "The Muslim Mother Theresa," *Huffington Post,* October 1, 2012.

22. Sarah McGregor, "World Bank Gets First Measure of 'Unequal' Somaliland Economy," *Bloomberg,* January 29, 2014.

23. Maximilien Von Berg, "A Very Unhappy Birthday for Somaliland," *National Interest,* June 6, 2016.

24. Ismail I. Ahmed, "Remittances and Their Economic Impact in Post-war Somaliland," *Disasters,* 2000, http://onlinelibrary.wiley.com/doi/10.1111/1467–7717.00154/abstract.

25. "Saudi Livestock Move Boosts Somaliland Economy," *IRIN News,* November 10, 2009.

26. Latifa Yusuf Masai, "Somaliland: 'Our Passport Not Yet Valid as Travel Document to UAE,'" *Somaliland Sun,* September 5, 2015.

27. "East Timor Profile—Timeline," *BBC,* March 1, 2017.

28. "Kosovo Profile—Timeline," *BBC,* March 3, 2017.

29. Edith M. Lederer, "Montenegro Becomes 192nd Member of UN," *Associated Press,* June 28, 2006.

30. Jeffrey Gettleman, "After Years of Struggle, South Sudan Becomes a New Nation," *New York Times,* July 9, 2011.

31. Crawford, *The Creation of States.*

32. "Non-Self-Governing Territories," in *The United Nations and Decolonization,* UN.org, http://www.un.org/en/decolonization/nonselfgovterritories.shtml.

33. United Nations, *Charter of the United Nations.*

34. United Nations, "Declaration on the Granting of Independence to Colonial Countries and Peoples," 1960, http://www.un.org/en/decolonization/declaration.shtml.

35. Quoted in Morton Halperin, *Self-Determination in the New World Order: Guidelines for U.S. Policy* (Washington, DC: Carnegie Endowment for International Peace, 1992), 15.

36. Organisation of African Unity, *OAU Charter,* May 25, 1963, https://au.int/sites/default/files/treaties/7759-sl-oau_charter_1963_0.pdf.

37. African Union, "Constitutive Act of the African Union," July 11, 2000, http://www.achpr.org/instruments/au-constitutive-act/.

38. African Union, "Constitutive Act of the African Union."

39. Yuval Shany, "Does International Law Grant the People of Crimea and Donetsk a Right to Secede? Revisiting Self-Determination in Light of the 2014 Events in Ukraine," *Brown Journal of World Affairs,* Fall–Winter 2014.

40. *Human Security Report 2013: The Decline in Global Violence; Evidence, Explanation, and Contestation* (Vancouver: Human Security Press, 2013).

41. Steven Pinker, *The Better Angels of Our Nature* (New York: Penguin, 2011).

42. Van Creveld, *The Rise and Decline of the State,* 350.

43. Bill Adair and Angie Drobnic Holan, "A Distortion of What Obama Said," *Politifact,* February 21, 2008.

44. Parag Khanna, "Breaking Up Is Good to Do," *Foreign Policy,* January 13, 2011.

45. Gettleman, "South Sudan Becomes a New Nation."

46. Ty McCormick, "Unmade in the USA: The Inside Story of a Foreign-Policy Failure," *Foreign Policy,* February 25, 2015.

47. McCormick, "Unmade in the USA."

48. Ken Silverstein, "Why Is South Sudan a Hellhole? Blame George Clooney," *Gawker,* February 6, 2015.

49. Peter Robert Woodward, "Somaliland Wants to Secede—Here's Why Caution Is Necessary," *Conversation,* September 8, 2016.

50. Freedom House, "Freedom in the World: 2017," https://freedomhouse.org/report/freedom-world/freedom-world–2017.

51. "Somaliland: Democratisation and Its Discontents," *International Crisis Group,* July 28, 2003.

52. Ann Scott Tyson, "U.S. Debating Shift of Support in Somali Conflict," *Washington Post,* December 4, 2007.

53. Jason Beaubien, "Somaliland to Trump: Take Us Off Your Travel Ban," *NPR,* March 10, 2017.

Outlier: Land of the Free

1. "Balkans: Czech Man Claims to Establish 'New State,'" *BBC,* April 16, 2015.

2. Joshua Keating, "The Man Who Would Be King," *Slate,* May 21, 2015.

3. "The Birth of Sealand," Sealandgov.org, 2017, https://www.sealandgov.org/about/.

4. Stephanie Boltje, "World's First Custom-Built Floating City to Rise off French Polynesian Waters," *ABC News,* January 16, 2017.

Chapter 4. The Dream of Independence

1. Nick Danforth, "Forget Sykes-Picot: It's the Treaty of Sèvres That Explains the Modern Middle East," *Foreign Policy,* August 10, 2015.

2. Quil Lawrence, *The Invisible Nation* (New York: Walker, 2008), 13.

3. Quoted in David McDowall, *A Modern History of the Kurds* (London: I. B. Tauris, 1997), 203.

4. Lawrence, *The Invisible Nation.*

5. McDowall, *A Modern History of the Kurds.*

6. "War in the Gulf: Bush Statement; Excerpts from 2 Statements by Bush on Iraq's Proposal for Ending Conflict," *Reuters,* February 16, 1991.

7. McDowall, *A Modern History of the Kurds,* 370.

8. Lawrence, *The Invisible Nation,* 52.

9. Joseph R. Biden Jr. and Leslie H. Gelb, "Unity through Autonomy in Iraq," *New York Times,* May 1, 2006.

10. "Full Transcript: President Obama Gives Speech Addressing Europe, Russia on March 26," *Washington Post,* March 26, 2014.

11. Will Dunham, "Kerry Condemns Russia's 'Incredible Act of Aggression' in Ukraine," *Reuters,* March 2, 2014.

12. Quoted in Halperin, *Self-Determination in the New World Order,* 68.

13. Halperin, *Self-Determination in the New World Order,* 12.

14. Serhiy Plokhy, *The Last Empire: The Final Days of the Soviet Union* (New York: Basic Books, 2014), 200.

15. Plokhy, *The Last Empire.*

16. Halperin, *Self-Determination in the New World Order,* 33, 2.

17. Sean Guillory, "Dermokratiya, USA," *Jacobin,* March 13, 2017.

18. "Tensions Continue between Kurds After Sinjar Violence," *ARA News,* March 8, 2017.

19. " 'I Am a Big Fan of the Kurds,' Says Donald Trump," *Rudaw,* July 22, 2016.

20. James Miller, "Why Islamic State Militants Care So Much about Sykes-Picot," *RFE/RL,* May 16, 2016.

21. Asli Bali, "Symposium on the Many Lives and Legacies of Sykes-Picot: Sykes-Picot and 'Artificial' States," *American Society of International Law,* September 28, 2016.

22. Michael Rubin, *Kurdistan Rising: Considerations for Kurds, Their Neighbors, and the Region* (Washington, DC: American Enterprise Institute, 2016), 24.

23. Sharon Behn, "With Lamborghinis and Rooftop Sushi, Why Is Kurdistan Broke?" *Voice of America,* July 26, 2016.

24. Josh Gerstein, "Was Biden Right?" *Politico,* June 13, 2014.

25. Jeffrey Goldberg, "The New Map of the Middle East," *Atlantic,* June 19, 2014; Robin Wright, "How 5 Countries Could Become 14," *New York Times,* September 28, 2013.

26. "Marked with an 'X': Iraqi Kurdish Forces' Destruction of Villages, Homes in Conflict with ISIS," *Human Rights Watch,* November 13, 2016.

27. Sara Elizabeth Williams, "Destroying Homes for Kurdistan," *Foreign Policy,* July 23, 2015.

28. Rodi Said, "Syria's Kurds Rebuked for Seeking Autonomous Region," *Reuters,* March 17, 2016.

29. Liz Sly, "U.S. Military Aid Is Fueling Big Ambitions for Syria's Leftist Kurdish Militia," *Washington Post,* January 7, 2017.

30. Wes Enzinna, "A Dream of Secular Utopia in ISIS' Backyard," *New York Times Magazine,* November 24, 2015.

31. Abdullah Öcalan, *Democratic Confederalism,* Kindle ed. (London: Transmedia, 2015), locations 71, 226.

32. Martin Chulov, Julian Borger, and Saeed Kamali Dehghan, "US Military Rushes to Defuse Looming Crisis in Kirkuk After Iraqi Army Advances," *Guardian,* October 16, 2017.

33. Jane Arraf, "After Iraqi Kurdish Independence Vote Backfires, 'I Do Not Regret It,' Says Barzani," *National Public Radio,* November 7, 2017.

Outlier: Out of State

1. "UN Warning over 12 Million Stateless People," *BBC,* August 25, 2011.

2. United Nations, "Convention Relating to the Status of Stateless Persons," 1954, http://www.unhcr.org/en-us/protection/statelessness/3bbb25729/convention-relating-status-stateless-persons.html.

3. UN High Commission on Refugees, "Addressing Statelessness," 2012, http://www.unhcr.org/publications/fundraising/51b1d61db/unhcr-global-report-2012-addressing-statelessness.html.

4. Joshua Keating, "How Come American Samoans Still Don't Have U.S. Citizenship at Birth?" *Slate,* June 5, 2015.

5. Max Bearak, "Theresa May Criticized the Term 'Citizen of the World.' But Half the World Identifies That Way," *Washington Post,* October 5, 2016.

6. Gellner, *Nations and Nationalism,* 6.

7. Atossa Araxia Abrahamian, *The Cosmopolites: The Coming of the Global Citizen* (New York: Columbia Global Reports, 2015).

8. Harry Cooper, "Malta Slammed for Cash-for-Passport Program," *Politico,* August 17, 2016.

9. Margalit Fox, "Garry Davis, Man of No Nation Who Saw One World of No War, Dies at 91," *New York Times,* July 28, 2013.

10. "Mos Def to Face Charges in South Africa over 'Passport,' " *Al Jazeera,* January 21, 2016.

11. Abrahamian, *The Cosmopolites,* 9.

12. Deborah Amos, "Syrian Babies Born to Refugees Face a Future in Limbo," *NPR,* July 24, 2014.

Chapter 5. The Country Vanishes

1. Intergovernmental Panel on Climate Change, "Climate Change 2013: The Physical Science Basis," 2013, http://www.ipcc.ch/report/ar5/wg1/.

2. United Nations Framework Convention on Climate Change, "Republic of Kiribati: Intended Nationally Determined Contribution," August 2015, http://www4.un-fccc.int/ndcregistry/PublishedDocuments/Kiribati%20First/INDC_KIRIBATI.pdf.

3. Chris Mooney and Joby Warrick, "How Tiny Islands Drove Huge Ambition at the Paris Climate Talks," *Washington Post,* December 12, 2015.

4. Laurence Caramel, "Besieged by the Rising Tides of Climate Change, Kiribati Buys Land in Fiji," *Guardian,* June 30, 2014.

5. "World Leaders Call for Action at Paris Climate Talks—As It Happened." *Guardian,* November 30, 2015.

6. Arthur Grimble, *A Pattern of Islands* (London: Eland, 2011), 55.

7. Kenneth R. Weiss, "Kiribati's Dilemma: Before We Drown We May Die of Thirst," *Scientific American,* October 28, 2015.

8. Sophie Foster, "Kiribati," *Encyclopedia Britannica.*

9. David Wolman, "This Place Is the Bomb," *Salon,* August 31, 2008.

10. Philip Shenon, "A Pacific Island Nation Is Stripped of Everything," *New York Times,* December 10, 1995.

11. David Brown, "Diabetes Becoming Alarmingly Common Worldwide, New Study Finds," *Washington Post,* June 25, 2011.

12. Intergovernmental Panel on Climate Change, "17.3.4. Adaptation and Adaptive Capacity," http://www.ipcc.ch/ipccreports/tar/wg2/index.php?idp=637.

13. Milan Ghandi, "Shielding the Ants from the Elephants," *New Internationalist,* December 8, 2014.

14. "Island Claimed by India and Bangladesh Sinks Below Waves," *Associated Press,* March 24, 2010.

15. Ishak Mia, "Climate Change, Sea Level Rise and Conflict Resolution of South Talpatti/New Moore Island," *Peace and Conflict Monitor,* July 15, 2013.

16. "Island Claimed by India and Bangladesh Sinks Below Waves."

17. Nick Miroff, "Venezuelan Troops Invaded Colombia This Week. But Just a Little Bit," *Washington Post,* March 24, 2017.

18. Elaine Kurtenbach, "Vanuatu President: Storm-Wrecked Country Must 'Start Anew,'" *Associated Press,* March 15, 2015.

19. Roger Harrabin, "Cyclone Pam: Did Climate Change Cause Vanuatu Damage?" *BBC,* March 16, 2015.

20. Mark Leon Goldberg, "A Country Was Nearly Wiped Off the Map This Weekend," *UN Dispatch,* March 16, 2015.

21. "Turning the Tide: Small Island States Lead, Innovate for Climate Solutions," *World Bank,* April 29, 2016.

22. Carl Bialik, "Ukraine's Population Challenge," *FiveThirtyEight,* May 17, 2014.

23. Edward Hugh, "The Suitcase Mood," *A Fistful of Euros,* May 7, 2013.

24. "President: If Emigration Is Not Stopped, Latvia's Existence Will Be in Doubt in 10 Years," *Baltic Course,* March 26, 2013.

25. James Ellsmoor and Zachary Rosen, "Kiribati's Land Purchase in Fiji: Does It Make Sense?" *DevPolicyBlog,* January 11, 2016.

26 "Tuvaluans and i-Kiribati a Promised Home in Fiji," *Radio New Zealand,* July 3, 2017.

27. R. H. Van Gent, "A History of the International Date Line," University of Utrecht, 2008, http://www.staff.science.uu.nl/~gent0113/idl/idl.htm.

28. Nicholas Kristof, "In Pacific Race to Usher in Millennium, a Date-Line Jog," *New York Times,* March 23, 1997.

29. John Conroy, "'Sceptical' Murdoch Laments 'Windmills and All That Rubbish,'" *Australian,* July 14, 2014.

30. Brian Oliver, "Pacific Islander Dances to Raise Climate Change Awareness," *Reuters,* August 15, 2016.

31. Published in Kanishk Tharoor, *Swimmer among the Stars* (New York: Farrar, Straus and Giroux, 2017), 69.

32. Maxine Burkett, "The Nation Ex-Situ: On Climate Change, Deterritorialized Nationhood and the Post-climate Era," *Climate Law,* 2011, https://papers.ssrn.com/sol3/papers.cfm?abstract_id=2372457.

33. Jenny Grote Stoutenberg, "When Do States Disappear?" in *Threatened Island Nations: Legal Implications of Rising Seas and a Changing Climate,* ed. Michael B. Gerrard and Gregory E. Wannier (Cambridge: Cambridge University Press, 2013).

34. Ben Quinn, "Migrant Death Toll Passes 5,000 After Two Boats Capsize off Italy," *Guardian,* December 23, 2016.

35. "Drought Threatens More Than 500,000 in Honduras-Red Cross," *Reuters,* October 22, 2014.

36. "New Zealand Deports Would-be First Ever 'Climate Change Refugee,'" *Agence France-Presse,* September 24, 2014.

37. Charles Anderson, "New Zealand Considers Creating Climate Change Refugee Visas," *Guardian,* October 31, 2017.

38. Peter Teffer, "Climate Refugees Coming to Europe, Juncker Warns," *EU Observer.* September 9, 2015.

39. Adrienne Cutway, "Officials Want South Florida to Break Off into Its Own State," *Orlando Sentinel,* October 21, 2014.

Conclusion

1. *Human Security Report 2013.*

2. Leo Tolstoy, *War and Peace* (New York: Vintage, 2008), 1129.

3. Dominic D. P. Johnson and Moncia Duffy-Toft, "Grounds for War," *International Security,* Winter 2013–14.

4. Joshua Keating, "Why We Fight (over Land)," *Slate,* March 28, 2014.

5. Frank Jacobs, "Winston's Hiccup," *New York Times,* March 6, 2012.

6. William Easterly, Alberto Alesina, and Janina Matuszeski, "Artificial States," *National Bureau of Economic Research,* May 2006.

7. "Putin Reveals Secrets of Russia's Crimea Takeover Plot," *BBC,* March 9, 2015.

8. Daria Litvinova, "Separatists in Ukraine Declare Creation of New 'State' Malorossiya," *Telegraph,* July 18, 2017.

9. "Address by President of the Russian Federation."

10. Somini Sengupta, "Vote by U.N. General Assembly Isolates Russia," *New York Times,* March 27, 2014.

11. Yuval Shany, "Does International Law Grant the People of Crimea and Donetsk a Right to Secede?"

12. "Canada Mocks Russia's '15th century' Arctic Claim," *Reuters,* August 3, 2007.

13. Vivienne Walt, "France's Marine Le Pen on Brexit: 'This Is the Beginning of the End of the European Union,'" *Time,* June 28, 2016.

14. Halperin, *Self-Determination in the New World Order.*

15. Raf Sanchez, "Barack Obama Tells Scotland: Stay United," *Telegraph,* September 17, 2014.

16. "Scottish Independence: Barroso Says Joining EU Would Be 'Difficult,'" *BBC,* February 16, 2014.

17. Abby Innes, *Czechoslovakia: The Short Goodbye* (New Haven: Yale University Press, 2001).

18. Gottlieb, *Nation against State.*

Acknowledgments

I must first thank all the people quoted in this book, who took the time to share their views, stories, and wisdom with me.

I've had vague ambitions of writing about this topic for a long time, and the fact that my fairly nebulous concept was ever translated into an actual book is largely thanks to the guidance of Lauren Sharp at Aevitas Creative Management and the careful editing of Jaya Aninda Chatterjee at Yale University Press. Thanks also to Mary Pasti and Robin DuBlanc for their invaluable work in preparing the text for publication.

The reported portions of this book would never have been possible without the help of the fixers and translators I worked with. Yusuf Mohamed Hasan, editor of the *Somaliland Sun,* got me into all the places I needed to be in Hargeisa and a few where I probably shouldn't have been. From government ministries to refugee camps, Hisham Arafat was a phenomenal fixer and perceptive guide to all things Kurdistan. Not much goes on in Kiribati without the knowledge of Pelenise Alofa, national coordinator of the Kiribati Climate Action Network, proprietor of the Kiribati Health Retreat, and participant in so many other initiatives I lost count. I was enormously lucky to have the chance to work with her.

Abram Benedict, grand chief of the Mohawk Council of Akwesasne, went out of his way to welcome me to his community, and

Doug George-Kanentiio spent an enormous amount of time acquainting me with Iroquois politics and history.

Jason Andrew was the best traveling companion and reporting partner anyone could ask for in Abkhazia and I look forward to our next adventure—toddlers in tow this time.

I'm enormously appreciative of my colleagues at *Slate* for their flexibility and generosity in allowing me to pursue this project. I am particularly grateful to my editors Allison Benedikt and Chad Lorenz; the editor of *Future Tense,* Torie Bosch; and the editor in chief of *Slate,* Julia Turner.

Thank you to Cara Parks and Nathan Thornburgh of *Roads & Kingdoms* for their support, and to Mitch Moxley for his excellent editing on my report from the World Football Cup.

Thank you to the Somaliland national football team, led by Ilyas Mohamed and Guled Aden, for kindness and generosity in two different countries. Thanks also to Mohamed Khadar for the warm welcome in Hargeisa.

Ethan Porter and Jacob Brogan provided enormously helpful comments and guidance on my earliest draft of the book.

More people than I can probably remember provided helpful guidance and support along the way during the reporting and editing of this book, but a partial list would have to include Christian Caryl, Uri Friedman, Marya Hannun, Mark Hay, John Hudson, Ian Kalman, Siobhan O'Grady, Dayo Olopade, Gregory Stone, Ben Walker, and David Wilkins. Thanks also to Kevin Alexander, Charlie Sohne, and Emma Dumain for their friendship and encouragement.

Will Dobson has now hired me at two different publications and I owe an enormous debt to his questionable judgment.

Thank you to Jean Ende and Michael Keating for instilling in me a love of travel and learning, and for indulging my interests ever since I decided to do a fourth-grade research project on Luxembourg.

Thank you most of all to my wife Miranda for her advice, support, and reassurance; and to my son Thomas, who was born while I was in the process of writing, for the inspiration and frequent distractions. I love you both.

Portions of this work were previously published in the following articles by the author:

"Coming to E-Stonia," *Slate,* June 16, 2015.
"The Unrecognized," *Roads & Kingdoms,* June 15, 2016.
"Make Liberland Great Again," *Slate,* January 20, 2017.
"The Refugees I Met in Kurdistan Were Not Threats," *Slate,* January 30, 2017.

Index

Page numbers in *italics* refer to illustrations.